KISS OF THE IMMORTAL
-Immortalized Book One-

MEGHAN JONES

Cover Design by May Dawney Designs
https://maydawneydesigns.com

Editing by MaryBeth Ryman and Roxana Coumans

Prologue

"This one." The vampire, her crimson eyes glowing with delighted hunger, purred the words, a slight wetness in her mouth.

She was a tall woman, with flawless, pale, almost-marble-white skin. Youthful, she looked no older than twenty-something. However, an immortal one's appearance means nothing. The skin-tight black dress she was wearing complimented her hourglass figure, and the low-cut front exposed her ample breasts. Despite her seemingly frail and thin body, she was incredibly strong and fast. A vampire, depending on their age, could easily lift a car and just as easily throw it, killing someone. They were incredibly fast, but not everyone was blessed with certain traits.

Some were special, gifted even, with powers no human could hope to possess. This one has long, straight silver hair which nearly matched her eyes, as though one reflected the other perfectly. Her shoulders were covered by golden pauldrons formed for her body and decorated with accent detail of thorned roses along the edges. Her wrists were laced in gold, the metal smithed in a fashion that had the bracelets appear as a rope wrapped around the immortal's body.

The feral captive stood in the back of the cell, filthy from dirt sweat and mud, refusing to clean themselves. Their clothes were torn, and dried blood crusted on the shirt's side and near the collar. Despite the cleanliness of the cell, its latest occupant made a point to make it as vile as possible. Feces was smeared on the walls in an act of defiance and rebellion in the only way possible. Words spelled out to show the deep-seated hatred felt by the captive, despite their age.

If one thing was taught, it was to never show weakness or submission to the vampire. After a few days of the repeated offense, the guards left the cell and its occupant alone, not bothering to clean it and thinking it a better punishment for them to live in their own filth as humans have done for thousands of years anyway. This time, though...it was different. Today, they cleaned the cell and the captive was warned of the loss of numerous meals if they dirtied it again.

Losing meals was the worst thing because without them a human would not have the strength to fight back. At the young age of seven years, nearing eight, nutrients were vital to proper growth and they intended to have a long life of it.

Breathing heavily, the captive's muscles flexed and tightened, prepared at any moment to attack. Held behind their back was a sharpened stone, a shiv made by the repeated rubbing against the concrete floor of the cell. Formed by pulling out part of the piping for the sink, the captive was careful to keep their handiwork hidden. By using the area under the partly unseated sink, the captive was able to hide the marks of sharpening by moving the sink when the guards came. A few times they were almost caught, but surviving this long was because of skill, not luck.

It had been months since their imprisonment and everyday was preparation for escape. How many guards were there total? What are their routes? When were the meals? How did they bring them in? When did the sun rise and fall? This recon their father had taught them before he left to join the resistance. They were supposed to be safe, supposed to have no chance of discovery. They made rules and followed them in order to keep hidden. What happened? It was still fresh in their memory, replaying over and over. With the anger and the rage, the seeds of hatred were sown. They were deep in the woods, far from any civilization or known vampire camps. There was no path but what the animals of the forest created and the family of humans left no evidence, no footprint of their presence, and yet they were found.

Found...and killed. Except one, only one: the captive. But why? Why did it have to only be them? Everyone they had ever known or loved was gone, killed by the vampire- and yet here they are, about to be sold to the highest bidder. The captive had heard that there are only three things that happen to a human when among vampires: they become traitors and sell out their own, they are killed outright, or worse become livestock. The captive did not want to die, but if the only other options were either of the latter two, they would rather be dead. Living as livestock, as a slave, was not living at all! To be the food to these monsters was a fate worse than death and as a human it was their duty to fight until the end to keep that freedom.

But right now they were not free. Right now they were caged like an animal...so they would act like one.

The cell itself was a concrete box. Only one side was not stone but a thickened acrylic-like glass, strong enough to resist numerous attacks but still allow for viewing of the "merchandise." Though there were two lights in the cell, the occupant managed to break one, darkening the back of the cell. No one wanted to deal with the feral animal so they left it be. These were viewing cells, used to display captives to potential buyers. The normal routine was that an ideal captive would be moved here after processing and a few days or weeks in the main captivity area, but this captive was special. For the safety of the "merchandise," they were placed here from day one to remain separated from any and all other human contact, except those placed in the cell parallel to the captive. That one was not kept occupied for long. Many people came and went, and in the eyes of each it seemed the fire of resistance, the will to live, had all been extinguished.

Not this one.

The transparent wall opened and, of the four standing outside the cell, one entered: a dog of the vampire- a traitor human who became a servant to the immortal. He held a collar and chain, wanting to make their own kin a slave. How ironic of human history for this. The captive's heart raced, but not in panic- they shifted their bare feet, placing one heel to the back wall. If they were to take from the captive again it would not only be the captive's blood shed this night. Or was it day? It was hard to tell as this cell, like the others in this section, was underground, cut off from the outside world. The only reason the captive could tell night and day was by the difference of the temperature of the concrete. This was a trick taught to the captive by another prisoner...before he was bought and taken away, that is.

The guard came closer. "Don't make this difficult," he warned, shaking his head and mentally pleading for this troublesome brat to for once not make his life hell.

The guard lunged at the captive. The prisoner kicked off the wall, going past the guard's reaching arm and using the shiv to open the side of his neck. Blood spilled on the ground from the shredded artery but the vampires wasted no time, grabbing the captive before the guard's body hit the ground. The guard grasped his neck trying to stop the bleeding, pleading for help from the vampires who ignored him. No mercy for the weak.

Grasping the captive's wrist, the vampires squeezed until the captive yelped and could hold the shiv no longer. Struggling against the inhuman strength of the immortal, the captive dropped the shiv to the ground. During the fighting and resisting, the immortal woman made her approach with a soft chuckle.

"I like this one," she said, grasping under the captive's chin and raising their eyes to meet her own. "Such *fire* in her eyes."

The captive, a young girl, glared and she jerked her chin away. She bit down on the vampire guard's hand and a trickle of blood lined the edge of the child's lips. The vampire guard grabbed her, ripping her off of his hand, then threw her to the ground on her stomach, pulling an arm behind her back and pushing her head into the ground.

The vampire woman's mouth curled in an amused smile. "And quite a bit of fight left in her," she said, looking at the restrained captive forced into kneeling. The woman motioned for the child to be raised up.

Grabbing the collar and chain from the side of the dead human, the vampire clasped it around the young girl's neck and tugged on the chain, jerking the girl forward toward her.

"You are mine now, *body and soul*."

Chapter One
A Dangerous Game

Fifteen Years Later

The rays of the rising sun are the most beautiful sight. It seemed all the colors of the rainbow painted the sky, illuminating the global canvas with its light. She loved this time, when the day began as the brisk, frosty morning dew collided with the heat of the sun. The chill reminded her of life. It was a feeling that relaxed and eased her, especially when her body ached, it cooled the heat she felt within. It was this way many mornings, her routine when called during the night. No one but a few servants and the guard were up now.

Vampires and sunlight were not a deadly combination. Those bedtime stories were false propaganda for humans to believe they had a chance. Humanity never had a chance, not against the immortals who swept through human defenses in less than three years. The world was theirs now, over a decade strong and their domination has not wavered. As the vampire reigns supreme, humanity is at the bottom of the food chain as second-rate citizens, slaves, and livestock. Against the vampire, there is little humanity can do to achieve victory. The immortal are stronger, faster. They have hidden

11

themselves in the darkness of world history, gathering their forces and resources until they could launch their attack.

Millions of people died or turned against their own and millions more suffered a fate worse than death.

This time was her time alone, her time to think for herself, to be by herself and this was the closest she ever came to freedom. It was short-lived, but it was the most precious thing she was 'granted'. Though she had late-night duties, she had normal tasks in the later hours of the day. That was not for many hours though, and right now she was relaxing, decompressing from the previous night. It was out here, in the light, where she felt the closest she would ever have to freedom. Beyond the limits of these grounds lies certain death; for fleeing, for trying to escape, risked being caught by the hunters again.

She sat on the roof of the Palace, which was usually off-limits to civilians and staff, but the vampires knew she would do nothing nefarious. What *could* she do? Plot against her masters? Commit suicide? They knew even she was not foolish enough because if she tried and failed, then she would certainly live to regret the attempt. Despite this life of a gilded cage, she refused to die. If she did, who would remember those who have died? Those killed by the vampire? Her survival here that was her fight, her resistance against the vampire ruler.

"You know when she finds out you're out here she's going to punish you."

Kira leaned back and took the offered bottle held to her. She looked at the top, then offered it back. He took his thumb and popped the cap off with little effort. Being a vampire was convenient for that alone. Bottle opener at one's fingertips.

The human woman shrugged, as she took a sip. "You make it sound like I try to hide it. That she hasn't already punished me." she said rhetorically, as she leaned forward with the bottle between her dangled legs. "Living day by

12

day..." Kira looked down at the bottle, "...Not knowing when it's my last."

Jake sat down beside her and then let out a sigh. "Such is the nature of the Game." he expressed, as he looked down at the grounds while holding his own bottle with his arm resting on his bent knee.

The Game is a common-tongue phrase referring to the delicate navigation of the social and political circle of vampire society. Politics and personal lives are the same, going as deep as a vampire's very blood and can be the life and death of one. A human has no place in the Game, no power, no influence--a piece of meat, livestock. And yet Kira was in the Game's heart, at the very top--the highest point for the bottom of the food chain. A rare and unexpected opportunity, but also the most dangerous place any human could be.

Kira took a longer sip, and the long sleeve of her flannel pulled up over her wrist with the movement. Jake saw the bruising on her wrist. "You *trip*..." He gestured with his free hand and asked with displeased sarcasm, "Or did you run into a pole again?"

"Actually, this one was my fault: I fell out of bed." Kira bumped Jake's shoulder with her own while taking another sip.

Jake raised a brow. "About your family?"

"No..." She shook her head. "About Eona."

"*Really*?" Her friend's voice filled with great surprise. "That's weird, you two haven't talked in--"

"About five years, yeah." Kira confirmed as she her temple then adjusted the scarlet scarf around her neck. She shut her eyes. "It was just a dream, but it freaked me out enough that I shot out of bed, legs got caught in the sheets and I hit the ground."

"You gonna be alright?"

Kira chuckled while she waved the beer. "Oh yeah, these help loads."

They both laughed.

13

Kira exhaled loudly. "Had Emily check it, it's fine. Tender, no ropes or cuffs for me for a couple days though."

A whistle from one of the roof patrols signaled that someone less than desirable of Kira's few freedoms was coming. Jake and Kira finished their beers and stood. He passed the empty bottle to his friend, then lifted her into his arms, jumped then landed on the ground in the gardens below. Away from the unpleasant guard, the two of them took their time around the garden and enjoyed the last of the morning dew before sleep called them both to their prospective stations.

"So, how does matchmaking go?" Kira prompted.

Jake rolled his eyes. "It's not matchmaking--I met with my fiancé last night. We had dinner." He stressed, "It was nice."

"And here I thought arranged marriages were an old school thing that only humans did." Kira sang with intended obliviousness, "Oh, the joy of being a human slave."

Jake stopped as Kira continued nonchalantly and disregarded the seriousness of her own statement.

"You're not a slave." Jake whispered. "Human or vampire you're a person, a person with a right to live and love like any other."

"That's a nice thought." Kira replied when she pulled her scarf down and reminded Jake of her predicament. "But we both know that's not true."

The Noble Vampire exhaled loudly while he shook his head. "I'm sorry... I wish there was something I could do."

"Jake, you're my best friend, you've helped me get out of more trouble than I can possibly think of."

"But you can't tell me everything because of Absolute Rule. I know and I hate it." Jake slid his hands into his suit pocket. "Can you at least come with us to the club on Friday? Bunch of us are going: me, Kaden, Mike, Jules, Hanna." He drummed his head for another name.

Kira shrugged. "We'll see, it's been getting harder and harder to leave lately."

"They think you're going to run?"

"They know I'm not stupid enough." The human frowned at him and gave the face he should know better than to suggest that. "Something's agitated her lately, and she's had me practically glued to her side."

"I hate to be the one to ask, but...is she...clingy?"

They turned the corner.

"Pfff, more like marking her territory," Kira answered, per usual she often compared the behavior of vampires to predatory animals.

Of course, she kept that comparison to herself, as she knew to keep her sharp tongue behind her teeth when in... *polite* company. She had to do that for much of her life, especially in the last few years. In the Palace every day was a fight for her survival. Every expression of her face, every motion she made, her body language, heartbeat, words spoken, all of it was an art- crafted, perfected, and sculpted all these years to ensure her survival. This art was constantly changing. Dynamic in its nature, the Game is not a force to be underestimated. Seeing the sun rising every day was one more victory, one more absolution that she had survived, but she knew better than to become complacent. She learned that lesson not once, but twice.

"I'll ask about Friday, but no promises."

Jake came in front and spun on his heels, walking backward with a victorious grin. "Alright! Don't forget I have to attend a Senate meeting tomorrow so I can't swing by till Wednesday."

Kira became quiet.

"Hey." Jake came around and wrapped his arm around her shoulder. "You're smart, cautious, and stealthy. That makes you far more dangerous than any vampire here."

They turned another corner then headed toward the Palace.

"Try to get some sleep," Jake said. He released Kira and went off to the side of the Palace then he disappeared after a few steps.

The sun had risen now, the light warmed the growing day. Kira walked up the rear steps of the Palace then looked over the river that traveled toward the mountains and the valley between. They built the Palace into the mountain, high above a city that lay below. Beside it, a waterfall fell from the cliffs above, creating a small pool in the back of the garden forbidden for use by anyone not given direct permission by the Master of the House. Perfectly defensible from any attack, anyone who tried would fight an uphill battle. It also made escape impossible for a human such as herself simply because she was not as fast or strong, and did not possess rapid regeneration. On raw abilities alone, going against them directly was suicide.

Kira survived differently. Then again, it was never her idea. She just went along with it. Looking out toward the back of the garden, she watched the sunrise over the horizon once more before heading inside. Years of living as a night owl and one's mind and body becomes wired in a certain way, and yet her nature as a human, a being of the light, has her yearn for the day. Even if for a few minutes, a few moments, it was a natural yearning for the sun. It seemed foolish to her now as an adult, but as a child she associated it with being afraid of the dark. Now she knew better. Now she knows the dark terrifies her and yearned for the day was nothing more than an instinctive impulse to claw from the darkness and to have that absolution of surviving another night.

She walked inside the massive Palace, a place she self-labeled as her cage, she took the time to memorize every inch of this place. From top to bottom, inside and out, even the off-limits locations and secret passages only the oldest of guards and servants who had lived and served this family for years knew about. She counted every step, knew the exact dimensions of every room, the distance between each door, the amount of steps, the number of doors and windows. She knew the name of every painting, every person depicted, their births, deaths and significance to immortal history. Kira learned every detail in order to survive and yet, she did not understand the workings of vampire society and only had a small introduction to their hierarchy.

She has lived in this palace for nearly fifteen years and in that time the furthest she has been are the pages of books, no farther than the limits of the city below. Under heavy guard she was never let out of sight, but where she had hoped to gain their trust, or their complacency of her existence, instead vampire society watched her. A human in her position was rare, unexpected, and very... unwelcomed. She has become the target of many hungry mouths, for more than who she stands behind.

The twenty-one-year-old woman passed a mirror and stopped to look at herself. On the outside, she looked like any other human woman living her life, a normal life without a thing wrong in the world. She wore torn blue skinny jeans, black sneakers, and a light black-and-grey flannel complemented by the scarlet scarf around her neck. Her long hair was raven black, as dark as night, and braided to the side of her head down the front of her collarbone. Her eyes were as blue as the sky, and reflected that she, as a bird in a gilded cage, would never rise to fly free. They stood out the most from her lightly bronzed flesh which showed her to be a mixed child. Not that anyone cared what color she was on the outside, only the red within mattered to *them*. She tried to copy what they would base a college student around her age off of pre-war magazines she had gained from the trash. The Master of the House did not care what Kira wore in her own time, but in 'polite company' (or just hers) there was an 'expectation.' To anyone on the outside, she looked like any other normal woman, but that was far from the truth.

Kira touched her neck, then walked past the mirror, trying to ignore the throb she felt beneath the fabric. She had learned to always trust her gut and her gut told her something

17

big was coming. Whether good or bad, she did not know, but what she knew was that she would stay out of its way, regardless. That was how she survived. That was how she saw the light of another day. She walked past a window to the outside and looked out to the city below. Even in the early hours of the morning, people were up and active. A few had gathered again, they picketted and protested outside the furthest gate to the Palace. Progressives: humans and ex-humans who think equality and coexistence are possible between humans and the immortals.

They're wasting their time, Kira thought to herself, her fingers touched the glass of the window as she watched them. *There's no such thing as coexistence with them.*

She continued on toward her room. This hall was empty now, safe for her. The Master of this house lived in these halls, as did Kira, which further added to the displeasure of the human's existence. She grabbed the knob to her room, Kira looked down the hall when she scanned for the presence of any. She saw no one, but that meant nothing when being hunted by a vampire. One second you could be alone, the next they pinned you against the wall with their hands around your throat.

Kira twisted her neck left and right, feeling stiff. She just wanted to sleep now, just go into her room and collapse on the bed. Doing just that, Kira shed her clothes and crawled into bed, she pulled up her covers and hoped that sleep would take over soon and that there would be no dreams tonight, especially about Eona.

The first series of drapes, farthest from the bed, pulled open. Then the third and fourth sets and the fifth set, the last, which was directly beside the bed, kept shut. Tea was ready on the nightstand on the left side of the bed: a morning breakfast comprising Crepes with questionably Strawberry flavored syrup, toast, and bacon with a tablet opened to the daily report all placed neatly beside the TV remote. Perfection. Every day she waited in the bed's shadow, hidden from the dwindling light of the sun. The Master of the house did not like to be awakened by the light of day. It is why the last set of drapes remained closed.

Many punishments followed before Kira mastered the routine, not even from the Master but behind the scenes by the head maid and Butler. They demanded perfection, drilled and beat into her that perfection until her knees and knuckles were bloody. Once blood was shed, however, their Master showed compassion to the human servant. That compassion did not come without a price and it is one Kira continues to pay day by day. It is also the greatest asset to her survival in the Game.

For Kira, the Pureblood Vampire who gave that compassion was known by the name of Carmilla Tepes, the Master of this house.

"Good evening, Lady Carmilla." Kira said, once positioned in the light of the windows.

"Ah, breakfast in bed." The Master arose, as she opened her crimson eyes to drink in the woman before her. "How thoughtful."

Kira jumped as Lady Carmilla pressed against her and eased the woman against the wall between the two windows.

"But I enjoy dessert so much more." The tall silver-haired woman slipped her hand past Kira's tailcoat top, slid around her waist and tugged her closer to match the immortal's curves.

The vampire's crimson eyes glowed with desire, her tongue touched her plump lips, eager to tickle the flesh of the human. The tender, sweet surface of her prey beneath her fingertips was so easy to tear into, so fragile, a delicate bird whose wings must be clipped. Her long hair cascaded down her exposed back and some fell over her shoulder, covering the lacy bra at the nipple. It had only been a few hours and still she wanted more. Lady Carmilla felt Kira tremble in arousal at her touch, a touch that never fails to instigate such a response. She smiled, pleased at her influence, but stepped back and returned to her bed. She raked her fingers through her curved hair as she reached for the tablet and brought her teacup to her lips.

"You can breathe now." Lady Carmilla teased as she sensed Kira's racing heart rate and rasped breath. "All good things come to those who wait." she added with a small smile when she heard Kira exhale quietly and calmed herself effectively.

Lady Carmilla read the data on the tablet while she sat on the bed, her silky pink lingerie all she wore without a single sense of modesty. Kira moved toward one end of the bedpost and grabbed the robe draped on the post then returned to the vampire's side. She held the robe open for the Lady to put her arms in the sleeves. The human cringed slightly as her wrist throbbed with a wrong twist. With Lady Carmilla temporarily clothed, Kira went on to the closet as she knew there was a Senator coming to meet with the Lady later in the night.

"What happened to your wrist?" The Lady asked, making Kira jump again as she tiptoed to her place in the doorway.

Kira bowed her head slightly. "I fell out of bed m'lady."

"Is that so?" Lady Carmilla asked as she strut towards Kira.

She gentle took the injured wrist into her long, slender fingers. "I hope that is the truth. Those of my staff should well know the consequences for harming..." She brushed her fingers along Kira's cheek and continued. "That which is mine."

The human shuddered, and a smile came across the vampire's face as she traced her finger under Kira's chin. Even the slightest touch, the smallest brush, is enough to get this woman flustered. A few steps more and the vampire can easily make the human putty in her arms. How delightful that

20

would be, such a treat this early in the night; however, now she needed to rest and recover to provide her continuously delicious service. Lady Carmilla hummed in contemplation, then walked past Kira to look at her own attire.

"You will take the rest of the night off." the vampire ordered. "Any who dare raise a hand to you in opposition will suffer the consequences."

"M'lady, it's just a bruised wrist. Doctor Sanders already—"

Kira leapt out of her skin as Lady Carmilla's intense gaze made a lump form in her throat. She bit her tongue before she jeopardized her life. One second, that's all it took, one whim of the vampire to decide she did not have any use for Kira any longer. She needed to prove her worth, her use, constantly, otherwise she would likely find herself at the dinner table.

"Forgive me. I spoke out of turn." Kira quickly apologized and avoided her Master's gaze.

Lady Carmilla shook her head. "You did nothing wrong. While your devotion to me is admirable, when I command you to care for your health, I am not to be questioned." She walked toward Kira and whispered into her ear, "Those who are disobedient are punished."

Kira swallowed.

"And we both know that I can be very creative in my punishments."

Chapter Two
Night on the Town

Kira slid one arm into her shirt, then the next.

"As far as your physical health is concerned, there is nothing unexpected." Doctor Sanders explained while she flipped through test results on the clipboard.

She sat at her desk across from Kira, her office lined with shelves of books in the medical field both modern and the great-great-grandfather of modern. The vampire set the clipboard down. She leaned forward and rested her elbows on the heavy dark-stained oak desk then dropped her head on top of her folded hands. Her youngest and most vulnerable patient came after discreet complaints of persistant throbbing in her neck. While the occasional pain is to be expected—an experience similar to 'phantom limb'--Kira's had shown increasing activity the last few weeks, more than in the last three years combined.

Stress would be the first initial cause, but Kira expressed no change in the normal level of 'doing everything I can to survive otherwise I'll be killed'. The doctor watched the human put on her shirt which covered the discoloring that marked her body in many places. Raised on her back were marks, a duller which meant they were no less than two days old. Wider, shorter lashes, even number; not on top of each other meant only six rounds. The lashes were not deep. A practiced hand did this, one who knew not only how lightly to make it for a human, but knew Kira's pain tolerance very well. What was permanent were the scars on her lower right back and upper left shoulder. Eight long discolorations dragged deep into her torso, used as an anchor once to keep one's prey still. The doctor expected those to remain with her for the rest of her life, however, they would fade and lower than discolorations than ugly scarring in the years to come.

Aside from the accident on her wrist, there was no other bruising, no evidence of mistreatment or abuse... not of the physical level. The doctor looked down at her files. The emotional and mental damage done to this poor woman was unimaginable, but of course, there was little the doctor could do. This was how Kira, a mortal, survived in a world ruled by the immortal. What Doctor Sanders could do was be an ear, be the only one she could count on. As an ex-human, she could understand humans better than those born vampires.

"But I imagine that's not why you're here." Doctor Sanders said, as she sat back and grabbed a prescription pad, "I'm prescribing some stronger anti-inflammatories and pain relievers---"

Kira turned around, rolling her sleeves up, "No thanks."

Doctor Sanders frowned, "Offer stands. You don't need to set up an appointment, just text me."

"She...how do I put this..." The patient rocked on her heels.

The doctor raised her hands, "I get it, don't have to explain."

Kira came around the chair and went to the couch near the window, across from the bookshelves. She plopped down, exhaling loudly, folding her arms behind her head. Kira looked at her doctor.

"Plans for tonight?" Kira asked casually.

Doctor Sanders shrugged. "It is the weekend, and I was planning on ongoing hunting. Young blood is always the sweetest when elevated by all kinds of —"

"Oh, shut up, you're a vegetarian." Laughed Kira, "Seriously, you got any plans? Me, Jake and a few of his friends are going out tonight, wanna go?"

"Carmilla is letting you unsupervised into the city? I remember when there was a time you weren't even allowed out of the Palace."

Fifteen years for the immortal is nothing. It is a moment passing by, a second of time to their eternal existence. Many, especially those who never knew what it meant to be mortal, distance themselves from that which changes, which ages. Doctor Sanders has been Kira's personal doctor since she first arrived and it has been a wonder to watch her change, to watch a lamb in a den of lions survive all this time... but not without a price.

She remembers it as though it were yesterday: being summoned to the Palace, seeing a feral, seven-something-year-old human girl in a destroyed room. One would think they unleashed a wild beast in that room; furniture thrown and destroyed, sheets torn, tied against the door handles, tied against the counterweight of fallen dressers. Windows broken, drapes all ripped down, pillows cut open. The doctor forced herself into the room and slipped through a small crack as the door pushed open. If the vampires wanted to, they could have easily gone in and subdued the wild child, but that was not the goal.

Doctor Sanders entered the room and found the child in the back of the room, near a window broken and pried open. She could get out if she wanted, but it was quite a ways down, even with the sheets tied together and thrown out as rope. That was a last resort, it seemed. The ex-human came in with a briefcase. She went toward the bed and brushed off fragments of glass and sat down.

"Tying the knobs with sheets, then using the heavy dressers you can't move as the counter-weight. Smart." The doctor, dressed in scrubs and her white coat, said.

Just as many other immortals, there were no imperfections in her marble skin, but unlike the other vampires Kira had seen, her skin kept its natural dark African tone, more human-looking, which made her judge that the woman was an ex-human. She had black and cherry highlighted hair, dyed from her natural black and long Box Braids she allowed to grow out over the years. Shorter than Carmilla in height, the doctor was more muscular in her legs and arms. Kira knew to watch for these details. Even in this state and cornered in the enemy's core, she remembered what they taught in order to survive. Her eyes were brown. Kira found it suspicious. She had heard about vampires able to hide their eyes somehow. Regardless of what color her eyes, Kira could tell: fangs, posture, vocabulary; vampire.

The doctor remained on the bed, "It must have been scary... being in such a strange place with all of them."

She saw the child in the corner, who clenched a shard of glass so tight her hand bled. Though dressed in fresh clothes, she did quick work to dirty and destroy them, the slave collar she wore still around her neck with a broken chain. The doctor stood up and sauntered toward the child whose face bore an expression just as fierce and hate-filled as the vampire's own so very long ago. When the doctor changed... she too held onto her hatred like it was her life raft in the open ocean.

"You don't have to trust me, but I'm a doctor." She looked at the girl's bleeding hand when speaking softly, "I want to help you, but if you don't let me... there's only so long I can keep them from hurting you again."

She watched the girl's eyes dart left and right in contemplation, and darted them repeatedly toward the window.

Doctor Sanders leaned against a flipped couch when continuing to maintain a gentle, mothering tone, "Your choice."

She could hear the rapid heartbeat of the girl, in panic, in fear, but she was not being reckless. She was not acting out of instinct. This girl was smart enough to think, even in a panic. They trained her to survive vampires and had been doing it for many years. Based on the little information she received, they had captured recently this girl and was the only one to be captured.

The girl cautiously stepped away from the door, "You're ex-human."

"Yes." The doctor nodded, "But unlike others... I didn't have a choice." She held her hand out, "May I?"

She dropped the glass shard and they let the flow of blood free, dropping on the floor rapidly. Doctor Sanders opened her briefcase, showing the girl the contents she explained everything she planned on doing and whether it would hurt. She first addressed the collar. It was the first to go. The doctor found deep ligature red that was rubbed raw and bled. The girl had fought and pulled so hard it broke the chain—impressive... and sad.

"My name is Doctor Emily Sanders." The doctor introduced herself as she used tweezers to remove shards from the child's hand.

The girl opened her mouth—the doctor put her finger over her lips, "Don't." The vampire whispered, "Whatever name you were born with, don't let them know, don't let them use it against you."

When she finished cleaning the wound, which did not need stitches, she wrapped it, "Never forget it. From now on, it will be the only thing you can call yours. If you want to survive... this place..." The vampire gestured to the room, "To stay alive, stay human, you'll have to play by their rules."

On the couch years later, Kira shrugged. "I learned to play the Game and I've played it well. Speaking of, you still haven't answered my question."

"I will have to politely decline. I have a meeting this weekend with a few colleagues."

"Damn, Em, you're always working. There is a thing called a 'social life' you know." Kira pouted as she rolled her eyes when she sat up. "I was hoping you'd hang out for once."

Emily smiled as she stood and grabbed a lollipop from her jar and tossed it to Kira, "Come on." She said before she dug into her pocket, "I need a smoke break."

On the roof of the hospital, they stood in the shadow cast by the entrance to the roof. Emily lit a cigarette, then offered one to Kira, but was politely declined. There were enough things in the world trying to kill her. Cancer was not something she wanted to add to the list.

"Now that we're out of the office, are you going to tell me why you really came?" probed the doctor as she pulled her brown hair back, the sides of her head shaved into a pattern.

Kira leaned against the wall, then slid down to her butt. "I needed to get out of that place." She relieved quietly, "I kept having that dream."

"About your attack?"

She did not answer.

"You nearly died, it's understandable and expected for there to be lasting trauma both physically and mentally." The doctor's side of the human's friend came out, but she did not come for a doctor's diagnosis, but a friend's ear.

"I feel like I'm slowly losing my mind, that I'm forgetting."

Emily took a long drag of her cigarette then blew the smoke up into the breeze above, "Can't say I blame you, having Carmilla on you twenty-four-seven—I would have torn my heart out if I had to deal with her."

"Honestly, she's easy. Once you get used to it, it's really not that bad. I could have ended up in a lot worse places." Kira said as she the fabric of the scarf between her fingers, "I'm alive, I've survived this long."

"This isn't living." Emily hissed as she threw the butt to the ground and smashed it with her foot, "Humans used like livestock, treated like trash, none of this should have happened."

Kira chuckled, "Starting to sound like a Progressive."

"Those naïve fools know nothing. Equality is a myth, so long as one has power over another, that's nothing, but a fantasy. Give both sides power, that's fair, that's equality."

"Like that'll ever happen." Kira shut her eyes, Emily joined her on the floor and when she settled, Kira rested her head on the Doctor's shoulder.

Jake and Kira were best friends. Emily, too, was just as close to Kira, if not closer. She had saved Kira countless times from when she was a child to when she almost died and instead of becoming one of them, she runs around with an interesting conversation starter on her neck. Emily never forgot what it meant to be human and was the one person who treated Kira normally, as a normal human adult and for one certainly understood as she stood in the shadow of a Pureblood. After all, if a vampire is not born, the only way to turn a human into a creature of the night is to be bitten by a Pureblood Vampire. Kira is the only known person spared from that fate and the worst part...it was not even Carmilla who bit her back then.

29

"I don't want to forget them, but it hurts to remember them, to remember what things used to be... the people I lost." Kira's throat tightened. "I haven't even heard those names in years and I'm forgetting their faces."

Emily leaned her head against Kira's. "I'm sorry I could never find the cabin. I know how much it meant to you."

"It's fine." The human woman said without care. She never expected the vampire to. She did not even try to hold hope she would have.

After minutes of silence, time Kira held onto with every ounce of strength, she knew she could not push her limits. She returned to the Palace, a car awaited her outside as usual, but it was not empty.

"Lady Carmilla..." Kira's open mouth showed her surprise, knowing for a fact the Lady should have been asleep—not that vampires actually needed to sleep—but to see her out in broad daylight was unexpected and very alarming.

"I had a meeting in the city and recalled you had an appointment with..."

Doctor Sanders walked from the hospital entrance to beside Kira, "Ah Lady Carmilla, what a surprise. I took you as a night owl." said the ex-human with intended sarcasm.

The Pureblood Vampire bit back her annoyance at the doctor's loose tongue and lack of respect. She was an irreplaceable asset that she could not afford to lose and knew it. Doctor Sanders enjoyed the times she tested the limits of the Lady's patience with her, the two of them bounded back and forth at another. Still, the doctor chose not to push those limits today, not with an innocent in between. Perhaps innocent was a stretch of a word for even Kira, but it was nearly accurate.

"Don't forget to take it easy, no extreme physical activities. Let me know if you need a prescription for those anti-inflammatories we discussed." She turned to Kira when she put her hands in her coat pocket and spoke loud enough for the Pureblood to hear.

Kira nodded before she went to the Lady's side because that would lessen the irritation the vampire had. She slipped inside the black-tinted car and Lady Carmilla kept to her side of the car. The immortal leaned against the window and looked out of it as though she were in deep contemplation. She still had an air of irritation, but it did not seem to be directed toward Kira or Emily. The human looked at the vampire, as she tried to read her face and understand whether she was in trouble or how involved she would be with the Master's frustration later on.

"M'lady?" Kira cautiously called out. "Is something wrong?"

Lady Carmilla glanced at Kira's reflection, "Why would you think there is?"

Kira searched for the proper way to speak without risking her neck... metaphorically and literally.

"You are not usually up at this hour. I was surprised to see you pick me up." Kira said quietly, fidgeted with her fingers in her lap.

"The meeting I had was unexpected and last minute. I thought it was convenient to take you home. Do you dislike this?"

There she went again. She twisted her words to have Kira dig herself into a hole with the only option to turn to the Lady for salvation. A trap that would have the wrong thing said result in a punishment all the while saying the right only tied her closer to the vampire. In this Game Lady Carmilla would win no matter what. Those are the kinds of games she likes and when the odds were against her? She would cheat to gain the upper hand and favor.

Kira frowned. "Of course not, it's just —"

A hand touched Kira's thigh which caused her to blush. Lady Carmilla smirked, a fang displayed as she watched the other woman's expression reflected in the window.

"It's just what?" asked the vampire, her hand traveled higher. "Tell me."

"Lady—" Kira struggled to say huskily as her heart beat escalated and a tingled heat gathered between her legs.

"Yes?" asked the vampire as she turned her head to Kira and watched the arousal fill the human's eyes.

Kira clenched the leather of the seat, "Please... we're —" She looked up to the driver.

Lady Carmilla hummed as she moved her hand from a sensitive place back to the center of the seat, "I hope you enjoy your time with your friends." The vampire said, the statement made Kira tilt her head in curiosity. Lady Carmilla has never concerned herself with Kira's activities outside the Palace.

"Er... forgive me if this is out of line..." Kira adjusted her scarf, "Next time... would you like to go?"

The driver raised a brow himself.

Lady Carmilla turned, surprised. Now Kira had the cards. She leaned toward the human, taking it under her chin and pulling it towards her, "If that is what you want." She kissed Kira until the human became flush, "Then I shall."

Kira followed Jake. They had taken his family's car, but the oldest one so as not to draw attention. The small group left the car. Kira was between three vampires. She looked to the end of the street, seeing a street motorcycle round the corner to the alley just as they were entering the club.

This place was popular, not top-class as the rich, powerful and famous would go, but popular for the local crew, especially the youth. It was the only club in the city that allowed humans, with or without an escort. The club was happily neutral as money was green no matter whose hand.

The sound of techno music pulsed throughout the building, vibrating the dance floor and electrifying the night. Kira held no fear of being hunted in the club, the rules of which and the bouncers ensured that would not happen. She branched off from their group, going to the bar to grab a drink. It would ease a few drinks and she had enough to dance, but not enough to be buzzed. No matter how many people, no matter how clear, no matter how many witnesses, she was never safe. Though Jake would do nothing to put her in danger, nothing was certain and in a world ruled by the vampire, everything became permitted.

Everything done and said was to survive, to make it to another day, but these outings allowed her to remember that even if it was out of reach, there was a life to be lived. She won't ever forget the taste of freedom she once had and how she would fight for it for the rest of her life.

From the bar Kira ordered a light and simple drink, vodka with sprite and a splash of cranberry. Despite her choice of light drinks, despite her thin stature, she was very much a heavyweight. Something she learned to develop as soon as possible in order to avoid... unpleasant situations. Thankfully, Lady Carmilla had no interest in a drunken stupor and was quite fixed on consent.

After she grabbed hers and a tray full of orders, she went to her group and played distributor. She bought the first round of drinks with her given credit card. Though she promised herself to keep her wits about her, Kira had too much fun to keep one-hundred percent on top of her bearing.

A few drinks more than she planned, and she was one more from breaking the line of tipsy and drunk. At her next turn to buy drinks, she opted for water as she recognized her error too late, though knew it was never too early to work to avoid a hangover. As their friends danced in the club center, Kira kept besides another human and talked with an ex-human and another human. It was a relatively safe place, when away from the others.

"And what is a beautiful woman doing here, instead of on the dance floor?"

Kira turned to the woman who came beside her, a vampire. She had short blonde hair shaved on the sides of her head with her hair styled back. She wore a black leather jacket opened to show her torn sleeveless shirt, her torn skinny jeans gave a 'biker girl' and certainly 'bad girl' appearance. Kira thought she may be the motorcycle rider she had seen earlier, which, she admitted to herself, was quite an appeal. Still happily buzzed, Kira indulged the mysterious vampire's desire for conversation.

"Catching my breath." Chuckled the human.

The woman smirked, "I can make you chase it all night."

Kira choked on her water a bit, "Wow." She wiped her mouth. The vampire handed her a napkin, "Well played." Kira commended.

"Well, you did walk into it." The vampire shrugged as she continued to wear a smirk on her face.

Kira nodded, "Yeah, but you're barking up the wrong tree with me."

"Ouch, not even going to give me a name?"

The human chuckled once and leaned back against the stool at the bar. "I'm off the market."

The vampire pulled a stool up, sat and ordered herself a beer, then asked if her amazing conversationalist wanted a pop.

"Who says I want another? Maybe I was just looking for someone to talk to?" The drinks arrived, and she slid the unaltered glass of Coca-Cola to her bar mate.

Kira looked at her for a moment and searched for signs; posture, hands' movements, facial expressions, even how many times one would blink. She did this to every new person she met, less with those she knew because she was already well-versed in reading them. This woman... whoever she was... Kira felt she could trust her, felt she was safe with her. That was something she has not felt in a long time. Maybe it was the alcohol, but she did not care. What was the worst that could happen? Lady Carmilla's scent was all over her. She was property already marked, and no lower vampire was stupid enough to take a bite out of her. Kira being this reckless was only because of that assurance... then the only thing that truly protected her in this world was the very thing that cages her.

"You the one who rode on the bike earlier?" Kira began.

The woman nodded. "You like bikes? Built her myself, a bit of a hobby of mine I picked up abroad."

Now Kira's interests became peaked. If anything could get her chatty, it was talking about the outside world.

"I was in Germany for a while. I stayed with my dad and went to school. During the weekend I could ride to four different countries in a few hours if I wanted to and the beer—" The vampire looked at the bottle, "The beer there was amazing, you humans certainly know your shit when it comes to that."

Kira bobbed her head. Not that she would know. She knows less about human history than the vampire one. Not that it mattered. It was their world now and they rarely remember the losers in history. Still, she was alive. She was here and now to remember her own history and that of her family... she owed them that much, as long as she lives long enough to remember them.

"Why did you come back?" Kira asked curiously, as she took the pop and sipped it.

The vampire's cheery demeanor lessened some, "I have a few things I need to take care of, get some things I left behind when I left."

Kira stared at her glass. "Must be nice to have something to go back to."

"K!"

Only one turned to Jake.

"Ready to head out? The others are well..."

Kira and Jake looked at their trashed friends. Kira threw back the pop and set it on the bar. "Yeah, give me a second."

She turned to the vampire woman, "Sorry I have to go."

"Still no to a name?"

Kira gave a sad smile, "I'm sorry... even if I gave it to you, I doubt we'd ever see each other ever again. My mistress...is quite territorial."

The leather-clad vampire smirked again, "So am I." She winked, pecked Kira on the cheek before taking her beer elsewhere.

Kira frowned a bit. This woman clearly though it would be good to be friends with her, but Lady Carmilla would never approve. She deemed most women around her threats, whether being protective or out of jealousy Kira could not have female friends whether or not they were straight. She gravved her coat and rushed after Jake to help carry one of their drunken friends out of the club, watched by the biker vampire as she sat at the bar.

"See you soon."

Chapter Three
Unexpected Reunion

An arrow hit a bullseye with expert marksmanship and precision and split the opposition's arrow right down the middle. Jake sighed while he shook his head and tapped the end of this bow, before he tossed it on the ground and went to the weapon rack. He grabbed the loaded crossbow, aimed and shot it, his bolt split his adversary's arrow in half.

Kira chuckled, when she rose her bow. "That's cheating." She released the string and broke Jake's bolt in half as she pushed the bolt's head and her own through the target.

An icicle shot out and punctured a hole through the target supseqently destroying all the arrows.

"No, *that's* cheating." Jake raised his gun-gesture finger and blew over the tip like he was a gunslinger.

Some vampires are different, even from their own kin. There were few blessed with gifts. Special powers vary from one individual to another, manifesting in what's thought to be the reflection of a vampire's soul. At least in theory. Elemental-based abilities, such as Jake's, who manipulated and created ice, are rare. If they do manifest in an individual, they are often of Noble or higher blood. This leads to the accuracy of the theory that the less human DNA a vampire has, the stronger they are and more likely to manifest these abilities.

Kira has seen almost every ability possessed by the staff of the Palace, but Lady Carmilla is the only exception. It was no question of whether she had power. As a Pureblood, one at the highest level of all in their society, but not once has Kira seen a particular ability to be shown. When one survived the Game it often meant they had the greatest power and the strongest blood. Lady Carmilla's position and blood alone did not secure her rule. Kira was certain she had one and often wondered if it differed from any other. Nearly all manifest physically as something: ice, shields, and laser-cutting weapons, acid; Kira had heard of someone having the ability to manipulate emotions, another to tamper with electronics, but in all the years she has spent with the Lady... nothing. Kira drew her bow and shot another bullseye at an intact target.

"Remind me not to piss you off." Jake raised a brow. With a smirk, Kira drew another from her quiver and another and another. She sank one arrow after the next in each target. Three targets popped up, another launched in the air. Every one of them hit in the center.

Jake huffed, "Where the hell did you learn how to shoot like that?"

Letting the bow rest at her side, Kira looked behind to see if anyone was nearby.

"My dad taught us." She answered quietly.
Jake tilted his head, "*Us?*"

Suddenly the staff of the Palace rushed around and pratically sprinted towards the main entrance. The guards listened in on their ear pieces, adjusted their positions and left the gardens without protection. Kira and Jake looked at another, then began to head inside to find out what happened. Two guards came in front of them and blocked their path.
"Her Majesty's orders: you are to remain in the garden." Said one sympathetically.

Jake was free to go and he promised to find out what was going on and let her know. Once he left and was out of earshot, one of the guards cleared his throat.

"Our orders are to keep you in the garden." One nodded to the other, "But your activities are your own, no matter how high in the garden it may be."

Kira turned around and ran to the largest tree in the back of the garden. She pulled the bow over her shoulder and proceeded to climb what she often referred to as the Old Man. In the branches of the ancient oak the human pulled herself onto a large comfortable branch that faced toward the front of the house. There was a gap in the thick branches. The leaves allowed the perfect view of the front courtyard and the valley below and unless someone had been here themselves, would never know its existence. The perfect view and the best hiding place.

The sound of a motorcycle roared above the walls of the garden. Kira positioned herself then saw staff members line the entrance of the Palace, the motorcycle in between two armored Suburban, many armed guards who bore colors other than the Palace. That would only mean their loyalties lie with a different house, but while their colors were different, the sigil on the guard's shoulder was that of the Imperial Family; the House of Tepes. From where Kira sat, the SUVs blocked the make and model of the bike. The rider wore a full helmet, threw their leg over and until she saw the familiar leather jacket Kira did not recognize her.

The rider removed helmet, her short hair undisturbed by the full-faced protection. Lady Carmilla stood at the top of the stairs. She walked down with heavy steps and a happy smile. This behavior was often when she greeted someone who either annoyed her or who had interfered in her affairs. Still she seemed happy to see the biker, annoyed, but still happy. *No...no, that can't be.* Kira's mouth dropped open. As she watched the two vampires enter the mansion, Kira rapidly climbed down and skipped several limbs before she jumped off the last branch to the ground. Kira ran as she tossed the bow to the side; Jake came out and was almost bulldozed by the human.

"Kira, wait." Jake grabbed her by the shoulders, "Before you go in, the one who came is--"

"Eona?"

They released Kira from the garden and she and Jake zoomed, with the vampire's speed, into her room then locked the door behind. Back and forth she paced she asked Jake again whether Emily had answered and again he tried to call her only for it to go to voicemail. She paced enough to make a dent in the carpet, and her heart rate sped up. Her neck bothered her as she pulled off the scarf and tossed it onto the couch that Jake sat on.

"How the hell did I miss it!" Kira questioned with great frustration. "I saw her! I talked to her last night, and I didn't even know! How the fuck--!"

Jake rubbed his head, "Hey don't be so hard on yourself I didn't even realize it was her."

"You didn't even see her!" The human argued against.

"Okay." Jake held his hands up in surrender. "Okay, so she's back; I mean Lady Carmilla *is* her aunt it's not exactly unusual for family to see each other. Just..." He rocked his head side to side, "This family happens to... have similar tastes."

Kira shot a very nasty and threatening look at him. The hairs on the back of his neck rose.

"She hasn't been back in five years." Kira gestured as she calmed her tone, "Hell, she stopped talking to me altogether three years ago."

"Then why are you freaking out?" The man shrugged a sigh, "Okay, so Eona is kinda your ex--" He bit his tongue when she saw Kira open her mouth to shut him up, "It's been five years! People change, people grow up, grow out of certain things you know! I mean vampires are different, we kinda..." He scratched the back of his head, "Bond for life--" Jake realized his rambles did not help and stopped, "But you're fine, its not like you're Mates, you're like friends-with-benefits with Lady Carmilla..."

Jake looked at the panick and guilt on Kira's face.

"Unless she knows..." He stopped himself and stood, "Nope! Nope, don't tell me; I don't know what you don't tell me!"

The human woman finally dropped on the couch where her friend once sat, and grabbed the side of her head and before she pushed back. *Please let this just be me overreacting.* She remembered the warm peck on her cheek, the fuzzy rest that lived on her even now. Surely, Eona did not recognize her either. She asked for Kira's name. She could actually not have recognized or remembered the human. In a perfect world, it was just coincidence. Eona was just trying to hook up with someone and it was a human; which is her type... apparently that runs in the family.

Clearly Lady Carmilla did not like Eona's sudden return—she though back, Kira wondered if that was who she was meeting with yesterday. It would make sense, but there she went again: jumping to conclusions. That was not how she survived, how she won the Game. Facts, facts save her, facts and the skill to navigate the complicated relationships that are immortal society. She could emerge out of this unscathed, with her life and status as a human intact. She needed to be calm and composed, to be the quiet submissive to her vampire master. Survival here is what mattered, not the events of the past.

They were children back then, and people changed in five years. Clearly Eona did... otherwise Kira would have recognized her... but did she subconsciously? She felt unusually calm and relaxed around her, safe even amid the bar's chaos, so maybe she really recognized Eona, but her brain had not caught up with her body. *No, wait, that doesn't sound right.* Kira groaned in frustration.

41

"What's the gameplay then?" Jake asked, looking at his phone.

Kira dropped her arms in her lap with a loud *clap.*

"I don't know." She sighed, already exhausted from the stress, "Obviously Lady Carmilla knows something is up, otherwise she wouldn't have kept me in the garden when Eona came. Safe bet is probably to just avoid being alone with Eona; stay glued to Lady Carmilla's side, so she doesn't suspect anything."

Jake agreed, "What are the chances that Eona still wants to be as close to you now as you two were then?"

"I do not know." Kira rubbed her aching neck, her hand covering the hot markings, "But if Lady Carmilla gets upset over me, then I'll be killed or worse."

"I honestly wouldn't be concerned about that." Jake said nonchalantly, "Think about it, if she wanted to kill you she would have already and probably years ago. Although it would be interesting to see a jealous Lady Carmilla."

"Thanks." Kira glared at him with dagger-eyes, "Real comforting."

The vampire chuckled, "You know what I just remembered?"

"Oh, enlighten me." Kira growled sarcastically.

"You know who else is here since Eona is? Your favorite person: Wolfgang!"

Kira fell over onto the couch, grabbed a pillow and screamed into it. Jake listened as she muffled a yell of something in between of 'that fucking asshole' or 'fuck that fucking asshole'; something along those lines. The Royal Protector, Wolfgang, was the senior most commander of the personal protection detail of the Tepes Family and Bloodline. He protected the previous head, whom Kira knew very little about, save for her being Eona's mother, and now he protects Eona.

Normally he would have stayed beside the current head of family, but considering their relationship... Wolfgang went with the Pureblood Princess when she departed. He was less a fan of humans than the general vampire population put together, he believed them to be weak, greedy insects by nature. He did not care what humans did so long as it did not involve vampires, which had Kira's presence in the palace an eyesore for sure.

A knock on the door was a servant calling for Kira. Jake opened the door, and the butler entered.

"Her Majesty calls for your presence." He said with nervousness.

Jake leaned against the door. "How bad is it?"

The butler turned to Jake. "No one enjoys being caught by surprise."

"Her majesty, even less than most, got it."

The butler nodded, turning to Kira, "I suggest you make haste, she... will not want to be kept waiting."

Kira shot up and sprinted, grabbed her scarf rapidly wrapped it around her neck—Jake lifted her into his arms and nearly instantly moved them to the throne room, they stopped just outside the side door. Kira fixed herself best as she could. She was still in her training attire and looked less than presentable, but Lady Carmilla would not be unhappy if she knew Kira changed for the 'unexpected' arrival of a guest. Jake gave a thumbs up. Not being summoned himself, he knew better than to enter when not called for.

The throne room was massive in the East Wing of the Palace. Its massive hall was open, cold stone support pillars lined the far sides of the room carved out of the mountain sections of the Palace were carved from. At the back of the room, where Kira had entered from a side door, was a large staircase ascending to the stone throne where the monarch of the vampire world sat. There Lady Carmilla sat, her golden dress pouring over a few of the steps where she had come from. She finished tasting a glass of blooded wine, setting the glass on the stone arm rest as she spoke.

"Ah, Kira, my dear, come join me." Her Majesty Lady Carmilla Tepes beckoned.

43

Though they saw another off the corner of their eyes, Kira dare not look. She bowed her head to the royal Pureblood Vampire and kept her eyes down as she climbed the stairs and arrived at the throne in moments. Lady Carmilla smiled, pleased. She looked at Kira's leather armguard and finger tab, which showed much wear and use. The sign of a hard worker and someone who practiced a great deal. She could only imagine what for.

Dressed in a single-sleeve athletic shirt and shorts, Kira wore this for practicality when training, her weighted vest over her chest and forearms to increase her overall strength and stamina. Though Lady Carmilla did not care for Kira to grow overly muscular, she was happy to allow her pet to have athleticism. Stamina is a human's greatest asset.

"How was your practice fair?" Asked the vampire.

Kira smiled. "Very well, my'lady, though... I had a bit of a hangover. I still beat Jake." That last part was a lie, but as she wore sunglasses it helped to make it a convincing lie.

Kira had long practiced the art of deception. Though not even she could get any significant lies past the Empress. Minor, innocent white lies were easy to get away with. At least as far as she could tell.

Lady Carmilla chuckled, "It often amazes me how humans can excel at things beyond a vampire. Wouldn't you agree with Eona?"

The human's heartbeat increased. Kira turned to see the vampire below, then felt the Empress's hands around her waist, like a serpant slithering around its meal to come.

"You remember my niece, Eona, don't you? You two grew up together for some time when you were younger." Reminded Lady Carmilla.

She kept the storm of her emotions at bay and bowed slightly. "I do. It is good to see you, Lady Eona." She knew exactly what Carmilla was doing: 'she is mine'. Just like an Alpha predator, she marked her territory and challenged this known predator to dare lay claim to her property. When Eona was younger, she never dared raise a hand to her aunt. She obeyed, did what was told and expected of her. When her aunt brought home a human girl around her age, she told Eona to become friends with her, to teach her and protect her from those not of the Tepes bloodline. Eona thought her aunt brought her to be a playmate, but she did not want to play when she was extremely vicious when Eona first approached.

It took time for the human to be near Eona, to even utter a word or two other than a hateful way of saying 'vampire'. Eona had asked Doctor Sanders, the first one to successfully tame the beast, how she could understand just a little of the reason for the human's resentment. Carmilla told her to name the human as she wished and as she refused to tell it herself, not that it mattered. Eona thought long and hard and consulted Doctor Sanders about what to name the girl, a name not to mock, not to pity, but something she could grow to be proud of.

"I am curious. You never specified why you came back. I thought you enjoyed the European Territories?" Lady Carmilla asked, moving her hand and stroked Kira's lower back.

Eona nodded. "I did promise I would come back after my studies were finished. As much as I loved the countryside, I missed you and my home." The younger Pureblood continued, "With the growing conflicts with the *Reich,* I thought it best to return and lend my help."

The Reich? Kira wondered, she heard the name in conversations passing, but knew little more than them being a faction of vampires led by a rogue Pureblood. Apparently, they had caused more trouble and stir even before the vampires declared war on humanity almost twenty years ago.

"And we always welcome you to your birthplace with open arms. I wish you would have notified me sooner. I would have planned for you." Lady Carmilla said with a sigh, her hand slipped to Kira's back and under her shirt where her fingers brushed Kira's bare skin.

45

Kira did well not to make it obvious, but the redness of her face was something beyond her control.

"I wanted to surprise you." Eona said with an innocent smirk, as she started the Game, "Besides, I wanted to ride my bike, can't do that and surprise you easily."

Lady Carmilla grew tired of the conversation. "I imagine not. Shall we continue this over dinner this evening? You must be tired from your journey and no doubt you are eager to explore your home."

Eona agreed, saying she would head to her bedroom in the meantime. She left the throne room which only Kira and the Empress remain. *Oh, I have a bad feeling about this.*

"Finally." The Empress pulled Kira into her lap, and had her meet the crimson eyes of the vampire, their faces inches apart.

Kira straddled the other woman unexpectedly. Despite the stiff, cold stone of the blocky throne, Kira could have her knees pressed on both sides of the immortal and propped herself partly raised by the bounce of her legs. She blushed anytime she was in this position as she was not used to looking the Empress directly in the eyes. How things went between them meant this was not a normal position.

"You have been awfully quiet." The Empress purred into Kira's ear, her hands reached around Kira's waist and firmly grabbed her butt.

The human averted Carmilla's intense eyes.

"Are you concerned about Eona's return?" Carmilla asked.

Kira shakily replied, "Why—would I—be?"

Carmilla's hands traced the human's inner thigh. Causing the girl to quiver.

"Y-you are the master of this house--" Kira shrugged to hold back her voice.

"It is good you remember that." Carmilla said as she pulled off the scarlet scarf and let it drop on the ground.

On Kira's exposed neck were pulsing vessels filled to the brim with her sweet blood. Beneath her tender flesh was the crimson currency of life, and this human had the most delicious of them all. The smell of thick cherry blossoms is a delectable nectar that only the finest quality blood may produce. How amazing it was that such blood became produced by a human woman with no immortal lineage. Not that it mattered whether or not she did. The highest quality meals belonged to the Empress and her alone, as was her right to rule and that would not be denied to her.

Carmilla brought her lips closer to Kira's neck. Her tongue ran across a major artery from the human's collarbone to the middle of her neck. Kira fought to keep her voice down. She braced herself against the Empress's chest and tried to keep herself up as the vampire's hands and tongue slowly traced the lines of her body.

"Never forget who you belong to." Growled the vampire, one hand came up from under her arm and reached across to grab Kira's neck as her other hand slipped between the woman's straddled legs.

A sharp inhale signaled the failure of Kira's strength. Unable to hold herself up, she collapsed her weight onto the Empress, her legs shook as the other woman's fingers pressed between the damp lips.

"You—are—*mine*." Carmilla's honey-thick words entered Kira's ear surged throughout her body. The immortal's mouth opened as pearly fangs extended, moments from enriching herself with the other woman's nectar before a knock on the throne door interrupted.

Kira panted and shook on Carmilla's lap and was mere motions away from coming undone.

"Carmilla..." Called Kira in a desperate plea.

As much as it pained Kira, Carmilla was equally restless from being unable to finish. The elder eased the younger back and brushed her thumb over the straddled woman's bottom lip.

"Tonight, do not expect to sleep in your chambers." Carmilla whispered again as she eased Kira off her lap.

Kira retrieved her scarf, the servant nodded in obedience the left out the side door as hungry eyes watched every step, listened to every heart beat until she was out of range. Once away, Kira, out of breath, stopped in the hallway then leaned against the wall to regain some of it. At the very least, to lessen the heat it threw her into. *I hate it when that happens*. Kira cursed. Even if it was survival, that was the pleasant part of it, at least much better than what other masters would put her through.

It was pure coincidence that Carmilla found out about her, and Kira's, shared orientation. Not hidden as a secret, Carmilla herself had shared her bed with men and women alike, which she had been famous for in time past, apparently. The Empress learned of Kira's preference in women when she had passed the bar where Kira, Jake and Emily frequented when Kira turned eighteen. While taken out of context, what Carmilla had actually seen was a truth or dare bet between a friend of Jake's and Kira. The two women won free drinks for the rest of the night.

After that, Carmilla started her pursuit of Kira until they were where they were today. Unofficially, by vampire standards, seeing as they had not killed yet her, Kira was the sole concubine to the Empress. The longest standing one for certain. In the past Carmilla had a reputation for being a Praying Mantis of partners. Kira was different, though. Kira endured no mistreat nor abused and was neither discarded nor killed. So long as she obeyed and did what was necessary to survive, Kira believed she would live quite a long life for livestock. That is... until Eona decided to suddenly show up. Hours went by, the night went on and many retired early. It was the weekend, but all engagements, significant events and any meetings under the narrative of Eona's arrival became postponed. An excuse was all it was. As the activity of the Palace died down, Kira left her room. She walked down the hallway and jumped when she was Eona stood against the wall, her arms crossed.

48

"Good evening, Lady Eona." Kira bowed her head slightly.

"Guess I don't need that name after all." The blonde-haired woman chuckled lightly, but her humor had no effect on Kira, "Come on we're friends, don't start with that 'Lady' shit."

Kira put her hands in her pajama bottoms, her top covered by a silky, thin robe. She kicked an imaginary rock, "You knew my name, there was no reason for you to ask." She said as she ignored Eona's last statement.

Eona shrugged, "I was hoping you'd recognize me and realize I was messing with you." She said, a little disappointed.

"Forgive the memory of a *human*. You changed from the last time I saw you." Kira apologized formally, mockingly.

"Likewise." Eona frowned, "You and my aunt were never that... *close*."

Kira huffed, "Things change."

"Apparently. Attire for late night strolls for one." Eona appeared in front of Kira and looked up and down the shorter woman, "I never took you for the silky lingerie type."

For a moment Kira contemplated whether or not to tell her off, to throw in her face years of anger directed and caused by Eona. She decided against it, at least for now.

"Maybe if you had stayed, I wouldn't have been."

She walked past Eona and reached her destination a few yards later at the last door the vampire wanted to see her enter. Without a second glance at the other vampire, Kira opened the last door at the end of the hall and entered. Inside, she found herself in the Bed Chambers of the Empress, a cozy, comfortable room filled with the finer things life offered. Expensive Egyptian cotton with velvet sheets, many aged wines, a fireplace; luxury furniture made by the best of carpenters; even the drapes were a thick velvet that blocked out all light. A large TV hung over the fireplace, a comfortable couch the perfect distance to warm and illuminate a room. In the far corner was a large master bathroom, complete with a large tub and glass wall in a shower. It had three shower heads.

The bed itself was custom, large and sturdy. They bolted it to the ground and wall for stability, but the bed's structure still allowed for some motion. At each of the four bedposts, to include an additional one at the center of the headboard; something built seamlessly hardware into the frame for ease of use and access. Though... use was only on special occasions, Kira doubted that would be on the list of *her* preferences. At least not tonight.

Kira looked to the fireplace and saw the Empress as she sat in a lone chair and held a glass of red wine that lacked certain *additions*. She had watched the human since she entered the room and patiently waited for her arrival, though expected a later arrival. Someone must be eager.

Chapter Four
Complicated Relationships

Carmilla sat on the bed. The small human curled close to her. Poor dear was worn out by their adventures that she fell so deep in sleep, not once has she stirred. The vampire smiled greedily, her slender fingers traced the woman's shoulder. Evidence of their activities decorated Kira's body like seasoning on a meal. Markings that made clear this woman belonged to another, something certainly on Carmilla's mind as she made them in the night.

Usually she would not have gone this overboard. The vampiress was truly quite subtle in her bedroom life. Not that she cared what other people thought, but simply did not care to have people gawk and stare at her possessions, no matter for what reason. Last night, however, one had eyes for what was hers. Yes, Eona's interest in Kira has clearly not changed and while in her niece's absence it did not matter, her presence now, was certainly an annoyance.

Kira turned over in her sleep, her bare back to Carmilla who now had a view of part of the human's scars. The four raised discolorations on her shoulder healed well since their unfortunate creation. The markings on Kira's neck too were visible, a slap in the face to the Empress of the one time she had the human out of her sight. Despite the setback, it worked wonderfully in her favor, a situation easily manipulated that resulted in the eviction of an obstacle with little effort. It aided in the long run as well—no matter how many times Kira was bitten, even by a Pureblood she would not turn.

In the short-term that boded well for Carmilla, but of course, with humanity came mortality to several causes. Disease, injury; the Empress intended for this one to live as long as possible, so long as she remained hers, at least. With consideration of Kira's actions and willingness, she had a petty concern for that before, but now... Carmilla wondered if Eona's presence would cause a fracture in that devotion.

Kira was no fool however, despite her attempts at concealment, the Empress knew many things. She was smart enough to know how to survive. Despite being a human, she had also done well at navigating the Game. While being in the Empress's bed had many political and...pleasureable advantages, what was absolute was the unsaid protection it created. No one would dare lay a hand on the Empress's property, no one at least who valued their position or life.

Eona was a different story because she was Tepes Blood, the daughter of the former Empress; Carmilla's younger sister. The current Empress could not send her away and she would never seek to harm her. Frankly, Eona was her beloved niece and she loved her like her own daughter. Despite public opinion Carmilla loved her family and though her younger sister gained the throne originally it was not as though the current Empress even wanted it. Eona and Carmilla were very close, but the incident five years ago caused a drift for personal and family reasons.

A light knock on the door annoyed the Empress. She moved out of bed, careful not to wake Kira as she dressed in a robe. When she opened the door, she found one of her advisors, Galen, an aged Ex-human whom Carmilla turned to long ago for his skills, leadership and prowess in warfare. Her devoted and loyal servant, that was even without Absolute

52

Rule, this man would never betray her. He came with information about the *Reich* others were not privy to—a letter sent by one of her many spies.

Galen glanced inside, past the opened door and saw the human asleep in the Empress's bed.

"Shall we continue this somewhere more private?" He suggested.

Carmilla shook her head as she read the note, "No, she's asleep. When did this arrive?"

"I just received it less than twenty minutes ago; I was reading it on the way to you. What is your will, my Empress?" The ancient warlord asked with a small bow of his head, "If this information is to be believed, even our SpecOps division will make no difference."

Carmilla shook her head as she ushered Galen inside. "I scarched every hole, every crack and found no sign, no evidence of he or his followers. How could he return without even a whisper?"

"Perhaps more are loyal to him than we initially believed?" Suggested Galen, "We always knew he had many followers in the past."

Carmilla nodded, "Yes, but the mass majority were executed, not that my sister bothered to listen to me when it came to looking for any remnants."

"What if the stories are true? What if he truly cannot be killed?"

Carmilla hissed slowly, "Anyone can be killed."

"We thought he was." Galen pointed out.
The letter was closed, and a match struck, burning it into nothing.

"Keep this between us for now until we have evidence. No matter my power or position, if I do not have all the Council with me, it will be difficult to amass the resources and labor in a short amount of time." Carmilla commanded, "I will not make the same mistake as my sister. I will not lead us into ruin, we will not fade, we will emerge stronger than we have ever before."

Galen bowed, "We already are because of your Majesty. No more hiding in the shadows of man, no more going around their rules. This world belongs to the Vampire, to the Tepes family. This I will give my life a thousand times over to ensure."

With a smile, Carmilla thanked Galen and he left the room. Kira kept her eyes shut, continued to pretend to be asleep because she would be likely be in a lot of trouble if she heard something she should not have. Who were they talking about? Who was so powerful that Carmilla was frightened of? How dangerous were they to threaten vampire-kind and if so, why not tell the others? If they were an enemy of the vampire... were they an ally of humanity? Could they turn the tide? Could they save humanity from enslavement? Within those thoughts, an uneasiness came as an idea. *Would Eona be safe?*

The bed behind her sank some. Carmilla had returned, and she felt the immortal's hand on her neck. Her cool palm eased the heat the markings made. This heat has grown the last few days and dried out her throat. Kira nearly sounded in complaint at the vampire's removal of her hand until she felt a rustle as Carmilla came closer. She gently turned Kira onto her back. The human did not dare open her eyes: and played that she was asleep made no movements.

For a moment she heard nothing, but then a strange sound, a puncture of something, sounded. The sound made when something sharp stabs or presses into something soft, organic... the sound made when Carmilla bites into Kira. But she felt no pain, nor pleasure, so what did the Empress bite into? She felt Carmilla touch her mouth with her fingers, then felt the vampire press a kiss against her. Something else... something warm, liquid. Kira could not control the race heartbeat created by her panic, but she knew how to play it off.

She pretended to stir awake. Carmilla was close to her face as she withdrew and wiped her mouth with her sleeve. Kira blinked a few times to clear her vision. A real yawn escaped

"Carm..." Kira mumbled as she rubbed her eyes, "Do you need..."

"It's alright." The Empress chuckled when she eased Kira on her back after an attempt to sit up. "Go back to sleep."

With a lazy nod, Kira rolled toward Carmilla as the vampire pulled the blanket over Kira's shoulder while she shut her eyes and tried to go back to sleep and forget what she saw on the Empress's sleeve. *Blood.*

With a blown puff of smoke, Emily held the cigarette in her mouth when she sat below Kira.

"You're certain?" The doctor clarified while she visited after she saw a very veague message from Kira earlier.

Kira nodded. "It couldn't have been anything else. I just don't get why. I mean, what does she gain from giving me blood? I haven't told anyone about the symptoms."

"This is the Empress we are talking about." Emily deduced when she gestured to her own neck. "She knows more than she lets on, much like yourself."

With a frown, Kira refused to believe Lady Carmilla had any knowledge of her recent symptoms. She has given no sign, has told no other besides Emily, and Emily is the one vampire she knows she can trust to beat Absolute Rule. In the past couple weeks, ironically since Eona's return, the pain, burning sensation and dry throat had persistenly increased. Initially, she believed it to be her imagination maybe lingered effects of her nighttime escapes, or simple stress, but Emily dismissed them all.

"You don't think it's the Stigma, is it?"

Panic set in.

The markings on the left of Kira's neck were not an ordinary tattoo. The cross-enjoy inking with four daggers into

55

each corner surrounded by long diamond-shapes, one attached to the circle in the center, making a keyhole shape. This tattoo called the 'Stigma' was a special and ancient technique that controlled ex-human or insane vampires from going on rampages or becoming Bingers. Though the technique is rarely used in the modern day, it was used heavily, especially when ancient Pureblood created mass armies of newborn vampires and needed to control them. Changed from its original purpose, this Stigma is the sole reason Kira has remained human.

When Kira was sixteen, an unknown Pureblood attacked and bit her where the Stigma now laid. For a human, being bitten by a Pureblood meant becoming a vampire, but Carmilla wanted to avoid that, so she commissioned the doctor and her experimental technique and the results were satisfactory.

"Are you doubting my ability to keep you safe?" The doctor asked.

Kira quickly apologized and assured her that was not what she meant. Emily told Kira that they have tested her technique many times and the success of its purpose was indisputable. The only thing that could fault its effectiveness is if someone intentionally tampered with it. Lady Carmilla's blood in truth should cause the Stigma to be stronger, not weaker. Something else, something internally might be interfering.

"You think *I* could be causing it?" Kira asked

Emily and Kira walked into the garden. "You know, this is the first time you have ever asked about the Stigma."

Kira shrugged, "I didn't care until now. I'm human and that's what matters, but if something is wrong..."

"The original version of the Stigma acted as a type of contract between a Pureblood and their vampire servants. While a Pureblood's inborn ability to control a vampire lies with Absolute Rule, there are ways to fight against it or even the involvement of a different Pureblood's order." Began the doctor's explanation.

The original Stigma ensured that the contracted Pureblood's orders were not overwritten and gave true control of an individual to them. Whenever activated, the vampire had no free will, but this was mainly to ensure a vampire did not go rogue and either betray their master or succumb to insanity for several reasons. It helped to prevent unnecessary bloodshed, but a mass decline in its use occurred over the years as the vampire population became lessened. People did not get turned as often and some immortals choose death over eternity.

Doctor Sanders took the original Stigma and used it as a base for a different Stigma, a 'lock and key'. It suppressed vampire powers useful for containment, but also to prevent a human from being turned. Of course, the ladder was less likely. Most humans who were turned before the war did so willingly. The previous Empress had strict rules about adding to the population and most did not disagree. Competition in the Game was fierce enough as is without adding more to the pot.

"So if the Stigma was unlocked, then I could turn?" Emily hesitated to respond, "Think of it like cutting out a tumor, but in this case, since yours can't be cut out, it's like putting walls around it instead."

"But some tumors can spread..." Kira tilted her head curiously.

"Some, not all. The Stigma is fulfilling its purpose, that's what matters."

Kira noticed the doctor did not give her a defiant yes or no. She chose not to push.

"As for the Empress, I imagine she wants to control the Stigma, or influence your vampire because I refused to give her the key." Emily said with a puffed prideful chest. It made her patient laugh. That sounds like something Carmilla would do. She cannot stand when something was not in her control. Especially if it belonged to her. Why go through all this secrecy, though? She was the Empress, Kira's mistress; she could do whatever she wanted and the humans would have no power to stop her. *That's not the only reason blood's passed though.* She though to herself as she remembered things Jake had taught her, things she had learned about the vampire.

It did not explain her increasing symptoms, though, it left her with more questions than answers. Emily knew Kira was unsatisfied with their conversation, but knew there was nothing more she could say in the lion's den unless she wanted to raise an alarm. Whatever spies the Empress had sent to monitor Kira and her, they would learn nothing of value other than a woman's curiosity and maybe her skill of appearing asleep.

Suddenly Kira turned around. Emily stopped and looked behind to see Eona as she rounded the corner. *I didn't even sense her.* The doctor glanced at Kira.

"Doctor Sanders, it's been a while!" Eona exclaimed with an enormous smile as she walked up to the two of them.

Emily put out her cigarette butt, then pulled out another one before she lit it.

"It has." An exhale of smoke followed the doctor's words, "Five years? You've grown. I seem to remember you wearing dresses, not riding bikes."

Eona chuckled, "Dresses were always my mom's thing, not mine. Besides, it's hard to wear a dress when you do as much traveling as I do."

"Hm." Emily sounded without interest, "Indeed." She turned to Kira, "I'll see you later. Text me for once, will you?"

"Phone goes both ways, you know."

Both women gave Kira an odd look.

"What?" She shrugged as she walked away. "It's not like I've had the same phone for almost ten years."

"Ouch." Emily chuckled at Eona, "She *really* hates you."

Eona sighed, "Subtly isn't her strong suit."

Emily turned and walked to the exit of the garden, "You have no one to blame, but yourself. Which also means only you can fix it." Emily waved. "Good luck with that. Kira isn't known for her forgiving nature, not that you would know."

Kira heard her name called, but ignored it and walked quicker as she heard the caller some closer.

"Leave me alone Eona, I'm too tired to deal with you."

It was the middle of the day and few people were awake. Eona was the opposite of the rest of the house; she enjoyed being awake during the day, to walk in the sunlight, often taking rides to the city on her bike just for the hell of it. She rode an older bike, built herself it was a combination of *Harley-Davidson, Royal Enfield* and *Triumph*. Together they made a street bike around 1400cc in power. Not that Kira bothered to remember, but she overheard Eona when she talked about it to one of the staff who also rides in passing. Instead of talking to a staff member, or another vampire, she persistently tried to be alone with Kira. Not that she had been successful until now. She was just as careful as Kira, not wanting to draw attention from her aunt, the Empress. The day was once the only time Kira had to call her own, now overruled by yet another entitled Pureblood. Worst of all, they were close at once.

"I can't imagine why." Eona shot out as a response, a direct, 'I know what you do at night.'

Kira stopped, turned and jabbed a finger at Eona's chest, "For your information, what I do is none of *your* business."

"Only *who* right?" Eona's sharp tongue fired back.

"Fuck you."

"Not until the first date, Doll."

Kira turned red and not from embarrassment.

"What do you want, Eona? You haven't spoken to me in three years. Why the hell are you trying so hard now?" Kira stopped, crossed her arms and tapped her foot impatiently, "Is that how prideful Purebloods apologize? Harassment?"

Eona frowned, "Last time I checked, you were the one who stopped writing —"

"Oh, don't you give me that bullshit!" Kira practically shouted, "I wrote a dozen times after you stopped replying and I never heard a damn thing! You cut me off!" She jabbed her finger into Eona's chest harder and caused the vampire to back up. "You're the one who left! You don't get to suddenly come back and think that we're just going to go back to being friends and all just like that! I'm not a vampire, I don't just get to forget and be merry, that's you, that's all you, not me!"

Kira groaned loudly, "You know I thought we were friends, I thought we were close." She shook, "I felt normal, I felt like a person, not a slave; I was able, for a moment, to forget the horrors you vampires put me through; then you just left! No goodbye, just a half-ass: 'I'm going to study abroad for a few years'. Do you have any idea how that made me feel!"

"I couldn't stay —"

"Why! I mean, I know I'm just a human, I'm just livestock to your kind —"

Eona stepped forward, "That's not at all what I believe!"

"Then why! Why didn't you tell me, give me an explanation, instead of making me feel it was my fault all this time!"

Kira panted, out of breath, her neck was on fire, her throat dry, she couldn't take it anymore. She stormed off. Jake, who appeared behind and shook his head as his friend ran inside, grabbed Eona. They remained in the garden by the Old Man, they used to climb as children. In the Palace they were the only kids as born vampires were not common. Jake was the oldest by a year, followed by Eona and ended by Kira who was the only one who knew her real birthday. As kids, Kira and Eona sometimes shared birthdays together because of how close they were, but often it was behind closed doors. Their own secret birthday celebration just the three of them.

Slaves did not get to celebrate their birthdays, sometimes they would forget their birthdays altogether. Though Jake and Eona never treated Kira as a slave, nor as less than them. She was their friend. Sometimes they even forgot she was a human and could not do what they did. Jake created snow in the ballroom, turning it into an ice-skating ring while Eona used her gift of air manipulation to push her and Kira around. They were not human and vampire, slave and master, they were children. But even children can learn the ways of the world.

Jake let Eona's arm go.

"You need to give her time." He advised.

"Every second I wasn't there, every year that passed was time she had to become entrapped by my aunt." Eona clenched her jaw, hints of her fangs showed through bared lips.

The Noble Vampire looked down, "Kira did what was necessary to survive."

"*Necessary*." Scoffed Eona. "It was *necessary* for me to leave and look where we are."

"It's different for her. We can't possibly understand her position or how she feels. We were never human." With shame at a cause he had no part of, but will haunt him all his life, Jake continued, "Kira watched her family be slaughtered by vampires, *our people*, made an eight-year-old kid see that. Every day is a battle for her survival. She has to do whatever means necessary because she knows in an instant they can kill her and is powerless to stop it."

The Pureblood Princess walked to the tree and felt the hidden carving. "So our friendship...is just a tool for her survival?"

Jake laughed, "You clearly didn't listen if you think that's true. Kira isn't angry at you for being a vampire, she's angry because her friend vanished without a word and left her alone."

"She had you."

61

"Yeah." Jake nodded, but not in agreement with the entire statement, "Yeah she did, but I wasn't the one that disappeared."

Eona huffed, turned around and leaned against the tree, "Kira said that I stopped writing and that she sent me a dozen letters after, but I got nothing. "

"So someone stopped your letters from reaching her and hers from reaching you." Jake scratched the back of his head, "That's a brief list."

"Two guesses who." Eona growled.

"Okay, so let's say it's the latter. She would have to have planned for years." Jake gestured, "If she had done that, she wouldn't have introduced the two of you in the first place and besides, they didn't become—intimate until Kira was eighteen." He shrugged, "I dunno Eona, that seems like a really roundabout way if that was her original intention."

She bobbed her head side to side, "I don't think it was the original intention, but certainly after she was bitten."

"Well, it's convenient when a Pureblood biting a human doesn't turn them. I mean, if keeping Kira human means so much to her, why did she bring her in the first place?"

"I dunno. Something's missing. My aunt is a bit of a traditionalist against humans, but she's not a sadist. Something is different about Kira. My aunt does nothing on a whim."

Jake rolled his eyes, "I really hate to say this, but... honestly, it might do more harm to Kira to separate them as things are. Your aunt has questionable morals, yes, but Kira is honestly doing really well, she's never once been mistreated by her."

"A kingdom of corpses is no kingdom I want to be a part of. And Kira is alive yeah, but as what, a sex slave? As a toy to a master; that's not living, that's not freedom; a gilded cage is still a cage."

Jake agreed with what Eona said, but tried to change things with words and pretty thoughts does nothing. Their society is to rule with power and Eona did not leave all this time, just to twiddle her thumbs. She went to learn, to train, to be stronger. If she wants to be a worthly Empress, she must prove her worth and challenge to the old ways is not a child's tantrum. Eona needed to prove that she is not only a force to be reckoned with, but has the support of her people, just as Lady Carmilla did when she began the war after the previous Empress's murder.

Kira was the innocent bystander in all of this, a human woman who tried to survive the new world order. If she so much as breathes wrong, she could be killed. Kira has her battles to fight. Her vampire counterparts have their own. For her sake, for her safety, Eona could not force a separation between her and the Empress because despite the two being family, the word of the Empress is indeed law. With, of course, a few holes, Jake has been more than happy to expose.

"First, I need to find out why my aunt is so fixated on her. It can't be just because of her blood."

Jake pondered for a moment, "Well, maybe it has something to do with Kira's past before I brought her here. I mean, are there any records of her parents? Maybe she had connections before the war started or her family did? She could be a bargaining chip."

"Considering we don't even know her real name, that's a possibility."

"Wait." Jake shook his head and arms. "Her real name isn't Kira Nightraven?"

Eona shook her head. "I don't think even my aunt knows. She refused to tell anyone so...Emily and I gave her one."

Jake was quiet for a time. "Damn. Good job. Remind me to ask you to name my kids when I have some."

Chapter Five
Failure to Save

She loosened the scarf and exhaled before she leaned forward, her knee bounced up and down as she waited anxiously. She had not expected this of herself to request such a thing. In fact, she was certain that if she was successful, her life would be in the greatest amount of danger than she thought herself capable of putting herself intentionally into. Whether Lady Carmilla would protect her was unknown, or even if this request of the audience would be taken seriously. But one thing was for certain, whatever Carmilla was afraid of Kira knew to be afraid of too and if she could get ahead of that fear and that unknown enemy, then she would survive yet again.

This, at the very least, she could work to get ahead of. An unknown enemy that she should not even know about; the question is how to deceive the Empress to accept without suspicion. Why her 'pet' was suddenly asked to know about the immortal's society, their workings, their plan; she would ask the Empress to put her trust into livestock. Kira hoped that her years as an obedient 'pet' would at least have her not question her motivations.

Perhaps she could be honest, to a degree. Omit some truth was not a lie, so long as they did not ask her directly. Even if suspicion was assumed, they had well versed Kira in innocent deception, a skill impeccable to her survival; at the moment, was being tested truly by Eona's presence. *This is the best way—if I can stay by Carmilla's side even when she leaves the Palace, I'll be safer than being here with Eona.* Kira thought to herself as the door opened. Three vampires left and passed her while only one bothered to glare at the human.

She heard her name from within; the door left ajar by the mistress's order as the others departed. Kira took a deep, nervous breath, her knees weak with anxiety and fear. If this went the wrong way, Carmilla could get the wrong idea about her intentions and all the years she spent to build a relatively good relationship would fall into shambles. *She has to trust me at least a little, but maybe I'm wrong, she's a vampire after all.* She did not want to have her name called a second time so Kira quickly entered the office.

She turned around and softly closed the door with one hand on the doorknob, the other braced on the door's surface. Whether it was courage, or stupidity Kira turned around to Carmilla. Behind the sleek, modern desk there were three holographic screens projected in front of her master. Though they were relatively transparent, Kira could tell the vampire's focus was not on her, which made her relax slightly, but also worried she would not be taken seriously.

Carmilla flipped through paperwork in front and to her side and alternated between the physical and the projected. For a moment she said nothing and thought Carmilla had either ignored her presence, or was otherwise occupied. Kira admitted she rarely saw the Empress at work, not on anything professional. Their time together often involved... less clothing and certainly less paperwork. As of late, Carmilla's summons of Kira to her bedroom had accumulated in number. Not that the vampire's consumption of the human's blood had. Why this was, Kira did not know.

"Your heartbeat is elevated." Carmilla said without looking at Kira, "It only beats this way when you are nervous."

Kira cursed internally. *Shit, I thought I could hide it.* Nervously, she tried to gather the courage to speak, but there was a lump in her throat. She was scared, terrified even of speaking to Carmilla in a manner that did not involve the human succumbing to the vampire's embrace. This was the first time she had attempted anything beyond that, and the instinctual fear of what the repercussions might be began to override her attempts at self-preservation in a new way. Carmilla noticed this. She stopped what she was doing and stood and came around her desk while she closed the distance between the two of them.

"What is it?" Asked the vampire, her hand gently Kira's cheek.

It barely calmed her.

"Lady Carmilla..." Kira clenched her fist, "I... I want to be of more use to you..." She finally managed to get out, "I... want to help you..."

A light chuckle came as the vampire used her finger under Kira's chin to raise her sky-blue eyes to meet her own crimson.

"What is it you wish to help me with?" She smirked, her voice low and smooth, "I am not thirsty, but my hunger for you is... constant."

Kira, normally able to control some of her reactions, quickly turned red.

"I-if that is what you wish..." she said and accepted that either she was not being taken seriously, or Lady Carmilla did not understand her meaning.

Not satisfied with the answer, Carmilla tilted her head curiously. There was something more she had come here to discuss. From the beginning, it was out of character for her to start contact between the two of them. At first, she thought it had something to do with Eona, but it seems she may have happily been mistaken.

"Satisfying our physical needs is not why you are here. Is it?" Carmilla asked out right.

Nervously and slowly, Kira shook her head as she averted her eyes. She was right to be nervous, to squirm under the vampire's touch, but this intrigued that same vampire. It was incredibly rare that Kira asked for anything, at least to the Empress directly, normally any of her wants and needs met by secondhand awareness and reports from other sources. It was the Empress's subtle way to win over the human's loyalty and affections, something more indirect than she would have gone for any other, but it was necessary.

She desired something more than a slave.

"What is it you wish?"

Kira bit her lip. "I want to learn." She finally forced out, "About vampires, how you rule; how you came to rule. I want to know you better."

"You wish to know *me*?" Carmilla asked with surprise, but it was apparent this was a pleasant surprise.

She smiled seductively as she whisked Kira's arm up and down, "But we know one another so well already."

The slightest touch was enough to raise the goosebumps on the woman's body, but there was something else in her eyes. Kira obeyed shyly, all orders and commands Carmilla gave in and out of the bedchamber. She melted in the vampire's arms at the lightest touch, the dirtiest words. Even the gaze of the immortal was enough to make the human weak in the knees. This time... Kira fought against her body's natural weakness to Carmilla and tried to keep firm.

"Lady Carmilla... I've been in your care for the last fifteen years, I've learned a lot, as a human in your world." Kira started and found her confidence, "I want to be of better use to you, that maybe somehow even as a human I can be useful."

Carmilla stepped back and leaned against her desk with intrigued. She thought of Kira's words for a few moments, but there was little to consider.

The Empress tilted her head slightly. "You are familiar with the Game?"

Kira nodded.

"Even for an Empress, the Game is an important tool to control the Council and Pureblood houses." Carmilla began, gesturing for Kira to sit in front of her.

It is called the Game because of the play of power between houses. Marriages, offspring, wealth and influence; these are things that drive a Vampire House to rise in stature. The highest, of course, are Purebloods, the purest of vampires, who have never had a single trace of human DNA within them. Therefore, their individual power is substantial, granting them abilities such as Absolute Rule: the ability to compel other vampires to obey all commands. Purebloods, the perfect vampires, are few, their rich blood and immense power sought after by lesser vampires.

In the immortal hierarchy next comes Noble Vampires, those who are born vampires either from other nobles or sometimes Purebloods. They are strong, having impressive abilities, though not as Purebloods. Following are Ex-humans, vampires born human and turned into a vampire by a Pureblood. They rarely exhibit abilities on par with that of Nobles Purebloods, but the exact understanding of what vampires can exhibit abilities is still inconclusive.

There is a level even lower than Ex-humans, one that almost any vampire can reach if they fall prey to their own nature. They call them Insane: a broad category those who have lost their minds by starvation, loss, binge-eating or contracting something from their prey. They have lost their sense of self and they overwrite their original personalities, devoured by their animalistic instinct to hunt, kill and feed. At their core, vampires are predators, after all. Once an immortal degrades to an Insane, they rarely return and are often hunted down and exterminated.

Carmilla looked at Kira's covered neck, protected by the scarlet scarf, "A human bitten by a Pureblood faces only two genuine options. Turning or dying."

Kira hesitated.

"But... there is also another type of vampire: any specific level does not classify them because it is more of a state of mind than physical. A vampire who goes into this state of mind is treated as incredibly dangerous and a threat to humans and vampire alike. We call them Demons."

Demons are immortals who give into their Desire, the predominate emotion of any individual vampire which can change, but often does not. It is a state a vampire allows themselves to fall into and is when they allow themselves to be controlled by their Desire or inner vampire. These personalities are often opposites of the immortal's original; usually, it becomes dominated by that single emotion. They do not just consume blood, but flesh, bone, vampire and human alike. Demons can be one of the most dangerous beings in existence, as vampires already feel emotions nearly ten times harder than humans. A Demon who becomes ruled by a single one can triple it.

Carmilla seemed saddened by their mentioning, "Vampires who become Demons... almost never return to who they were."

"They change that much...?"

Bounding her head side to side, Carmilla answers, "Some people are capable of change, while others... become who they were meant to be."

At age sixteen, Kira had lived many years in the Imperial Palace, she became close friends with Eona and Jake. They were the only ones within each other's age and played together often. Though the staff and guests showed their dislike, Kira's actions and reactions when guests were present were different, when they were alone and it was just the three of them, they were all equal.

Back then, Eona wore dresses and skirts. Her hair was long and silky. Kira would often sit behind her under the tree and braid it while Jake sat in the tree. There was nearly nothing the three did not do together. Eona and Kira were thick as thieves and caused a good deal of mischief. They were never caught, not with Eona's speed and Kira's knowledge of staff schedule and habits and worked as a stand-in during the summer vacation.

As they ran through the Palace they found every secret passage and hidden compartment in the ancient castle. They discovered secrets long forgotten or never known, but by the original architect. They would sneak out during the day, explore the river and forests above, followed the streams until they found the small lake a mile away, even though there seemed to be its own trove of treasures. Jake and Eona swam in the freezing waters, while Kira often stayed in shallow was and then they watched the sun set over the horizon, the creatures of the day retreat before the rulers of the night emerge.

They had small picnics, talked about everything and nothing, watched the clouds roll by, the seasons change, the city illuminates the valley. This special place, a cliff overlooking the palace beside the waterfall, was special, known only by Eona and Kira. There they camped for a couple hours, told other secrets, shared some memories of pasts neither would return to. It was easier to connect with someone when they shared the same pain of the loss of a mother.

Kira had forgotten the pain she suffered from all those years ago, forgot the daily struggle to survive for over two years when the war began. She forgot humanity lost; she forgot what she lost, and lived a life like a normal child would have. She and Eona were closer than others. Their shared interest in many things only brought them closer, which reinforced their feelings toward another.

That secret cliff was where they affirmed their feelings, but kept them in secret. Innocent people who only wanted to love and cherish another; there was no human and vampire, no master or servant, simply two people in love. Kira thought she could live a happy life, to grow up and the three of them would always be together.

That is what she thought.

One fateful night, a houseful of guests had the human safely tucked away in her room. They did not forbid her from leaving, but she had long grown into the habit of not being present with other guests. Originally, it was to avoid her becoming a meal of another vampire, but after a time, they did it as a force of habit than with a purpose. There were many times when she left with no problems before, the hunger in her stomach had her leave for the kitchen.

There were many more guests than Kira originally thought. She found she could not make it to the kitchen unseen this way and used a passage found in Eona's room. She had done this many times and saw as it was on the way back to her room; it was not a problem. On her way, Eona's aunt, Lady Carmilla's voice, echoed out.

Though Eona and Kira were close, Lady Carmilla was not someone she liked to be nearby alone. The Empress often had these eyes of hunger toward Kira, a desire she did not quite understand. She slipped into a nearby room, Kira silently backed away from the door and hoped that her presence would go unnoticed. The Empress's words were indistinguishable, but they easily recognized her voice, a chuckle as she spoke to another unknown woman. They stopped for a moment. Kira heard the door jingle. Her heartbeat quickened. The door opened partly, but it stopped. Lady Carmilla's voice was more easily heard through the ajar door, then it opened, the Empress was mid-kiss with another woman in the doorway.

Kira held her breath. The one vampire was too deeply engrossed in the Empress's arms she did not notice the human, but the Empress she did. It was not the fact that she saw two women kissing, but it was the confirmation of the rumors Kira had heard about the Empress's...affairs. Two crimson eyes locked on two stunned sky-blue, their intensity not angry, not violent, but inviting. That same hunger Kira recognized was present, but while the woman in the Empress's arms was focused on the Pureblood, they did not return her the same. It focused the Empress on Kira.

"Let's go to my room." Lady Carmilla said though at the moment Kira did not know whether she spoke to her or the vampiress the hung on her.

Carmilla stepped back and kept eye contact until she closed the door, their footsteps quickly faded as they went down the hall to the Empress's bedchambers. Kira exhaled loudly and sucked in replacement oxygen, breathless from more than just a lack of breathing. The human shook some, the intensity of Carmilla's eyes as unnerving as ever. *I hate when she does that.* She clenched her jaw and looked out to the moon that hung high in the sky through the window. She wanted to wait a little longer before she headed back. After a time Kira walked to the window to look down at the people below.

From behind, the door creaked. Kira turned—black took her vision. She was on the ground, and scurried back as she kicked her feet that slipped on the blood drenched floor. She forced herself back with one arm, her other clenched her neck hard. They pulled heat from her limbs. They grew cold as that same heat rapidly escaped her neck and coated her hand in its wetness. Kira Panted heavily as she struggled to keep her eyes open, her vision went in and out as she saw another person who stood in the shadows, their crimson eyes overpowered her identification of their face.

Pain burned at her neck. Her heart beat so hard she thought it would break from her chest. Harder. She clenched her neck, she coughed, spitting blood from her mouth as the wall hit her back. The sting and burn of pain shot up throughout her back, as her blood soaked her clothes and then stained the wall she leaned again. She had nowhere to go, no strength to fight. *I'm gonna die!* Kira remembered the helplessness she felt as she watched her family be massacred, remembered it was the vampire, remembered that she was human and that to them she was nothing more than food. *I don't want to be one of them!* Glass was beside her from a window she did not remember being broken. She reached for it, but her vision blurred.

She woke up in bed, her neck wrapped, Doctor Sanders beside her as she spoke to Lady Carmilla.

"Ah." The Empress sensed the awakening, "You mustn't move."

Kira ignored it and sat up, her neck screamed in agony, as though someone had poured liquid fire down her throat. She grasped her neck instinctively. Doctor Sanders eased her grip free and explained to Kira that she lost a lot of blood and became severely wounded.

"I—I—w-as—a—tat—cked!" She struggled to speak.

Lady Carmilla nodded, "Yes, a Pureblood attacked you, fortunately Doctor Sanders was able to stabilize you."

"Hey, hey, it's okay." Emily soothed when she came over and verbally talked Kira down, "You're okay, you're safe. I was able to prevent you from awak--turning." She said, "You're still human, but you shouldn't move in your condition. The Stigma is working, but you lost a lot of blood."

"St-igma—?" Kira tried to get up, Doctor Sanders tried to hold her down, "What—what does that mean!" She resisted, the doctor realized that Kira was about to become erratic and called for sedation, "What does that mean!" She shouted.

Lady Carmilla grabbed Kira by the sides of her chin and forced her to look at her, "Stop fighting." She commanded.

Kira glared. Carmilla grabbed her arm and stopped her from swinging. "Stop fighting and I will show you."

Emily hissed, "She almost died! You can't force her to obey, she's not your servant!"

"And you're not her mother." The Empress shot a dominating look.

The human breathed heavily, quickly, her useless resistance of the vampire subdued, her arm and face were let go. Carmilla reached to her neck. Kira hesitated and instinctively jerked back while she protected her neck. For once, the vampire did not force the human to obey. She grabbed a hand-held mirror instead off the dresser.

"See for yourself." Carmilla said. She held a mirror to the human.

Kira swipped the mirror and looked at her bandaged neck. Doctor Sanders slowly and delicately unwrapped her neck to reveal a crossing, dagger tattoo.

Kira left Carmilla's office with a sense of pride and victory. She had convinced Carmilla to allow her to learn of the government and was told that a part of these lessons would be done first-hand. Experience was the best teacher. Kira's attendance of social events would be a drastic change to her presence among those of the Game. They may see her as a threat, but a well-protected one. No one would dare raise a hand to the Empress's property, but the vampire must not show weakness. Many would take having Kira at her side as a show of favoritism.

While favoritism and the opinions of the Council mattered not to the Empress, their resources, assets and support did. They needed to remain united and avoid factions, avoid internal wars and struggles for power that their enemies may see as the moment to strike. Some may even take it that Kira is a soft spot for the Empress, a weakness. Though the truth of that must not be made known it nevertheless put Kira's life is in danger. It was her choice. Though Carmilla enjoyed she got to keep such a treasure to herself, she enjoyed the opportunities Kira's presence would bring. No longer would she have to keep her in the Palace like a secret, safe kept from others, instead she would be beside her and always within eyesight.

Outside, Kira felt a sense of nostalgia come over her and visited a place she had not in a long time. The old tunnels and passageways remained untouched by time, unused in her absence, but she remembered them like the back of her hand. She was above the Palace now, which overlooked the entire valley as the dawn came to greet the valley. This was her favorite time, her alone time, when the colors of the sun painted the skies a beautiful canvas.

She was not alone.

"I thought you forgot about our spot." Said Eona.

Andddddd there goes my peaceful morning.

Kira stood up from the cliff's edge. "Consider it yours. I was just leaving." She said in one breath, her words visible in the morning chill.

She passed Eona, but the other woman grabbed her by the arm and kept her from going any farther.

"Kira... I don't care about this spot, I care about you." Eona said.

The human looked at her arm. "Huh." She jerked free. "Could've fooled me."

Eona followed her back down to the wine cellar that saw little traffic. There they had privacy, uninterrupted, but too loud of raised voices and it would quickly grab attention. Especially in a house full of vampires. Yet in this house, the Tepes women were as different as night and day, and Kira was right in the middle. Between a rock and a hard place.

"Please, Kira, give me a chance —"

"To what?" The younger woman stopped, not bothering to turn around, "Not explain why you left? You know we never figured out who stopped writing to the other first." Kira's tone was mocking. She turned and leaned her back against one of the pillars to finally looked at Eona as she crossed her arms. "Do you even know what you put me through? Does your entitled, prideful, Pureblood, arrogance even comprehend the consequences of your actions?"

"I couldn't stay." Eona frowned. "After you were attacked...it's hard...for a young Pureblood to control their thirst. I was afraid I'd hurt you."

Kira blinked, "Hurt me?" She uncrossed her arms and marched right up to Eona and jabbed a finger in her chest, "You did more than hurt me."

Eona stepped back as an angry Kira advanced and explained, "I tried to protect you. I thought my aunt would leave you alone."

"This isn't about Carmilla!" Kira slugged Eona in the chest. "This is about *us*!" Kira choked on her words. "You weren't there! I needed you and you left!" She slammed both her fists into a cornered Eona. "I was alone and had no one to turn to! I almost died and the one person I was closest to, the one person I needed, abandoned me! *Carmilla* was the one who protected me, who saved me, not you!"

She beat her fists against the vampire. The intensity of her fists lessened as the woman's heartbeat raced and her legs weakened. Eona held her up and grabbed her arms which kept her from dropping to her knees. It was her fault, she left unexpectedly, just after Kira was attacked, but there was no choice and telling the truth was not an option, not yet.

77

"I'm sorry." Eona said.

Kira stepped back and pushed off Eona's chest. "You think you can come here and apologize, thinking everything —"

Eona grabbed the back of Kira's head and pressed her lips against the other woman. Her other hand grabbed the younger's waist and pulled her into her. Kira's arms froze in their place and her entire body tensed up as the vampire's tongue exploring the inside of her mouth. For a moment, they parted. Kira tried to catch her breath, caught in a spell cast by Eona. Again, Eona went forward, her lips plump and wet as her tongue assaulted Kira's own. It was intense, pure passion, different from lust entirely. It was deeper, hungry for emotion, for heart and mind.

It felt wrong.

Kira pushed Eona back and covered her mouth with a gasp. What the hell was she thinking, what the hell was she doing? *No, no, that did not happen! That can't happen!* Kira stepped back.

"I made the mistake of letting you go once, trying to protect you. I won't do it again."

Chapter Six
Health Hazard

As she laid on her bed, Kira crossed her arms and rested them over her eyes. She had a pounding headache, which persisted now for days that rarely had her out other than at night. A persistent dryness made her throat scratchy. She overheated routinely when she tried to sleep which led to many restless days. To her, fortunately, there was little activity in the Palace and even Lady Carmilla had not called for her presence for the last few days. She sent servants to give her books and records to study on. Kira was thankful that she had taken the human's request seriously. Though was surprised it was that the Empress allowed for it, she felt a little better knowing there was more than a physical relationship between them.

Despite her headache, Kira was happy to have something to keep her busy, to keep her mind occupied. Without distractions, every thought returned to the wine cellar, returned to Eona, to her lips, her tongue—and how different it was from when they were younger and how wrong it felt. Kira shook her head and huffed and tried to think about something else—that something else somehow became Carmilla. Heat crawled below her waist. *Fuck*. She groaned, as she crossed her legs, turned over and buried her face in her pillow. *Fuck. Fuck. Fuck. Why did she have to do that?* She clenched her pillow then yelled into it. *It was easier just to hate her.* When she turned onto her back, she stared at the glow-in-the-dark stars taped to her ceiling. *What the hell am I supposed to do now? She's not gonna stop and Carmilla will never let me go.*

Kira sat up and rubbed her throbbing neck. The Stigma felt hotter than her body. Her phone's screen lit up; a message from Emily:

U still feeling sick?

Calling what she feels 'sick' was a bit of an exaggeration, more of increased symptoms from their last conversation. It was worrying, but not something she wanted to describe over the phone. She did not want to leave a trail, leave evidence to cause worry... or a threat. The last thing she needed was for someone to plant a seed of doubt in the Empress's ear, or spread a rumor among the Game that threatens her position at the Empress's side. Kira held her head in her hands. *I need to be careful.*

She looked down at her phone, another message lit up the screen.

U alive there?

Kira chuckled and grabbed the phone as she typed her response:

Yes, to the first, barely to the second. Headache is killing me. Finished the meds you gave me already.

A minute later, Kira's phone buzzed with a phone call.

"I'm coming to get you. Be outside in half an hour." Emily said, the wind blared into the phone. She must be in her convertible with the roof down.

Kira grabbed her jacket and began to leave when she stopped and stared at the scarlet scarf folded neatly on her dresser. She sighed as she grabbed it. It was her safety blanket because of who it was from, no matter how much time passes or what they ever did. *I never could really hate her.* She wrapped it around her neck and went into the hallway, careful to shut the door silently. The moment the door closed, something dug into her back. Her scar burned, her neck was dry as a desert. She clasped her hand over her throat and nearly collapsed on her knees, but could prevent it by grabbing the doorframe. *What the—*

The sound of wood splintering caught her attention. Kira looked at the door frame and yanked her hand away. Wood broke, the wall partly indented which matched where her fingers were. A cold sweat went down her back. She stared at her hand, wide-eyed and without belief how she did that.

"Kira?"

The human shot up. Eona tilted her head as she wore concern on her face. Her eyes alternated from a frightened Kira to the wall at the back. Kira clenched her teeth then forced herself up before she fixed her hair and braced herself against the wall. Her breathing was heavy through her nose and she ignored Eona's calling. She took a single step—all the strength in her body was gone and she fell. Eona caught her just before she hit the ground

"Hey!" Eona exclaimed, about call for help.

Kira grabbed her arm.

"Don't you fucking dare." The human threatened, "Emily is already on her way—I just need to get to her. Don't say a word."

With mixed emotions, Eona nodded as she helped Kira to walk downstairs. The moment the car arrived, the vampire moved the human instantly to it, the roof already up and slid Kira inside first before entering herself. Emily's eyes widened. Eona made her intentions clear.

"Go."

In the hospital, they kept Kira in Emily's private office and patient room adjacent. Quickly she removed her shirt, to her reluctance, but Doctor Sander's orders, Eona helped her undress her upper body. It was the first time Eona had seen the Stigma, a substantial source of guilt and pain for her. Kira was right. No matter Eona's justification, she abandoned her friend and ran away. The woman's closeness to her aunt, their relationship, was because of her absence, and it was no wonder. Kira was a human alone in the Palace, nearly dying because of a vampire and then later cared for and comforted by the one person who could give absolute protection to her from others.

It was survival, Eona told herself. Kira had no choice but to accept that protection and the cost that came with it. Those feelings were only admiration, appreciation towards the one who protected her. Eona hoped to herself that if there were feelings between them, it was not like what they had shared. She hoped that those feelings between her and Kira had not disappeared. She did not think they had. After all, Kira constantly wore the scarf she had given her.

"Not a word." Kira growled, an ice blanket over her upper body.

Eona nodded silently.

Kira glared, "I mean it, not a fucking word to Carmilla or Jake.""

With a frown Eona said without strength in her tone, "Do you really think so low of me? I would never do that and I would never make you sick—"

"I'm not sick!" Snapped Kira angrily, "Carmilla did nothing this—!" She panted, "This is from the son of a bitch who almost killed me!"

Eona jumped at Kira's raised voice. Emily entered as she brought with her a couple of medication bottles, a black, label-less bottle, a glass of water, and a mortar and pestle.

"If you two are done bickering like an old married couple —"

Kira gave the obvious look of being pissed at Emily's comment.

"Relax." The doctor rolled her eyes. "It was just an expression. I can hear you down the hall, unless you want Carmilla to find out these stays between the three of us."

At the table behind Eona, the doctor set down her ingredients. From one jar came sugar. From the black bottle, the doctor tossed three condensed powdery cubes of coffee and an additive. She mixed them together in the mortar until a fine powder, she mixed the concoction into water and mixed until dissolved. Brining the glass to her eye for visual inspection, she turned to Kira, offering the glass to her.

"Take this, the symptoms should go away for a while."

Kira downed it in two gulps. Making a disgusted face, "Needs creamer."

The doctor laughed, "Well, there is powdered creamer, so that should do the trick. The biggest thing is the coffee with cubes with my secret ingredient." She said as she shook the black, label-less bottle, "I've never given it to a human before, but it's not deadly, just not meant for you."

Eona looked at the bottle suspiciously.

"It's a suppressant mixed with other synthetics." Doctor Sanders explained, "Helps reduce thirst, strength— think of it as a vampire ability nullifier, well, experimental. It's easy to make. I can have an entire pack for you by the end of the week. Just drop one or two in your drink and the symptoms will go away." She said when she rubbed Kira's back.

"It can't be that easy..." Eona looked to Kira, "How long has this been going on?"

"Only the last couple weeks, started just before you came back to the Palace." Kira shrugged. "But today... that hasn't happened before."

"So crushing a door frame isn't normal?" The Pureblood looked back to the doctor. "I thought the Stigma was supposed to stop her from turning."

Emily leaned against the table. "This version was experimental to begin with never done on a human. I had to do a lot of last-second adjustments from the original brand. Be lucky it worked as a tattoo instead of a hot poker."

Kira took off the ice blanket, her temperature had returned to normal, though now she was cold. Whatever that special ingredient was, it did the trick. She felt instantly better, like cold glacier water was going down her throat, like she was being rejuvenated from within and it spread throughout all parts of her body. She was grateful, especially with how miserable she had been for the last few days. However, if Emily said that she was human and would not turn, then there was no need for concern. Curing cancer is not a painless endeavor and stopping a human mid-turn from becoming a vampire had never been done before. She would take what she could get and be grateful.

Eona's fierce protectiveness of Kira was unjustified and it would win no favors from the human, but...it differed from when they were children. Back then, Eona always obeyed what Carmilla had said. The Empress was foremost her family and one of her only living relatives. She was girly and shy, but adventurous; this version of her, this woman was confidante, protective, and unwavering. *You really changed.* Kira dropped her head a little. *We both did, maybe too much for us to ever be like we were before.*

Kira felt a buzz in her pocket and removed her phone from her pocket, seeing a message from Carmilla:

Where are you?

She needed to think of a convincing lie, fast.

With Doc Sanders and Lady Eona at the hospital. Doc called to have a quick exam to give me a prescription to help with some problems.

It was better to ask for forgiveness later than be caught in a lie.

What problems?

Carmilla responded instantly.

"Uh, guys, little help here?" Kira ushered them over to her phone as she stalled with another quick message meant to sound shy:

It's... embarrassing to talk about.

They read the message that followed from Carmilla:

You never have to be embarrassed about talking to me when something is wrong.

Emily grabbed the phone. "Give me that." She said with annoyed disgust, quickly typing a response. Hitting send, she gave the phone back, "There, that ought to be good enough."

Eona and Kira looked at the phone and the response sent to Carmilla:

Cramping.

The Pureblood looked away with a mixture of embarrassment and laughter while Kira slugged Emily, "How the fuck did you know I was even on! It ended days ago!"

Emily shrugged, "Short version: moms know. Long version: Vampires, humans each have a particular smell and... taste. It changes subtly depending on the state of the body."

Kira blinked a few times, "Meaning..."

"The more turned on you are, the better your blood tastes." Eona chuckled and winked at the mortal.

Kira rolled her eyes. "Figured that much from Carmilla. Tell me something I don't know."

Emily and Eona looked at each other smiling, then in unison, "You smell like Cherry Blossoms."

A car from the Palace came and picked up Kira and Eona. Much to Kira's dismay, Carmilla was in attendance. Sitting across from her aunt and Kira, Eona watched out the window, seeing the city pass by.

"Are you feeling better?" Carmilla asked as she pressed her shoulder against Kira then gently traced circles on the younger woman's palm.

Eona averted an irritated glance.

Kira nodded as she shook like the paper bag with a small supply of what Doctor Sanders had on hand. If there were any more fits, she would be okay for a few days.

Carmilla smiled, and leaned over as she pressed her head against Kira's.

"Good, your health is very important to me."

A scoff came from Eona.

"Is something about that difficult to believe?"

Eona waved her hand, "A bit; you know, the healthier she is, the more you can use her as your sex slave —"

Carmilla raised her hand—Eona's face went to the side, slapped with full force—by Kira. Both women were surprised. The anger, the fury, the fire in her eyes—it was not a front.

"Don't you *ever* call me that!" Kira shouted, "Whatever happens to me has nothing to do with you anymore!" She dropped back in the seat. Just as they arrived at the Palace Kira slid out, slammed the door and marched towards the garden.

Carmilla and Eona both watched her until she vanished behind the walls and remained in the car. After a few moments, Carmilla crossed her legs and adjusted her skirt.

"Must you be so obvious?"

Eona ran her fingers through her hair, "Must've learned it from you."

The Empress chuckled as she shook her head, "My, you have changed. I remember when you would listen to every word I say, look up to me like I was your god."

"Until I grew up and realized gods didn't exist."

"Ah, but that is where you are wrong. They exist, but I am not one of them. No..." Carmilla crossed her fingers and hung onto her knee, "I am Empress, the matriarch of all vampires. Blood or not, this includes you and I do not appreciate when someone else's eyes, or puts their hands on my property."

Eona bared her fangs. "Kira is not property. She's a living person."

"True, but she is human, one who is well aware of her place in our society. She is far cleverer than you give her

86

credit for." Carmilla said lightly, a smile came over the vampire's lips, her pearly fangs showed through, "She continues to surprise me after all these years."

"What do you mean?" Her niece asked in confusion.

"She protected you, Eona." Carmilla said with a hint of amazement at the woman's quick thought and reaction. Never has she done anything this defiant, this bold; it was new and exciting.

"Kira hit you first because she knew if she hadn't your punishment from me would have been far more severe." Carmilla opened the door. "I will warn you just this once because you are my family: *Kira. Is. Mine.*"

Inside the garden, Kira drew her bow and sank an arrow into the center of the target. Two targets popped up. Kira drew, shot one, drew and hit the next. Another popped lower. She dropped to a knee, hit the target, spun around and hit the next one that was shot into the air. She could be happy or sad, angry, pissed off; scared and she would always hit her target. Her father taught them the way of the bow to survive; hunting, surviving, by any means necessary. Any means necessary was difficult against a vampire. The only way it could kill them was by destroying their core, and that was difficult to destroy with their regeneration.

Fuck. Kira shot again and again and again until her target was Swiss cheese. *Fuck*! Another. *Fuck*! Another. *FUCK*! The bow string snapped, the archer clenched her jaw so hard her teeth ached, her neck burned again. She breathed out a low growl escaped from the back of her throat. She marched back towards the front of the firing line, she threw the bow on the ground and grabbed another as she drew the string back. She eased the tension of the string, then dropped the bow. Her butt followed as she hit the ground.

God fucking damn-it! Why did she do that, why did she impede the two of them? That was a death wish. Why bother? There were no feelings she had for either of them; she could not have feelings. This was about her survival. They were vampires, Pureblood vampires who took her family from her, who started the vampire-human war and brought the apocalypse to humanity. To them, she was a slave, nothing more. She was property, a plaything; livestock. Her father taught them to hate the vampire, to curse them, to fight until their very last breath and never allow yourself to be a slave. To him, death was the better option. That was not an option for her. Never, death was an end, death was giving up.

Kira leaned back and looked up at the sky.

"How does your hand feel?" Carmilla asked as she down the stairs elegantly, as though wearing a gown and attending a ball.

Quickly the human rolled onto her knees and bowed deeply her head against the ground as the Empress approached, "Forgive me, Empress!" She asked, exhausted, "Hit your niece, I lost my temper and--!"

The shadow cast by the Palace lights over the Empress hovered over Kira. Normally, if she was being punished, it would be now. She would feel a shift in the Empress's tone, but it was not here. She dared not look up, not break this bow. She needed to accept the punishment, turning the other cheek because that was how she survived. That was how she would always survive.

"How does your hand feel?" Asked Carmilla again, "Hitting a vampire, especially a Pureblood I'm told to a human feels like hitting a rock."

Kira hesitated, unable to figure out how to answer. "I — " She flexed her hand—oddly enough it didn't hurt at all.

Was the punishment to break her hand? To cut it off? Carmilla has always been one for creative punishments. It would not surprise her creativity would easily cross over to cruelty.

"It... doesn't hurt...my'lady."

A chuckle followed. "Seeing as you expertly murdered your target, whose face you imagined for that, I wonder?" Carmilla took the bow from the ground and held it in her hands.

She pulled at the string. "Your skill with the bow is impeccable." Carmilla plucked the string once. "Will you teach me?"

Was this a joke? Kira was uncertain. Slowly she stood, mouth gaped open somewhat. Was this a test? Regardless, she knew she could not lower her guard, else she would find herself at the end of the range with a few arrows in herself. That would certainly be ironic. With a silent nod, she agreed, requesting the Empress to load an arrow and drawback on the string and hold it. Looking at her posture and stance... Carmilla clearly was already versed in archery, yet still asked for Kira's tutoring. The Empress's unpredictability was making her nervous. A few minor adjustments and Carmilla let the arrow fly it stopped in the bottom corner of the target.

"I never was one to use the bow. Swordsmanship was where I put my time and effort in. Long before the age of the firearm, of course." Carmilla offered the bow to Kira, "I do however, enjoy watching a master perform."

Cautiously Kira took the bow then loaded an arrow. "Lady Carmilla..."

"Carmilla will do just fine." The Empress corrected.

Kira lowered the bow. "I'm sorry for getting angry... I know I'm just a human, I know I'm your slave, but I... I can't stand to be called that."

The Empress looked at the target, "It is true, in the eyes of society, and of the Game you are a slave, however, truth is often more complicated than black and white."

"I understand that more than people think, even as a human." Kira sighed quietly.

"It is true our... activities, may appear that as a master and slave to an outsider, but I had hoped that is not what you believe." Carmilla inspected an arrow.

Kira looked at the vampire, then drew her arrow. She released it and hit the target center mass.

"Truth is often more complicated than black and white." Kira repeatedly lowered her bow. "But what I believe doesn't really matter in the end."

"I disagree." Carmilla held the arrow out to the other woman. "I find your opinion quite fresh and different. A human whose heart was so full of hate towards the vampire now shares a bed with their Empress so passionately."

Chapter Seven
Outside the Cage

"New York?" Kira and Jake said together as they paused their meals as Eona pushed off the doorway and entered the room.

"My aunt is meeting with the human representatives at the old United Nations facility then from there we're heading to Germany for a Council meeting." Eona explained as she reached past Kira and picked up grapes for her plate.

She reached for the vine between the two—a fork came between and without even looking Kira stabbed the vine and kept Eona from taking the whole bunch. The human has always been very territorial about food.

Kira then turned her from Jake to Eona. "That's neat and all; what does that have to do with us?"

"You're both coming with us."

Jake spit out some of his drink as a half-eaten grape dropped from Kira's mouth.

"That's a terrible idea for one of us—" He raised his hands to Kira, "No offense."

"No, I agree—Eona, you remember I'm human, right? Having me there is like attacking a raw steak to me and throwing me in a literal lion's den." Kira exclaimed in slight panic.

Eona shrugged, "Despite our difference of opinion, my aunt and I both agree you will actually be safer with us than remaining here."

That's a matter of opinion. Kira growled to herself, as she rubbed between her eyes, "Okay, so let's pretend for a moment that I'm not freaking out over this: how long are we going to be gone?"

"At least two weeks, depending how long the Council meetings take—those you won't be present for... obvious reasons." The Pureblood answered as she took a grape from the stabbed vine and popped it in her mouth, "Who knows maybe I'll get the chance to show you where I went to school."

Kira's expression softened. *I'll get to see where she was all that time? I've never even been to a university before, let alone left the country.* She thought more, staring at her plate. *When was the last time I actually left the valley?*

She remembered few details of her childhood, but Kira recalled vast forests a change with the season; beautiful oaks with yellows, reds, and oranges that floated down from their canopies. Cold winters when the two of them played in the snow just outside their secluded cabin. They ate the rations gathered in the previous season: smoked and salted trout, deer; canned jam made from blueberries; wild turkey. Her mom had taught them how to survive nature, how to trap; she was a country girl through and through, however her medical knowledge of herbs was even more impressive.

Those memories followed Kira into her sleep. The forests of changing seasons as she chased her other self. Down the paths of the woodland roamers, squirrels, and deer; animals who created their own way without leaving obvious signs they ran. In front of her, her target jumped on a rock, then pushed off it and landed in a pile of leaves. She followed soon after, and landed on top. Laughter filled the air as they rolled from the pile and stopped on their backs as the leaves fell from the treetops then floated around them.

She looked to her right and saw her face smile back at her and the sun twinkled like stars through the forest roof. They laughed together—the next second was nightfall. She reached for her other self, her back was to her as blood soaked them. Their mom struggled to speak as a vampire grasped her tightly in his arms, like a predator clinging to their kill. His fangs were so deep into her throat the youngest could not even see his mouth.

"R—un..."

Her eyes full of tears, she forced herself up and she grabbed the broken knife she ran at the vampire with screams. Another grabbed the child by her hair and pushed her into the ground with sufficient force to break her lip. She did not stop fighting. Even as a third stepped on her hand, she refused to give up the knife. Her mother reached out to her, strength faded as her eyes rolled to the back of her head, her hand dropped with a soft *thud*. The child screamed like a wild animal, roared and fought as the vampires pulled her away from the cabin, their bodies left on the ground, the fire from the stove consumed the house.

She screamed the name of her other half.

Kira opened her eyes with a jolt. Jake had leaned over the seat, his hand on her shoulder as he has shaken her gently awake. He held concern in his eyes, he and Eona, but neither said anything. Carmilla sat across from Kira and locked her eyes on the human, but then returned them to her screen after a few moments.

"Are you alright?" Eona asked, her concern noticeable her voice.

Kira nodded, as she rubbed her eyes and stood. "First time flying." She lied partly, "Not sleeping well." She went towards the front of the private jet, where the personal bartender and steward prepared the in-flight refreshments and snacks.

"Is there something we can help you with?" asked one vampire man, with a hint of edginess and nervousness. Blinking repeatedly while she rubbed her headache away, "May I have some water, please—"

The vampire began preparing.

"Actually..." Her headache spoke for her. "Can I also have neat whiskey?"

Less nervous and slightly relieved, the bartender nodded as he handed Kira a bottle of water and her drink. "First time flying?" He asked as he watched the human down the alcohol in less than three gulps. Taking that as an unspoken need for another, he made a second and handed it to her quickly.

"Yeah..." Kira groaned, sitting at the barstool, putting her head on the table, "Can't say I'm a fan."

He chuckled, "It takes some getting used to, it's much better than it used to be."

"That is certainly true." The Empress commented as she appeared beside Kira as she set her empty wineglass on the bar to be refilled.

Kira turned her head still on the bar.

"Rather take a train." Kira said. "Safer."

"And what makes you think I wouldn't protect you?" Carmilla's statement caught Kira off guard, enough for her to not have a response. Just in time, the captain's announcement for their preparation for landing came over the intercom and everyone took their seats. As they landed in the airport, dozens of reporters greeted them, the Imperial Guard and other dignitaries coming to greet and kiss ass to the Empress.

Dressed in travel attire, a skintight black strapless dress, decorated with golden glossed beads. The Empress wore a neck golden ornament attached to matching shoulder pauldrons. It was often the Empress dressed in such attire when in publishing places, a traditional attire of the Empress for as long as the Empire has existed. Her silvery hair was lightly curled and free-flowing in the wind. Kira remembered how the Empress looked the day they met and how different, yet unchanging, their relationship has evolved since then. Their stations have not changed and yet... emotions certainly have. Yet despite their stations, here, in front of all, Carmilla has beside her a human woman.

Much to the matching of her master, they showed Kira to the world in a golden Maxi dress with batwing sleeves. A black shawl was over her shoulders and up the back of her neck, coming down the sides and curled around her arms. Her long, thick raven hair was pinned into a tight bun, restrained like herself. Carmilla had suggested Kira wear sunglasses. It helped to hide her shyness and embarrassment and though such an expression was delicious to the vampire, she selfishly desired to keep that expression for her eyes alone.

Eona Tepes, Princess of the Empire, niece of the Empress and daughter of the previous departed the plane next. She chose a fashionable pantsuit, her blazer closed, and her crimson dress shirt beneath catching the eyes of many. The young Pureblood was the one of the latest centers of attention, re-entering the spotlight of the vampire public and the Game. She made a bold statement and left an air of uncertainty and uneasiness.

In the Limo, Kira was glued to the window, watching the city skyscrapers, both new and old as they drove past. As the sun went down and the night life of the city came to life, the hotel they were staying in was in Times Square, in the city's heart, with sight-lines from New York City, to New Jersey to the Atlantic Ocean. They reserved the top floor for the Empress and her party.

A penthouse with four rooms taking the entire floor, the level included a large sky pool, hot tub with fire pit, all able to be privatized with retractable roof and walls. Equipped with a full kitchen, each room even had its own master bathroom with hot tubs, king-sized beds, mini-bars, satellite television on an eighty-inch television. A penthouse worthy of an Empress.

As soon as they entered, Kira dropped her bag on the couch then b-lined to the outside patio that faced the ocean though it was too foggy to see. Carmilla sighed as she held a hundred-dollar bill between her fingers and had it taken with gratitude by Eona.

Eona won their little bet.

"Guys you've got to come see this!" Kira called out, both women smiled as they agreed to a truce as they went out to the patio and saw out towards the waters, a colossal marble statue illuminated on an island—a recreation of the original copper one that had been retired for preservation reasons.

The shine and sparkle in Kira's eye. One would never imagine half an hour ago she was airsick.

"Which way is the ocean?" Kira asked eagerly, her head turning between the two women, one on each side of her.

Carmilla pointed toward the bridge and explained the river that led to the ocean where the statue on the island was. Like a kid in a candy store, Kira looked out in amazement.

"I've never seen the ocean before."

"You think that's amazing? You should see the Pacific. It's colder, but surfing is a blast." Eona grinned.

Carmilla chuckled, "I much prefer the Caribbean myself. The waters there are crystal clear that you can see almost twenty feet down."

Kira smiled widely. *I never thought I would live to see this.* She never expected to live this long, to have these opportunities, to be a slave, but one with such freedoms. She was a slave; she was a human living in a vampire's world, but she was alive. She was treated well, cared for, protected... maybe even had a future. *Maybe...I really could have a happy future.* For the first time in fifteen years Kira dared herself to dream, to think beyond a daily battle for survival, to have hope for something more, though it was a dream to think it would be without cost. This time, she would not forget, but she would not allow it to rule her.

A knock on the door alerted the others of their bags. Eona went to grab hers. Kira left to help, but was stopped when Carmilla called her name.

"I thought I might steal you away for dinner." The vampire whispered in Kira's ear as she wrapped her arms around.

Kira blushed, "*Now...?*" she whispered in question. Carmilla purred, "I...am...famished." She nuzzled into the woman's neck, "But that comes later." The vampire released Kira, "Come, change into something comfortable, we're going out for dinner."

When the Empress said casual, Kira had half a mind to dress semi-formal as she knew Carmilla's tastes. It surprised her to find the woman could literally make a blouse and skinny-jeans with lace-up boots look elegant. They took a rental car, something inconspicuous and drove to another skyscraper, yet again they took an elevator to the top floor. A restaurant of few people who kept their eyes and noses to themselves. Carmilla walked in front and Kira trailed behind as it led them to a secluded corner which overlooked Central Park.

"Whatever you want, it's my treat." Carmilla explained as she selected a wine from the server then took a menu from the server.

Kira looked at the food, but focused her attention on Carmilla. She acted differently towards her, more seductive than possessive, using affections rather than domination to win her over. It was more than sex, than physical touch. There seemed to be a genuine effort in connecting...like they were actually dating. Why was she going this far? Was she threatened by Eona? Did she know about their relationship back then? The woman clenched her fist. Of course Carmilla knew, if she did not before she certainly did now, Eona made it obvious enough, her worries for Kira were beyond that of a 'friend'.

"Lady Carmilla..." Kira asked. "Why are you doing this?"

The vampire continued to look at the menu. "I don't want you to feel I've neglected you." Carmilla said. "We will be very busy for the next couple weeks and I imagine you will be worn out from such publicity."

Or you want to remind me and Eona that you're watching our every move. The human knew those eyes, the possessiveness and desire. *You're marking your territory, not just for Eona... for anyone who'd look at me.* Kira looked back at the menu and did not realize that somehow these gestures made her smile—Carmilla did. She may have played the innocent fool, but it was only a mask, one of many she had worn throughout her life. Whatever Carmilla had planned, Kira knew to survive she would need to be on her side, but it had been progressively harder to tell the difference between what was her survival and what was becoming attached to the vampire. How could she not? For over a decade, she is all Kira has ever known. *I can barely tell the difference anymore.*

"Thank you." Kira said quietly, and she meant it.

Whatever the motivations, whatever game either was playing against the other, she truly genuinely felt gratitude. Consideration and thought like this... was not fake.

The servers brought the wine, a close mimic of Carmilla's eyes, its bitter scent mixed with something metal... but also sweet.

She raised her glass, "To us." The vampire smiled seductively, her foot brushed Kira's, "May our time together be as certain and eternal as the setting sun."

Kira's eyes widened and she blushed some. What kind of toast was that? She was human; she was going to stay human. She would grow old and age. How long until Carmilla lost interest? How long until she sought a younger, youthful vampire that could fulfill her needs for companionship? *I can't even predict what she's going to do next. Everything's changing so quickly.*

She raised her glass to meet Carmilla's toast, they indulged in their meals. Near the end, Kira was chewing on the last of her dinner when the server came offering dessert. Carmilla politely declined as she waved the server away. The younger stiffened her body, Carmilla had risen her foot to the human's inner thigh and caused a heat to swell further up. She bit back a moan and barely managed speak the vampire's name quietly.

Carmilla leaned her chin against her hand, "I had something else in mind for dessert."

In the penthouse, the door was not even closed before Kira was pinned against the door, their body weight shut it. Carmilla aggressively engaged in hungry kisses, her fingers easily navigated Kira's body and found under her shirt and removed it just as effortlessly. She cupped the woman's breast, a gasp escaped the younger's mouth, caught by surprise by the quickness in tempo. The vampire smirked, her tongue slipped into Kira's open mouth and caused another moan to be held inside.

The human created a space and needed a moment to catch her breath. Carmilla grabbed the hands that reached for her pants and moved them above her excited prey's head, then pinned them against the door. She lifted a finger and wiggled it back and forth.

"Ah, ah, eager are we?" A fanged grin showed their own eagerness to sink into their sweet treat.

Kira squirmed, the vampire's knee pressed between her thighs, holding up the younger's weight. One hand kept the hands above, another grasped the butt, then pulled Kira into the knee and rubbed her sensitive place in only a few strokes, before the vampire felt her pants become wet.

"You've become more resilient. Before, one stroke was enough to make you come undone." Carmilla said with pleasure, her words hot against Kira's exposed skin, as she stroked her tongue up the inked markings on the human's neck.

Kira pulled against Carmilla's restraining hand. The vampire purred, "Oh? Where did this strength come from?" She looked at Kira's hands, then down at the woman herself, a mischievous idea formed in her mind, "That won't do at all."

One moment they were at the door, the next, Kira felt her back against something soft, the master bedroom in the bed she barely gave a passing glance to when they first arrived. Carmilla still held the woman's arms up, but she sat up, her free hand dangled a pair of leather and velvet handcuffs on one finger. The woman beneath turned flush red. Though she had seen those before, this was the first time Carmilla had brought them out directly to her. The heat in her cheeks rose, her stomach sank as the wetness below her waist nearly broke through the dam that was held by crossed legs.

"Your boldness will someday get you into trouble." Carmilla chuckled.

Kira confidently smirked, tilting her head in amusement. "But not today?" She teased and tempted; the rabbit taunting the lioness.

The vampire's grin grew. "You are playing a *very* dangerous game."

"Heh." Kira chuckled, "Haven't we been playing all my life?"

"Oh no my dear, this is unlike any game you have ever played before." Carmilla leaned closer and traced her thumb across Kira's lower lip, "This is a game of complete and utter *surrender*, to trust in me and only me with every ounce of your being."

Her finger traveled down Kira's mouth, her chin, her bare neck, between her exposed breasts, around each nipple, stopped then hovered over her lips.

"Giving into your desires, to push aside logic and fear and indulge in pure and raw ecstasy." Carmilla smiled, "Entrust me with your body, your mind, and your heart."

Kira opened her mouth to speak, but Carmilla placed her finger over it to hush her a moment longer.

"Think carefully." The Pureblood said sincerely, "If you cross this point, there is no turning back." She held Kira's chin. "Whatever your answer, there will be no punishment: this is your choice and yours alone. *Yes...* or *no.*"

Kira looked at Carmilla, watched this woman, this vampire, the Empress of all immortals responsible for the war that spelled the end of humanity at the top of the food chain. She looked at every detail; Carmilla's silky, silver hair, its curls having been brushed out, which left faint remains of their previous style. It flowed down her back and over her shoulders and barely acted as a barrier to conceal her v-cut blouse, it was soft. Flawless marble skin, too all others it would seem as cold as stone, but Kira found that was not always the case. Being skin to skin, she was quite comfortable to the touch.

Carmilla was not the type to show emotions of care, compassion, kindness. She has her own mask, the mask of the Empress of the immortal: brutal, ruthless, benevolent; yet well-known for her priority of her people. And yet, despite this mask, she was kind to Kira, caring, passionate... loving, even. It was not always like this, this relationship, whatever it was, began rough. The defiant slave against their intolerant mistress, their beginnings were in anger and in hate and now... Kira felt sick when she thought about hating Carmilla.

Kira looked at this woman, a voice in the back of her mind urged her to decline, to turn away. Do not believe them, do not help them, do not turn your back on them, do not trust them and for the love of god never fall in love with one—or two. *Don't think.* Kira thought to herself. Carmilla's grip lessened, and she could bring her hands down. *Don't think about her, don't think about anything, just forget.* Forget and give in, just like Carmilla said: *surrender.*

Kira cupped Carmilla's face and brought her down to have their lips meet.

"Say it." Carmilla ordered as she pulled back.

"Yes."

Like the burning sun, Carmilla's crimson eyes ignited. She smiled, hungry; desire dripped out of her mouth. Her shirt came off in one fluid motion, she interlaced her fingers into Kira's. She dove in and kissed firmly Kira's entire self beneath the vampire, her hands free to explore the other woman without restraint. Carmilla sunk into the woman beneath, her thumb tugged on the waistband of the jeans.

"The moment it becomes too much, that you reach your limit, you tell me." Instructed the vampire seriously, telling Kira to say back to her what she said, Carmilla whispered, "Take them off."

Kira's jeans quickly hit the floor. She grabbed her briefs to make a work of them too, but her hand was snatched, pulled up, held against the pillow.

"I prefer to unwrap my present."

Carmilla released Kira's hand and then traveled lower as she gently eased off the briefs, soaked through from Kira's growing need. She kissed down the woman's neck and toyed with Kira's hard nipples, going between her breasts as she temporarily released one, her mouth taking the hand's place, as it continued down before she brushed over the woman's swollen lips. A moan escaped, just as the first finger played with her entrance.

"Carm..." Kira squirmed, "Please..." she begged.

The vampire looked up, "Hearing you call me like that..." Her finger circled slowly, "Makes me want to devour you whole." She smiled when she glanced down. "In fact, I think I *will* have a taste."

Carmilla crawled lower and eased Kira's legs apart as she settled between them. Her arms slithered underneath, coming up and over as she clasped the human's thighs in place. She kissed the tender flesh. Kira's sensitivity heightened to new depths. All rational thought gave up as her body's senses took over. The vampire's eyes watched the color of life flow hot toward her partner's sex, the sweet scent of cherry blossom that made her mouth water in anticipation. A sharp inhale followed the burst of pleasure. Kira's voice was music to Carmilla's ears, her own sex soaked by the sharing of this moment.

Carmilla licked her lips of her meal as she rose from below and heard the humming bird from Kira's chest. She slowly rose and straddled the woman beneath her as she ran her fingers through her hair and combed the gleaming star-light silver back. A single fang bit into the Empress's lower lip, her precious thick blood sought by all, unobtainable, undrinkable; the Holy Grail of the immortal race oozed, coating her lips.

Carmilla leaned down, their lips inches from one another, the immortal's intoxicating words resonated within Kira, "Now you... taste."

They kissed, fire raged between them as they exchanged the currency of life with one another. Kira's neck beneath the Stigma pulsed and surged throughout her being, but it was not painful, it collided and seemed to amplify her sexual desire and ecstasy. Her desire, her hunger for Carmilla satisfied, yet reinvigorated and she craved for more, for everything. Her body reacting on instinct, her hands took a mind of their own and gripped at the vampire's back, then dragged her nails down until she could seize the woman's butt. She clutched her prize and pulled Carmilla up into her hips which deepend the next kisses they shared.

Carmilla smiled without breaking their lip's contact, but a moment's pause allowed her to speak once more before she was engulfed in desire again, "*You are mine.*"

Chapter Eight
Victorious Losers

Eona leaned over an untouched cup of coffee as she held her head up with one arm propped up and stared off into nothing.

"You look like hell." Jake sipped a glass of orange juice having noticed she had not changed her clothes from last night.

They had gone to the bar together. After Lady Carmilla and Kira had disappeared, there was little interest in waiting around. A local bar near 14th to 28th Streets was just where they headed. Jake had hoped his friend would find a warm body for the night, someone to take her mind off Kira and her aunt's extra-curricular activities, but she was not in the mood to play fuck-boy. They drank, but neither got drunk and, with no interest in exploring the nightlife, they returned to the hotel, had a few more drinks in the bar before they called it a night.

Jake and Eona returned to the penthouse and found they were not the first ones to return. They were certainly the quietest.

Eona shot a glare just as Kira entered the kitchen. She walked, her steps careful and short when going to the fridge. When she opened the fridge, Jake shook the opened OJ and set it next to a clean glass. Kira looked at her friend, then at Eona, who turned her bar stool away and took her cold coffee and moved to the couch. Silently, Kira and Jake exchanged looks.

"Long night." Jake said as Kira poured her OJ.

She took a sip.

"Couldn't sleep with the choir next door."

Kira spat out her drink. Eona smirked and chuckled silently as she drank a sip of her coffee. With a bright red, Kira coughed and cleared her throat, "S-sorry..." She said sheepishly, "I didn't know we were that loud."

"Based on what we heard, I don't think you cared." Jake huffed in amusement as he hopped on the counter just as his toast popped out of the toaster.

Once the others had risen and dressed, they awaited their security team to call in. With the facility of the former United Nations being across the street, a vehicle was unnecessary, but it did not stop the Imperial Guard from making the block the most secure area in all the world. To the Empress, this was unnecessary and eccentric. Few could stand against her, and none of them were human. She chuckled to herself at that thought: Kira could resist her, but not very well.

This meeting of human representatives was nothing more than a formality, a publicity stunt to quell some of the civil unrest that continued since the war's end. It gave them a false sense of representation, of hope that their feeble voices would be heard. Humanity has become second-class citizens because of their own arrogance, as they had long believed they were superior; their arrogance, greed and pride, destroyed the world around them.

Vampires may be monsters, but only humans can become demons. The immortal's declaration of war was to take the future of this world from their mortal counterparts. To save it and themselves before humanity doomed them all.

As she looked at the streets below, Kira saw the crowds allowed to gather and protest the vampire's presence, their rule; the Empress's rule. Her sanctions and limitations of human movement and freedoms. Their legalization to be enslaved by their vampire overlords, to be drained and killed for 'unreasonable' defiance. Their rights stripped from them, their freedoms limited by laws and yet they were still freer. They could still travel, could still leave the county, love who they wanted, get the jobs they wanted. Kira's eyes shut as she let out a quiet exhale.

Humanity lost much during the war; children become adults at tender ages, mothers and fathers outlived their children. Brothers and sisters lost their other halves, forced to wander the new world with half their heart six feet under and the other half a broken shell of its former self. The humans here, today, hold on to the old ways, the old system of government where one could protest for change and it could very well happen, demanding social equality, justice. Pretty, empty words now; there was only one rule, one law: Empress Carmilla Tepes.

A part of me still wants to be like them. Kira thought. *To have freedom and choose.* She clenched the steel guardrail. *I wish I had a choice.* To choose to work, to choose where she could live, to travel and see the world, to connect with humans, to help them and love? Love was not something she held interest in, something she knew anything about. Physical attraction, sexual desire, that was not love, it was lust and *that* she certainly knew and enjoyed.

Kira's thoughts returned to the faint voices far below, their cadences and rally cries. She listened to them call for the chance of the abolition of slavery, of the degradation and discrimination of humans. In their hearts, they called for the death of the vampire. *Why do they bother protesting? Do they think they can really change something*? It made no sense to her to waste their time, their freedom, their lives when they knew nothing will change.

Maybe she could have understood them if her life had turned out differently, if the vampires had never found them in the woods that night. *What would they say if my family saw me now*? She thought as she tugged at the scarlet scarf around her neck. A pained smile cracked. *They'd probably be disappointed in me. Dad always taught us to fight; death was better than chains*. She turned away and headed inside to put on her clothes for the day.

Kira entered the elevator with Eona, and Jake, the Empress would go down later, and the idea was to paint a smaller target on the back of the Imperial Family and guests. For Kira herself, the only human among them, it was safer to be distanced from the Empress. Though she could easily protect the human, the chances of her being caught by an attack were significantly less than when beside two gifted immortals. Though she would not admit this, Kira was happy to be with them, to be with her friends again. She felt like she was a kid again, innocent, ignorant, that she had forgotten how horrible and unfair the world could be.

They entered the lobby, a small team of Imperial guards dressed in black suits stood between them and the door. Wolfgang was beside the elevator and followed at Eona's side, when they entered the lobby. He was an older-appearing man, still youthful in his immortal physique; he had thick, short military-cut hair, his suit slightly different from those beneath his command. Though a thinner man, he did not appear skinny as a body fit for a swimmer.

The Commander of the Guard began as they walked towards the doors, "It is my advice that you drop the dead weight."

"Deadweight can heal, you know." Kira rolled her eyes.

Wolfgang did not give her a passing glance, "And speaking out of turn."

Kira growled, "I see you haven't changed a bit."

Eona and Jake smiled.

The Pureblood vampire looked back at Kira, "You have." Was all he said before he turned back towards the door and continued his conversation with Eona. "It would be in our best interest..."

Kira tuned out what Wolfgang was saying and stopped just short of the lobby door. Jake noticed and stayed behind with her. He called her name, but she did not hear him. She stared off at the doors, the people's voices. They chanted against their treatment, against their enslavement, against the domination of monsters over them. Kira heard their voices, she heard the cries of a city burning. The screams of people as the vampire descended in the night, slaughtering all in their path, they fed on innocents without care as to age, gender, or race. She remembered them running, pulled, then lifted into their parent's arms as they ran to cover. The Red Night, the declaration of war and humanity's apocalypse.

She remembered watching the vampires' march, their armies stormed the city; she remembered them cloaked in gold and blacks. They were beautiful, like statues she saw in books at school, their reddened eyes were mesmerizing; Kira remembered as she watched and listened to the vampire's words. No others seemed to listen, but she spoke anyway, her eyes locking onto the human child as though she was looking at her and only her.

"Attention foolish humanity! We vampires take back our world and save it from you! Resistance is futile." Kira watched her, but did not understand her words at that time, but after The Red Night she did.

Kira's parents turned the corner, but not before the human saw their leader, one who remained unchanged for years to come. She remembered her clear as day and ignored anything else as that moment as she burned the memory of the woman she would meet years later. Kira remembered her crimson eyes, the elegant, golden pauldrons she wore and her long, silver locks pulled up into a ponytail. Years later, Kira could put a name to that face.

"Kira!" Jake shook her gently as he came between her and the lobby doors, "Hey, what's wrong?"

"I—" she shuddered as Eona turned around and back stepped. "I'm okay—just... I don't like big crowds."

Eona listened to the woman's heartbeat as it raced, the tremble she hid behind her back and stagger for breath. Something made her nervous, but the vampire doubted it was a crowd. Kira took a deep breath in. She stepped out, Jake and Kira flanked Eona. The Pureblood Princess remained in the center. Protestors, humans and ex-humans surrounded the hotel, those turned aggressively and against their will who sided with their former kin.

While she listened to screams and chants, Kira clenched her fists and dug her nails into her palms to distract her. Something, anything to distract her. *Shut up.* She clenched her jaw tight and fought her own mind from putting her back to that night. They were loud; they were aggravating; they screamed and yelled all for what? What did they think they could accomplish? The vampire would not listen to them, they would not bother to listen to livestock. *Shut up!*

"End—the—Em—pire!"

They chanted behind the barriers and guards, spewed profanities and threats. One broke through the barrier, grabbed Kira and pulled her into him. He looked into her eyes and saw their sky blue was nothing like the red of the immortal.

"She's human!" One yelled.

"Traitor!" The human held Kira tightly then was grabbed by the throat by Eona. Jake grabbed his wrist, and froze it by the touch.

Guards came in and took him away. Eona gently placed her hand on the small of Kira's back to comfort and ease her forward. Kira looked at the crowd, at their anger and frustration, trying to understand them, understand her own people and when she found she could not, that frightened her more than any threat to her life. She realized she had begun to forget what it meant to be human.

Kira stared down the street. One stood out in the mob. He was without words, without anger and frustration. He stared at Kira, with something else... curious.

"Hey." Eona leaned over, "I've got you."

The vampiress rubbed the woman's back some, "It's okay, I won't let anyone hurt you."

Kira turned away from the man and looked at Eona. Rather than the kid, the teenager she knew, Kira saw only Eona in front of her. A confidante, responsible, adult strong enough to make the words she said have truth and meaning. It differed from when they were younger. Eona was no longer girly, not rebellious, or complacent. It seemed they had switched roles. Kira eased closer to Eona, feeling comfortable, feeling safe, like she could even let her guard down again. *Don't*. She told herself. *Don't forget ever again. I'm not like them.*

What did it even mean to be human anymore? Has living with vampires, living with the very one who started humanity's downfall, somehow converted her to being more like *them* than human? Was being human physically all she could claim to be now? How long until even that eroded away? How long until these symptoms could not be suppressed, could not be hidden? Was she going to become one of them? Was she going to die? Maybe that would have been better, maybe...it would have even been better if she had never been born.

Inside the former headquarters of the United Nations, what was the symbol of diversity, change, and equality had been changed to almost a monument of humanity and the supremacy of the immortal. Humans from all around the globe, representatives, diplomats each here to convey their 'requests' and concerns in false hope of appeasing the Empress and getting back a small fraction of what was lost, what had been taken. If only on paper. Kira stayed close to Eona who conversed with a few dignitaries whom she had known and met in her time abroad.

Listening to the vampire, Kira realized that what Eona had said about studying abroad had been true after all. She was very formal. Her higher-educated speech and words were ones even Kira did not quite understand. Discussing climate change, economic policies, conflict analysis, Eona was extremely familiar with many details of current international events. Kira herself only knew of recent events, but the other woman was familiar with details and dates that seemed to lead up to the current news.

It impressed her with Eona and with that, felt slightly guilty about her previous biased against her and used her studies as her excuse to leave. Of course, she had to leave. She was the Princess, an important political figure and leader in vampire society, one who did not care to play the Game and held no fear in being a social outcast. She had complete confidence in her reasoning and power—it must have been nice to be born into such a position in society, but also a dreadful curse. Kira could not imagine having that kind of responsibility.

She felt out of place, self-conscious when she listened and added nothing, to be a trophy to parade around. Maybe that was not how Eona and Jake saw it or even Carmilla, but it did not help to make that feeling in the pit of her stomach go away. *Come on, you're here to learn. To play the Game better for yourself and to be useful.* Kira would smack herself silly if she were not in public. This was not the time to wallow in self-pity, to be self-conscious. She had a purpose if not for Carmilla, then herself. This was how she had survived this long, she listened and used what she heard to live another day, to win the battle and see the sunrise again.

As she left the safety of Eona's side, Kira did what she knew best—she became invisible. As a human in a vampire's world, sometimes being seen through, being ignored and underestimated, was one's greatest asset. Here with humans and vampires together, she became just another face in the crowd; when in Rome, do as the Romans. She stuck to the side of the room, Kira kept to a small crowd of people. She appeared as though she were a part of them, she looked around to watch and listen. She knew to not draw attention to herself, to not stand out and to hide in the shadows.

The crowds moved closer to the main assembly hall, the whispers of the Empress's arrival becoming the center of much anticipation. Kira opened her phone and shot a few messages to Eona and Carmilla and informed them of her wellness and not to worry. She eavesdropped on the languages she knew, Italian, English, bits and pieces of three others, one of them technically a dead language; courtesy of vampire education and one she allowed no one to know. Many conversations were about the coming policies, some the human representatives wanted to be changed, a few even agreed it was pointless to even attempt to discuss removal. Kira admitted to herself that inside the Palace it shielded her from many of these rules and did not know how restricted even 'free' humans were.

One conversation drew her attention. Two men and a woman. Rather than talking, they signed, and Kira knew exactly what they were saying. They had a time-frame, talking to another about people being in place and waiting for the signal. They were human, all three of them, and it took little for Kira to put two and two together. Kira looked at them, and they noticed her. She signed to them:

Too many vampires. Whatever you're planning won't work.

Granted access by one of Wolfgang's men, Kira kept near the media areas and blended in with them. Here she was just another human, invisible to the unsuspecting. Eona took the stage first and opened the discussion board to different topics to be mentioned, later announced the arrival of the Empress Carmilla Tepes.

"Twins... have always fascinated me." Said a youthful man, whose tone and words reflected a greater age than that of his appearance.

Kira hesitated at the word, her head snapped to the man whom she had neither sensed nor heard. With a built, muscular body, his clothes barely covered his size with an open-collared suit topped by a black overcoat. He had shoulder-length blonde hair combed back, two pieces on both sides of his face free to hang on the sides of his face. With brown eyes, Kira looked at every detail, every feature of his face and felt his eyes were the most out of place. They looked almost... fake.

He glanced down at her, "How different they can be from one another, the Empress and the previous are as night and day."

"You said twins?" Kira asked, the word fightened her greatly.

The unknown man nodded. "Carmilla and her sister, born only minutes apart. Yet the youngest inherited the crown rather than her, it makes one wonder how she must have felt at that moment."

She glanced at Carmilla, who answered questions from the assembly, Kira's eyes softened. "I... did not know."

"It was quite the anomaly. Vampires very rarely give birth to twins and for those born into positions of power, well...it is in the vampire's nature to take." Explained the man who Kira had a growing uneasiness about.

Something about him told her to either run as fast as she could or to curl up in a ball. He was powerful; he was *dangerous,* and Kira did not want to be near him. It was that kind of feeling that would kick her self-preservation into gear, having her flee for her life, to save her life, but she could not do that here. She wanted to signal someone, somehow, but what could they do? If this man thought to kill her, she would be dead on the ground long before anyone even realized they could not see her. Kira swallowed hard. Her neck burned, and she reached up and slid her hand beneath the scarf and placed her cooler palm on her burning flesh. Why was it acting up now?

"Vampires have a thirst that knows no end." He said, his tone neutral, his posture relaxed, "If you do not wish to be taken by it you would be wise to run."

Whoever he was, he had no fear of harm from anyone here, but why was he talking to her? Why did it seem like he knew about her? That he knew her situation?

Kira... played the Game.

"What makes you think I want to run?"

The man looked at her, "I see it in your eyes: the fear for your life, the desire to be free again, the right denied to humanity by the vampire." He leaned against the wall, "You fear being hunted again, to be chained and locked away like an animal."

"I'll always be in a cage." Kira said simply, "No matter how free I'll always have an invisible chain around my neck." Her fingers dug into the Stigma.

"Even if that may be true, this is also: the free choose, a slave obeys." The man countered as he saw the tattoo that is usually covered by the scarf.

Kira smiled a little. "You sound a lot like my dad, right before he abandoned us to go fight your people."

The man was quiet.

"Yeah." Kira glared some. "I know colored contacts when I see them. You were outside and snuck up on me without me noticing; for someone who advocates for humans, you've never been one, have you?"

"You... are just as perceptive as her." He said, the statement catching Kira off guard.

"Her?"

He walked away.

Kira followed, "Hey! What does that mean?" They left the assembly area. She reached out and grabbed his cloak and realized the moment she did, it was a mistake.

Her heart skipped a beat, her entire body froze in fear as an overwhelming force emanated from this man, this vampire. This was not the power of an ordinary vampire. Kira had not felt this fear since she was almost killed back then. She let go of the cloak, stepping back, her eyes widened in shock, trying to understand how she could feel this way, could feel this power; senses of a vampire's strength known only by one who is an immortal. The man turned around and faced Kira, his crimson cat-like eyes shining through the colored contacts.

"If you remain by her side, the day will come, when she becomes the very thing that destroys you." He warned darkly, towering over her, "You would do well to remember who and what you really are or you will suffer a fate worse than death." He leaned closer and whispered into her ear, one-word, one name, that shocked her to her very core.

He left her with those ominous words, telling her the very future she would experience, as though he had seen it firsthand. She watched him walk into the crowd, vanishing behind a passing duo. *How! How does he know that name!* Kira shook herself back into movement. *Who the fuck was that!* She turned back to the Assembly Hall and tried to understand what just happened, what it meant and why he seemed to not only know her, but to mention the Empress being a twin terrified her.

She went to one guard and asked for a radio to contact Wolfgang. The vampire scoffed at her at first and told her to run along like a good little slave back to her master. Annoyed, Kira turned to her phone and rapidly texted Jake.
EMERGENCY GET HERE NOW

He arrived in less than thirty seconds.

"I got your text, what's wrong?" He asked.

Kira grabbed him and pulled him toward where the vampire had disappeared to.

"There was a vampire, he had colored contacts, brown and black hair; he knew me! She explained, out of breath.

"That's alarming—"

"He knew me, me *before* the Palace!" She exclaimed frantically, "Jake, there shouldn't be anyone who knows that!"

The vampire hesitated. "I thought everyone who did was..."

"Dead!" Kira said with fear. "Everyone in my family is supposed to be dead, but he knew it, he said it out loud!" A loud commotion in the hall had them both inside their humans began arguing, shouting demands and outcries at whatever Carmilla had said. She stood there without a care of their thoughts, their desires. This was nothing more than a show, and there was no power here, no voice that she or the council would listen to. These people were nothing more than tools, humans who believed they could strike a deal with those far above them with nothing to offer. Kira turned to Jake, asking what just happened.

Empress Carmilla announced, by order of the Council a mandatory draft of humans to be turned into vampires for the Imperial Army in order to put down the human rebellions. There would be no exceptions, no way to buyout or bypass the draft. Everyone and anyone of the criteria would report to the prescribed duty stations to await transition. Of course, ample pay and benefits would be granted to those drafted, but they would automatically cast any who tried to resist or flee into slavery to be used in labor camps.

Kira could not believe what she was hearing, did not understand why this woman, this vampire, could be so kind and caring to her and turn around and do this. She did not know which mask was real, which one she should believe. The vampire had warned her, if she will do this to complete strangers, what would she do to Kira, who was closest to her? What would happen to her if Carmilla ever tired of her and cast her from her bed? She could not be turned. The only options were to flee or to die if that was so. What choice did she have but to continue to prove her worth, to continue to survive?

There was relief for Kira when she saw Eona and that she clearly did not agree to this. There was at least one person, one vampire within the Palace who was against this enslavement and degradation of humanity. What else did Carmilla think she should do to humanity? Was the war not enough? Was the pain, the loss and anger not enough; was there not enough bloodshed to appease her? Vampires have a thirst that knows no end. That man knew what Carmilla was going to do, like he had seen the future. Was he here to stop the Empress? He warned Kira of a fate she would suffer if she remained, but why warn her? A single, ordinary human?

"Jake..." Kira said to a concerned and ashamed friend, "Don't tell anyone what I said." She went into her phone and erased the message, "I'll tell Wolfgang about the vampire, but don't mention to anyone he knew my name."

Jake tried to convince her that silence about someone who seemed to threaten her life was a grave mistake. Kira would hear nothing of it. Whoever that vampire was, he was not there to threaten Kira, nor did he seem he would come after her. He wanted to warn her and by using her real name he knew she would take him seriously and it did more than just that. *He had to have learned it somewhere*. The human frowned as the Assembly was now in an uproar. *Who?* She searched her memories, dug through pain and anguish she barely could stand to relive, but knew there was no choice. She could ignore and turn a blind eye to much, but not this. *I watched them die with my own eyes. The cabin burned to the ground.* Who then? Who could know her real name? Know what name she was given? Know which house she went to?

The guards took action and subdued any humans who came too close to the Empress as she departed the stage. Kira watched her walk off, but she did not look back at the human. Why would she? She did not look for forgiveness, for approval. Kira was only human, a body to warm her bed, she was livestock. What did her opinion matter if she did not even mention this to her when she began teaching Kira about politics? What was she to the Empress? Why could she not understand, after all these years, what the Empress was thinking, what she was going to do? Everything else before was easy. She knew her habits, her likes and dislikes, but outside the Palace she seemed like an entirely distinct person. Or perhaps this was who she was all along.

Chapter Nine
The Last Stand

Kira remained quiet. She kept back and waited for most of the masses to leave before she tried to make it back to the hotel. If anyone planned anything they would remain back for recon, this was the time they would loosen their disguises and make mistakes. Well-trained infiltrators would not likely make them, but inexperienced ones would which it easier to find and follow them. After what Carmilla announced during the meeting, Kira knew in her mind protesting humans would not take that quietly and those who were less than peaceful would hasten.

It was not as though she had been completely secluded and protected from going on in the open world. Kira admits she had turned a blind eye. She had become complacent, docile; *domesticated.* Her parents trained them to survive. She survived by obedience because it was her best chance, but that life was not something that could last forever.

It was not a matter of if, but when Carmilla grew tired of her and when she did... Kira knew too much. Carmilla would dispose of, if not her, then by someone else who believed she knew too much; Wolfgang probably jumped at the chance to kill her. At least he would make it quick and be done with it, though having her neck snapped and body left in a ditch somewhere was less than appealing.

No. Kira thought to herself as she continued to watch the people, unaware the ringing in her back pocket. *They won't kill me. I won't be livestock.* She needed to break free from the delusion she would die peacefully. That was never an option, not for her, not as a human in the world of vampires and not being the property of the Empress of them. *Carmilla doesn't seem like she'll lose interest in me soon, but that can change in an instant.* If that were to happen, she would need help to escape, not just from a human, but a powerful vampire. She thought of Eona and a knot in her stomach formed. Logically, for the sake of survival, Eona Tepes was her best chance, the Pureblood Princess of the Empire. Even when Carmilla tossed her aside, if Eona still held any interest in her, she would try to take Kira for herself.

Why did the idea of using Eona make her sick? Eona could be her ticket out of death's doorway. They could persuade her to take Kira away from the Palace and then escape at the best opportunity. She could find her way into the human-controlled territories where vampire influence was held off by members of The Last Stand. Human resistance fighters dedicated to the freedom of humanity from vampire domination. Humans and ex-humans alike fought together to repel the Empire. Kira often thought their fight was meaningless in the end. Perhaps that was her bitterness toward her father talking. *I never saw him again.* She frowned. *But we never did know what happened to him.*

There were no letters, no signs or signals. He left, not even saying goodbye to his children before he left them alone to go play hero. They were left alone, left to be hunted, to be found. He said those woods were the safest than anywhere else they had ever been—that was a lie. Kira does not even remember his face, not that she ever tried to remember it, but his lessons, his training that prepared them, allow him to live on in here. They learned to track, to hunt animals and survive in the forests with little to nothing. To hide one's scent, one's presence, he taught them sign language to go without sound; Kira remembered he had tried to master slowing and even stopping his heart to avoid detection.

She never quite got that down.

The human rebellion known as The Last Stand or the LSA was without a doubt here in the city. They were likely in every city, vampire controlled or not, but with the Imperial Family's presence, the stakes were higher. Kira knew if she were to plan an attack, a vast city such as New York would be it. The block could be the most secure place on Earth, but it would not stop a sniper and there were more than enough people, human or former, willing to sacrifice their lives even for the chance at giving an opening to the Empress or even Eona. With both present, it makes the chances of at least one success greater, but also the possibility of failure greater than well, as assets would have to be divided to cover both if that was the plan.

What would she do if what she thought was correct? Who would believe her? The Imperial Guard gave her no regard. Wolfgang would probably rather see her be the first to get shot or thrown from a building.

Kira pulled her phone from her pocket and saw two missed calls and three messages. Two from Eona and one from Carmilla. How likely was it they would listen to a human based on a 'feeling'? Against their own professional guard, not to mention she had to try to avoid mentioning the vampire with cat-like eyes. He was someone Kira had every intention of learning more about, without their help, even if she had to use unsavory means to do it. It was mainly a matter of not getting caught.

Should she even say something? If Carmilla were to somehow die... Eona would become Empress. *There's no way they're too strong. There are too many guards.* Kira read the first two messages, conflict growing in her mind. Her neck irritated her, her fingers cold and clammy. If they died... she could run, she would be free and no one would hunt her down. The cage would be broken. Humanity could be free, and all she had to do was keep silent.

Why then did she find no happiness in the thought?

She clenched the phone and read the messages again when she walked outside.

Lady Eona:
    Jake and I want to go to the bar later. You in?
Another one proceeded after there was no response.
    You okay?
Lady Carmilla:
    When will you return?
Kira blew out a frustrated huff and looked up at the hotel.

"And you're sure about this?" Carmilla asked in contemplation, Eona stood with Jake beside her in the kitchen.

Kira frowned as she swallowed then took a deep breath.

"I'm sure. I—I know I don't really have evidence and the guard has everything covered, but—"

Jake came in, "But you know humans."

With a nod, "I know The Last Stand. I know they're willing to do anything to kill the two of you. All in the name of humanity's freedom." She was slightly ashamed of what she was about to say and admitted a part of her had thought this through, "It's what I would do."

Carmilla stood from the couch. She walked to Wolfgang and spoke to him in German. Whatever she said had him leave the suite and talk through his earpiece as he exited. The Empress came back from the door, toward Kira, who unconsciously stepped back in fear. She dropped her head down and averted Carmilla's crimson eyes. The Empress stopped in front of the human and did not take her eyes off Kira before she said to Jake and Eona.

"Give us a moment." She said in a tone of request rather than command.

Eona nodded and passed Kira and Carmilla, the princess and the human's eyes, met for a moment. The two left and waited just outside the door as there was a small sense of fear for Kira's safety.

Carmilla gently raised Kira's eyes to meet her own. Though Kira's sky blue held a raging storm within them, conflict threatened to destroy her from within, that storm was not eased she met the vampire's. At first Kira was fearfuly, but when she looked into Carmilla's eyes she did not see disappointment nor anger, but sorrow.

"I imagine this is not easy for you, knowing your sense of self-preservation often dictated your actions. Doing whatever necessary to survive the Game, no matter the personal cost, shutting off your emotions and hardening your heart." Carmilla said quietly, "You, as I, put on a mask to show the world, hiding our true selves even from those who have known us all our lives."

Kira was stunned and confused altogether.

"I often thought your growing obedience over the years was an acceptance of your stature in our society and another survival technique you used. I see now I was wrong. Your understanding and manipulation of the Game is unparalleled for one your age and kind." Said Carmilla as she gently touched Kira's exposed arm, causing goosebumps.

There was conflict in her that much was clear, the deeply seeded hatred and resentment of the vampire ingrained in every human. Hers was a scar even deeper. Her family slaughtered before her very eyes, bought like an animal, raised as servant, nearly killed and turned. And yet, despite all this, she stood before the Empress of the Immortal and desired to save her life. No other human with such experience would ever rationally make such a decision which gave Carmilla hope that this was a sign of something more.

Carmilla smiled affectionately, "I would hope that one day...you will come to trust me enough to show me your true self." The vampire said warmly, "After what you have shown me today, you have my complete trust and confidence." She said with warmth, "Thank you."

Kira thought this was the best time to get a better grasp on the situation and that she might in fact be safe to ask despite a previous decision.

"May I ask you something?"

"Of course." Carmilla stepped back and leaned against the back of the couch.

"Are all vampires' eyes red?"

The question seemed unusual, but then again Kira had interacted with a handful of immortals. "Born vampires yes. Ex-humans if they have transitioned completely, yes. Those were transition cease aging completely and look and have the strength, healing and speed of the average immortal. An exception lies only with an ex-human who has resisted drinking human blood. Though they possess the powers of a vampire, they age and keep the same color eyes they had when fully human." The Empress frowned. "Why do you ask?"

"What about a vampire with red, cat-like eyes?" Carmilla's face instantly changed; pure shock and for the first time in her entire life... Kira saw fear in the vampire's eyes.

"How—"

An explosion shook the building. Kira staggered back and forth and lost her balance. Carmilla caught her then pulled her into her body and held her tightly until the shaking ceased. The doors burst open, Eona appeared in an instant, Jake raised ice to trap the attackers. The Empress moved in front of the human and took her hand into her own, then moved her behind without releasing her grip.

"How many?"

Eona shook her head, "We don't know, communications are being jammed, three just came out of the elevator. They threw flash grenades at the same time as another device being detonated and killed two guards." She explained and glanced at Kira, "We need to get you out of here —"

Carmilla's grip tightened, "Kira is going nowhere, and my side is the safest she can be."

"This is not the time or place for your pride and possessiveness!" Eona snapped angrily, "It's dangerous. Kira isn't like us, she's—"

The surrounding air grew heavy, the power of two Purebloods thick and crushed those who could sense it in overwhelming pressure.

"I am fully aware what she *is* and *is not* Eona." Carmilla threatened, "You would be wise to remember the same." She emphasized the last part, and Eona's expression twisted into something shameful, enough that she could not even look at Kira again.

She did not know why Eona gave such a... guilty expression, but despite the anger, the fear in this moment, she hated that she saw this woman wear it. Kira broke free from Carmilla's grasp and came between the two women, her hands out to brace against them to keep them separate.

"Stop it, both of you!"

Wolfgang and the others entered the room.

Kira turned to Carmilla quietly, "She's right, I can't be here, and I'll just be a liability. If LSA realizes you're protecting me, they'll target me, trying to get to you. I can't..." She clenched her fists, "That's not good for any of us."

Carmilla frowned, "You have never seen me in battle." She grabbed Kira's hand and pulled her closer. "There is a reason I am called the Red Queen."

Eona hesitated.

"I'm not saying you can't protect me... I'm saying... I don't want you to be seen protecting a human, if people think you're favoring me..." Kira had already thought this part through, but Carmilla's desire to protect her was not what she expected.

She knew the Empress's opinion of their relationship exceeded a physical contract and that frightened Kira. She had deflected the subtle hints the vampire seemed to create and hoped that she was simply reading into something that did not exist. What she just said and did changed that, it... complicated things. If people noticed Carmilla's public displays of affection, they would see it as a weakness of the Empress and, without a doubt, Kira's life would be targeted just to get to her.

Kira could not allow those emotions to interfere with her survival. She had to be smart about this and had to somehow convince Carmilla it is her own idea to keep this changing relationship a secret. Any attempt to tell her outright would make her laugh. Her confidence in her abilities as an immortal would have her disregard Kira's lack of them.

Kira took a deep breath then explained a part of her method of survival: "I excel at the Game because I'm invisible. People don't notice me, don't target me and as long as I can keep going unnoticed I can gather information, I can warn you again of an attack like this." The human expressed as another explosion rocked the building.

Wolfgang came closer and removed from his overcoat a Desert Eagle pistol and handed it to Kira. She stared at him for a moment. He gestured the pistol in his hand for her to take it and she did. She her shirt and put it between the small of her back and her waist belt.

"There's an emergency exist—"

Kira walked past him and went to the bodies of the humans killed by the guards. Beside them were piles of clothes filled with the sandy ash of vampire remains. She looked at the bloodied bodies of the humans, their bodies full of bullet holes. Her stomach turned, but she had to ignore it. It was not the first time she had seen dead bodies and would not be the last, but it did not make it easier. Kira looked at the human, locked in ice, her head the only thing not locked in a prison of ice.

"Fucking traitor—" Though she wore a ski mask, it froze her mouth shut by Jake.

"What are you doing?" The Noblemen asked.

Kira found what she was looking for, an encrypted radio, functional and unaffected by the jamming device. She held it up to the vampire, then grabbed another from the other corpse.

"These are short-range radios, old ones that only match each other, but aren't affected by jamming." She explained, clipping one to her belt, grabbing the jacket of the human and pulling it off, "They won't be on the same channel, they'll probably change every few minutes, don't speak just listen or they'll dump the radios altogether."

Carmilla came out. Wolfgang and Eona watched in astonishment.

"How do you know this?" Wolfgang asked suspiciously.

Kira stood up, taking a sheathed knife from the corpse's side. She looked at it, seeing the red band around its handle, and attached it to her own belt.

"I wasn't born in the Palace." Kira answered flat as she put her hair up. She reached down looked at an exposed arm and saw a tattoo of a red band around her wrist.

She wished she had a bow and arrow. "Anyone who escaped the Red Night learned quickly how to survive." *That's how they tell their members, hmm?* She thought, discreetly as she dipped a a scrap of clothing in their blood. It would be used later to mark herself in order to avoid confrontation with actual members.

"Before the Palace, we avoided being caught by Human Hunters for three years." She said matter-of-fact and pushed back any memories of that time.

Survival was more important than memories long gone and a time that would never return. Right now she needed to get out of this building and needed to separate herself from the Imperial Family. No matter if LSA had not connected her to the family, it was only a matter of time; she needed to flee; hide her face so none would recognize her. *If I can get out of the building with no guards, then it would be possible*. Kira's face changed. *I could disappear in the crowd*. She thought of the bright blue sky, endless green fields, unbound; living outside a gilded cage. *If I leave here... I would be free.*

She thought of that, thought of the forests they once ran through, the snow they played in. She thought of being younger, of going to school, back before the world drowned in the blood and flame of the apocalypse. Deep within her, a thought surfaced, a feeling that coursed from her core, from layers beneath, pulsing the markings on her neck. If she left, she would never see them again. *Eh?* Her heartbeat pounded in her chest. *Am I... having second thoughts?*

That should not happen. She did everything to prevent the development of any emotional ties to them. She constantly reminded herself they were vampires, they were the enemy—they murdered her entire family in front of her, for god's sake! How could she possibly hesitate at what could be her one and only opportunity to escape? She should jump at the seams and yet right now she is hesitating? Her thoughts turned to the Stigma. *Did this...bind me to them?*

Carmilla stared at Kira, deep in thought, but then it changed. At first the vampire admired her confidence, her tact and her ability to analyze the situation and come up with a solution. She knew Kira did much of this to save her own life, but she also went against every fiber of her being to help them—self-preservation or not. She went against her fellow human and this woman was willing to sacrifice anything, do anything, in order to survive. Kira chose the vampire over humanity and that brought her one step closer to where Carmilla wanted her to be.

And yet, right now Kira's expression changed; a realization of something. Carmilla had a feeling it did not have to do with their current situation. She had touched the Stigma on her neck, hidden beneath the scarlet scarf. Something else was amiss. A great fear had taken her.

"If excelling at the Game means you being unprotected and in danger, I will not allow it." Carmilla commanded with no room for debate.

As Eona and Wolfgang spoke of exits, Carmilla placed a cool hand on the Stigma, "Stay close to me."

Defeated by the betrayal of her own body Kira nodded. She frowned, unsettled because her mind wished to flee, but her body did not or was it the other way around? It was easier to accept the Stigma bound her to the Imperial Family, to Carmilla, but Kira hated to think that it may not even be the Stigma.

It was easier to blame it, to use it as a cause for her hesitation in escape. Rationally, she should want to escape. She was a human, and they were the vampire. And yet, despite the atrocities she has seen, she herself has committed... a part of her did not want to leave, neither Carmilla nor Eona.

They made their way down the stairs from the Penthouse. The gunfire closed in with every floor they descended. Eventually the small band was forced to exit on a lower level, the stairs collapsed and another set further down being seen ridged with explosives.

Wolfgang glanced at Kira, who was only slightly affected by the danger. *She really knows what she is talking about.* He narrowed his eyes. *Based on her age, she would have only a couple of years of experience to learn how to evade Human Hunters. We were never able to confirm her origins and family beyond where she was captured.* The Commander took point, he dashed down the hallways, grabbed a human combatant and snapped his neck. *Not even her real name—has she been hiding it to hide her relation to the rebels?* The thought came to him: child soldiers were developed and used during the war. With the consideration she had killed another human being when the Empress chose her showed she was already equipped with some combat knowledge, her skills with a bow were impeccable and dangerous.

If she was a spy, she would act on orders far outdated and The Last Stand Army was not even formally formed till years after the war's end from survivors of military branches and freedom fighters. If Kira was a spy, she could not possibly act on orders anymore—since the beginning she had been trying to escape the Palace and now...she has not once gone against the Empress nor Eona. Still...it unsettled that both Tepes women have an eye for a single human.

A group of fighters threw a grenade from a hotel room. Jake threw up a wall of ice. Eona grabbed Kira and shielded her with her body as Carmilla raised her hand. The explosion was deflected; the humans came out, guns blared; Eona used her manipulation of wind to slow the bullet's velocity until they dropped. Carmilla caused the bodies of the enemy to twist and split. The sound of bone snapping and flesh tearing made Kira sick as she watche Carmilla manipulated their blood and rip it from the rebel's bodies as she screamed in pain and agony.

They were raised into the air, suspended by Carmilla, their blood controlled by the Empress. She pulled their veins from their muscles, wrapped it around their bones and arteries as she strangled them from within. Blood poured from all places; eyes, ears, nose, mouth and drenched their clothes. Kira watched their fate and was brought back to her past. She trembled in fear and covered her ears at the horrific sounds. Eona turned around and camping in front of the human as she blocked her eyes as the screams of fellow humans suddenly stopped. Limp bodies landed on the ground with a *thud*.

Eona uncovered Kira's eyes, and the woman shot an angry glare at Carmilla. The Empress cared not, whoever's blood she spilled, whoever she had to kill, no matter how many did not matter. No one touched or threatened what was hers, be it friend or foe. She would protect what was precious to her, by any means necessary, and ensure that fear rocked the core of the very ones who dared oppose. It was a message: the Empress is not to be trifled with.

"Sorry." Eona said, taking a step back, "Didn't think you wanted to see that..."

Kira took a shaky breath and opened her eyes before she swallowed and clenched her neck from ths discomfort she felt. It was a different kind of sensation than before, a craving, a hunger that made her mouth water and made her stomach twist.

133

"I've seen worse..." Is all she said when she walked past the Pureblood and glanced at the mutilated bodies of her fellow human.

She had to see this, had to accept the reality that she caused their deaths. In order to survive, she sacrificed them up, their lives were weighted less than her own. Maybe they could have lived, maybe not, but their deaths this way, by the Empress, were her doing. Kira knew this was the reality she had to understand and accept—accept that her choice had consequences. Either way... this was war. Innocent people will always suffer and die no matter what they did.

Another explosion, just below them, rattled the floor. The vampires staggered from the shake, a few lost their balance. Kira hit the ground on all fours. The marble cracked and snapped from the elevator and raced toward her. The floor gave way and collapsed beneath her. None could react in time and watched helplessly as it crumbled and Kira fell through, disappearing into the darkness.

Everything hurt, every step sent a jolt of pain in her body. She groaned in protest, partly opened her eyes, though her vision was blurred. Not much reached her, everything was fuzzy, her ears rang and her head pounded and a sharp pain in her leg could only be a break or fracture. It hurt to breathe. Raspy, only half her chest expanded with each inhale; a collapsed lung that was treated by a chest decompression needle already.

Kira tried to look up, tried to look at whoever, or whatever, carried her, but she could not identify them. All she made out was a glimpse of sky-blue eyes, before her consciousness slipped away and darkness took over. Her savior kept her close. The gunfire and explosions that echoed all around did not faze them. Humans and vampires alike raced past, but did not take notice of an unconscious woman being carried away by the unknown shadow.

Carried from the battle, the savior kicked open a door that lead to the hotel's loading dock.

"If you take her now..." said the vampire as he appeared in the door, "She still will not be free." He said, the figure stopped, "They will hunt her."

"I know." They said quietly, "But that doesn't mean I can't protect her... even if carrying her to safety is all I can do."

They set her down in a sheet basket and dug into her back pocket. Her phone screen cracked, but otherwise working. By now, the vampires of the Empire have likely already found the jammer and are destroying it. Sending a message now would have it delivered quickly, but allow enough time for the two of them to disappear. The man with crimson cat-like eyes remained in the doorway, awaiting the other to finish.

They sent the message:

    In the loading docks in a laundry
basket. Bring a doctor.

The members of The Last Stand destroyed much of the hotel, most of the rebels killed, though an unknown number escaped in the chaos. They failed their aim to kill the Empress and Princess, but they succeeded in their true mission: to show the world the vampires were not invincible and the Imperial Family was not untouchable.

Eona received the message first. She sprinted back inside, she found the loading dock and the scent of Cherry Blossom led her to Kira's location. She removed the top layer of sheets and found the unconscious human, her cellphone on her chest, her bloodied fingers and clean screen told Eona it was not Kira who sent the message. The princess shouted for a medic and an ambulance was called. Eona and Jake both rode while Carmilla handled the public. A live execution on television showed that the Imperial Family had prevailed now as they had in the past. Taken to a private hospital, Eona held Kira's phone in her hand and went through the messages and contacts.

Her own phone buzzed. She removed it from her pocket, a message from an unknown number appeared on her screen.

Keep her safe.

Chapter Ten
Inconspicuous Servant

"Stop rubbing it." Jake elbowed Kira as she rubbed the patch over her left eye. The woman stuck her tongue out, her hand dropped to her side.

Kira had sustained a significant amount of injuries when the floor collapsed: broken leg and ribs, a fractured wrist and arm. She had many lacerations, internal bleeding, and a broken eye socket. As though she had slipped through the debris, Kira narrowly avoided being crushed and fell many floors below, out of reach and out of sight. Far from where she had fallen, they found the human woman in the loading dock, hidden from anyone who was not told where to look.

Kira rolled her good eye, "Look, I didn't fall two-and-a-half floors to be told I can't scratch an itch." She frowned as she crossed her arms in her seat.

Jake handed her a beer, "Fair enough, Doctor Sanders did a hell of a job patching you up."

"Guess there's a couple perks to having vampire blood?" Kira popped the top.

The vampire chuckled, "Enough to join the dark side?"

Kira paused mid-sip and shot him a glare against a joke in poor taste.

"Sorry."

Kira stood. Jake dropped his head in his hand at the stupidity of the comment he made without thinking. She walked past Jake and Wolfgang, who glanced at her after she went back towards the end of the train. Doctor Sanders had indeed healed her, using her own blood. As a vampire who had not gone through a full transition, her blood would allow for a gentler, though slower, healing of the human's body. They mended broken bones in days, fractures in hours, there was no surgery needed, and scarring would not occur. Still... for a few days, Kira would be tender and sore.

In another compartment Kira sat as she enjoyed a view of the German countryside. Emily turned in the rotating chair to greet Kira.

"You feeling okay?" The doctor asked, as she extingushed a cigarette in the ashtray, "Still in pain?"

Kira shook her head, "No." She exhaled in frustration, "Just... a lot on my mind."

The sound of the locomotive and the ambient noise were enough to ensure no one would hear them. Emily gestured to the seat in front of her. Kira turned around to the door she came from and shut the blinds, before she went to the seat offered after. She flexed her hands in and out and felt her internal cup of fear and anxiety near a boiling point.

"He knew my name." She exclaimed as she clenched her aching jaw, "He knew my *real* name. That shouldn't be possible. I watched them die in front of me all except—" Her words lost their frustration and instead sparked an old, familiar feeling within her.

She had long suppressed it, long hidden it deep within her. It was irrational, unpredictable, and a fury of emotion that would threaten her chances of survival. *Hatred.* Hatred of the vampire, what they did to the world, what they did to her family and what they did to her. Against her best efforts, it was never fully extinguished. Those embers born

138

out of the past were always present, never truly gone. Kira had allowed those embers to dwindle to near ashes, until being attacked and nearly dying, but unlike before, she did not allow the fire to rage. She contained it, allowing it to be fed by her desire to survive. And now... those embers were being smothered by this chain, this stigma.

"This vampire, you said he had 'cat-like' eyes?" Emily asked inquisitively.

With a nod, "It's the first time I've seen or heard of a vampire with eyes like that, I asked Carmilla and she looked surprised... scared even." Kira calmed the growing heat in her chest. "I've never seen her scared before."

Emily tilted her head curiously. "And he came to you?"

Kira nodded silently as she thought about his words and the meaning behind them. The coincidences in what he said were no doubt targeted, meant to unsettle her and end the conversation with her name; it was to make her believe him. This vampire sought her out specifically, knew how close to Carmilla she was. He did not go through all that trouble just to warn her the Empress would eventually kill her. Not that that much was not already common knowledge. Kira had prepared and planned for that for a long time. *Oh.* She recalled another block in the road.

"I wanted to ask you about the Stigma."

Emily gestured 'go on' to Kira.

"You mentioned before the original version was to bind vampires to the one who branded them, right?" Nodding that she was correct in her memory, the human continued.

"Is it possible that 'binding' is present in the one on my neck?"

"Absolutely not." Emily sternly rebutted. "I designed it to ensure that a vampire will not roam free against the wishes of a human. Despite my state now, I too was once human, in another life."

Kira looked out to the window and watched the rolling hills race by as the train effortlessly and seamlessly glided across the railroad tracks. Kira said the word that more closely describes the state she believed herself in.

"What about being sired?" She mumbled, as she rubbed her irritated neck, "Not being bound in the obedience sense, but a physical apprehensiveness on being separated?"

The immortal doctor pondered over the term, her brown eyes deep in thought. *Now that I think about it... Emily's eyes are also a normal color. Carmilla said that means she's never had human blood, but she's pretty old.* Kira remembered the vampire never mentioned her actual age, but Carmilla and Eona both have mentioned the doctor being in their lives for a very long time. If that were the case, as a vampire not full-transitioned, she should still age and yet she is not. In her experimentations, did she stumble across a fountain of youth?

"When you say apprehensive...do you get sick when you're separated from Carmilla and Eona for a certain length of time or perhaps distance?" Emily questioned professionally.

Kira frowned. "Why would I get sick from being separated from Eona? Kinda, what I've been gunning for a while, you know."

"Humor me." The scientist in her emerged.

Discontent with the idea that she could actually be sired to Eona for whatever reason Kira continued, "In New York, I tried to leave, I was going to slip out with everyone busy fighting, but then..." She clenched the arm of the chair tightly, the light of the day suddenly cut off by the train's entrance into a tunnel.

"I hesitated, the more I thought about leaving, the sicker I got, like they attached my legs to lead whenever I ever made the attempt."

She thought about it more and wondered if her sacrifice of her own people was also a twisted loyalty.

Did this sire somehow corrupt her sense of self-preservation and intent of survival? Somehow, it seemed to taint and cloud her mind with an unnatural and unwanted desire to not be separated. She of all people trained herself to never allow this, to shut off her emotions and disconnect from what was happening around her. Her body was a tool, a tool to survive, that was never in question, and it allowed for her to do just that for years. Now that was no longer enough. Her mind was sharp. She knew how to play the Game and would use it for as long as possible.

The perfect opportunity came and yet... she did not take it, she could not.

Emily crossed her arms, "Are you certain it's a sire or... have you become attached to Carmilla herself?"

The armrest snapped, "Are you kidding me!" Kira shot up, "I could never—not with her—"

Without taking a defensive against Kira's anger she responded, "So its not about her being a vampire. So your body doesn't seem to distinguish a difference." Calmly she continued, "Emotions may have nothing to do with it, the Stigma physically altered your physic, it's possible that there are lingering effects of vampirism, but I think you are still here because you chose to be."

"Chose to be—why the hell would I *choose* this?" She released the broken armrest with a *clank*, "That's ridiculous!" Kira stood. "After everything they did—!"

Emily stood, her hands on Kira's shoulders and eased her down. "The Stigma needed a base, a power to counter your turning and a Pureblood against a Pureblood was your only chance."

"Meaning...?" Kira asked, heated, but sitting down.

"Your base... was Carmilla."

The sky-blue eyes flickered another hue, "What?" She gritted her teeth, "So what that what trauma bonded me?"

Kira shook her head rapidly and stood again as she paced back and forth. Carmilla never had an interest in Kira before she found out about the human's preference and that was not until she was eighteen. She took Kira from that cell and gave her to Eona to raise. The human child was like a new pet to give to her niece back then. *But...* Kira frowned, holding her sides. *Carmilla was there when I woke up, not Eona. Even if it was to warm her bed, she kept me around. She looked after me…protected me…why would she do all that?* She exhaled, frustrated. *Why does she have so much interest in me?* What was she brought there for, why would she stop Kira from being turned? Did she know who tried to kill her, was she protecting them? Her? *What the fuck is going on? Am I committed to Carmilla or are we, really…*

The shuttered door opened. Eona took a step into the train car, an awkward silence taking over.

"Yes?" Emily asked lightly. Kira too angry and frustrated to give an answer without snapping.
Eona's eyes wandered from Emily to Kira. "We're getting ready to arrive at the station. You guys coming?"

"We'll be there in a minute." Emily waved her away.

The door shut. Kira slammed her fist into the wall, breaking the wood. She growled, frustrated more than the fact that she didn't feel that. What was it really between her and Carmilla? The two of them could not possibly be; it was a sire; it was a synthetic bond, a fake. She and Carmilla could never be. It was nothing more than physical attraction; it was only friends with benefits, there was no emotion, no care; she was a blood bag to her dessert; the next warm body.

"Addressing that concern at a later date, with more privacy, the vampire you met: I doubt he means you harm." Emily changed the subject, "I wouldn't believe anything without proof, but maybe you should hear him out." She rubbed her head, "It could help you escape this place."

Kira looked at her, confused.

"If he is who I think he is, he will cross paths with Carmilla and that alone shows either his determination or desperation. Both are dangerous." Emily said, concerned, "I don't want you to get hurt."

Kira held out her arms in a hyff, "I have nothing. I'm no one. Killing me does nothing."

"Maybe Kira Nightraven isn't who he's looking for."

The train slowed, screeching to a halt, gravity having them lean forward.

"Either way..." Emily stood as she collected her bag, "He'll probably want to meet with you again."

Kira was ledt alone to think on Emily's words. She began to walk to the other end of the car, opposite of where everyone else was. *What could he possibly want with me? My family wasn't anyone important; dad was a soldier and mom was a nurse. I'm the only one left and I've spent my life in the Palace.* She thought about her past, she could scarcely remember anything before the Red Night. At the tender age of four, they threw her into hell on Earth and she knew nothing more than how to survive.

If it's not about my parents, then is it about Carmilla? Eona? He's not warning me out of the goodness of his heart. He wants something. Was it to drive a rift between them? An angle could be to use her closeness to the Empress to somehow blackmail her into trying to assassinate her? If that was the case, could he be working with someone within the Council? It was not a fairytale. Plenty of the members are not thrilled with how Carmilla leads nor her choice of... partners.

Based on her research and discussions with Carmilla, the Council's support of her is greater now than that of the previous Empress. Eona's mother died shortly before the vampires declared war on humanity. Kira says 'died', but rumors still circulate that her death was never truly clarified: murder. As this was often one of the main reasons for the war—humans attacked first. There are very few ways to kill a vampire, the only certain way is to destroy their core.

That's certainly a justification for wanting to kill the Empress. Use her human partner, easy scapegoat; blame the Last Stand; harder crackdown on human regulation. If Carmilla were to somehow be killed, no matter by what method, Eona is the next in line. It would crown her Empress and rule the Empire. *That wouldn't be a bad thing.* Kira thought, given Eona's personality then and now, she treats humans rather fair for a Pureblood of the Imperial Family. Is someone aiming to make her Empress then? She is not someone who can be manipulated or controlled, though. Eona is a progressive who may even dissolve the Council, which defeats the purpose if the goal is to keep or gain power.

If not about them, then it's about me. Again, that makes no sense. Is there something about my family I didn't know about? What relevance would it have now, though? The only option Kira saw was to wait, wait and see, wait and allow her new cat-eyed acquaintance to find her again. As unsettling as waiting for a blind spot was, she knew he was not foolish enough to meet with her when she was heavily guarded. He would wait when she was alone or vulnerable.

The door to the train car opened behind her.

"I know, I know I'm coming, Em —" Kira turned, expecting Emily, but was faced with another.
Wolfgang shut the door behind him. "Expecting someone else?"

"I'd rather jump off a roof, but knowing you, you'd do the favor of throwing me." Kira glared with her one visible eye.

The Commander chuckled, "Is the worst all you expect of me?"

"Well you are an ass." She said with a scowl, "And I'm smart enough to know which one is next in line to take a stab at me."

Wolfgang laughed as he walked toward her. He was a Pureblood Vampire, just like the Tepes, Eona's father, and the widow of the late Empress. Extremely protective of his daughter, he has eliminated anyone and anything that would so much as lay a hand on a hair. Devoted and loyal to the Imperial Family, he has served the Tepes for a very long time and from what Kira remembered he was one of the eldest living immortals in the world.

Wolfgang had never liked Kira, in fact he thought Carmilla's taking of her was to set an example to others. He thought she would die quickly, just as many of the Council

144

Members, to make a cruel game of how long a human would last alone in the halls. It surprised him the day he went with her to gain a human pet, that she had done so for Eona rather than for her own amusement. Despite his disapproval of having a human companion... it relieved him as a father to see his daughter happy. She rarely smiled since her mother had died.

"Then this should come as no surprise when I say: do not get caught anywhere alone, especially during the Council meetings." Wolfgang said as a formality rather than a warning, "It would be troublesome if you were to be mistaken as a snack for another."

Kira crossed her arms. "I can take care of myself, thank you, and I've done that for quite a long time."

"The Palace is nothing compared to the rest of the Council; you were sheltered."

"I know how to play the Game." Kira said firmly. Wolfgang scoffed, "A human has no place in the Game —"

"Which is why I learned how to play." The human pointed out, "You've been gone for a long time, so you still remember me as a kid—I've grown a lot since then and I'm not as naïve as I was. I've learned how to go unnoticed, how to be invisible because now that's how I'm going to survive."

The vampire tilted his head in curiosity, "You think you're going to be cast out."

"I *know* I will. I'm human, I have a time limit, I'm only as valuable as the services I can provide and a warm bed cools faster than information." With great seriousness and certainty, Kira cast out any lingering thoughts of the Stigma, the unknown vampire and the sire.

"You overestimate my value if you think otherwise." She added.

Wolfgang walked toward her. "As a human? No. It is you who underestimates your value, not for *what* you are, but *who* you are, to *them*."

People disembarked from the train and filled the slightly illuminated station. It was near sunset now, the coming darkness a sign that the vampire's natural environment was coming. Prowling the night, no human would be safe as it stalked them as the prey they were. Kira knew this feeling of stalking, feeling it all her life. Her years in the Palace had not numbed nor dulled her to that fact. She did not grow weak behind tall walls and a cushioned lifestyle. A warm bed did not soften her to the reality of what was just outside the window. Kira may have turned a blind eye to the treatment of other humans, but it did not mean she did not learn from it.

"It changes nothing..." Kira said as she walked around Wolfgang, "I'm living on borrowed time."

Eona and Carmilla departed the train first out of formality. Greeted by a few Nobles and Purebloods, they headed to the armored limousine accompanied by the Imperial Guard. Kira watched them leave from the train and waited until the servants boarded, tasked with retrieving belongings. She joined their ranks after she changed her attire to street clothes of a lower servant, with more formal attire for later in the evening. This is where her personal mission would begin, she needed to learn the servant routes and routines, and see where the guards of the castle would be posted.

Hohenzollern Castle is the ancestral home of the imperial family of Germany from more than a hundred years ago. In Baden-Württemberg, Germany, it acted as the meeting place for many council meetings before and post-war. While in the past the architectural blueprints were public knowledge, it ceased to be accurate. Many modifications and alterations took place in the interior to accommodate the immortals; their needs and wants, interior decorating, and such. Regardless, it did not make it impossible to know what lurks within—Eona ensured she would not go blind and where there were historical castles, there were forgotten secret passages.

As she aided the immortal servants, Kira noted immediately that there was not a single human among them. As she helped load the luggage, she also noted a few Imperial Guard remained stationed at the train, while this was not

146

unusual for security, she noticed one broke off and followed as she and the servants finished loading the truck and hopped in the bed. Half-expecting the ride to be silent with the vampires glaring at the one who did not belong, it surprised her they engaged in conversation during the thirty-minute drive. Still, she was not alone. Trusted staff members from the Palace were with her, aware of the decision to keep matters of the Palace within those walls.

"It's surprising to see a human as a part of the Imperial staff." Stated by an immortal woman, youthful, giving her forwardness, it was likely she was newer and younger.

Kira thought it wise to answer for herself, "A slave is not worthy to be employed by her majesty. Her benevolence in allowing me to work and live is payment enough." She recited, this not being the first time she has said the line.

Kira kept her eyes down to show submission, something her fellow staff members did not allow to go without defense.

"She works well for a human. Despite her physical disadvantages, Kira is one of the fastest learners we have ever had." Defend Edward, an ex-human who came to the house not long before Kira.

The others nodded in agreement. This helped win the staff in the truck over, but it was a pre-game. The real challenge was to continue her invisibility, working silently, inconspicuously while she gathered the information she sought. Carmilla had briefed Kira on which council members to pay closer attention to. There were twelve, each seemingly older and grumpier than the next. Nobles and Purebloods eager to play the Game, it is rare they have a new face. When the previous Empress died, Carmilla's place on the Council was left open, but she quickly awarded it to her niece Eona before she even sat on the throne. It did not win the new Empress any favors.

They took the visitor's belongings to the back of the castle, the servants filed in, then they took baggage to the rooms set aside for them. It was a significant advantage to know which vampire was in which room, especially to know which to avoid. There were some on the Council who enjoyed playing with their food before eating it. Others set their slaves out into the halls without a collar to be easy pickings for the wandering vampire out for a morning snack. Kira was very grateful that the Empress was her mistress now more than ever.

To avoid that, Kira wore a collar with the Empress's Sigil and applied also applied makeup to cover up the Stigma as though it were never there. This collar was a thick leather, a ring was at the base of her throat, seeded comfortably in the curve. To both sides was the Imperial Sigil, fashioned like a belt on the back of her neck. They tied the scarlet scarf around her waist. She could not part with it, but she needed the collar to be visible.

They would serve dinner in the next hour. Kira found a place to change. She removed her bandages and noted most of her injuries healed. Afterwards, she followed the staff to the kitchen, receiving an order from one of the head maids to take tea to the Empress's Chamber and took the tray. She took a cart and rolled through the previously mapped hallways, which unfortunately had her cross one of the drawing rooms where she was stopped by a vampire's who stood in her way.

"Ah." The vampire curled a toothy smirk, "What a treat you are." He said with a hand on the cart's end to keep her in place, "I wonder how sweet."

Kira lowered her head in a bow. "My lord, they have tasked me to bring tea to her majesty. If I may, she doesn't like to be kept waiting?"

"Oo, how tangy, a little fire in you." He hummed, as he opened the top to inspect the content, "I'm certain our Empress would not mind if one of her subjects takes care of their needs to better serve her." He reached to her hand, but was grabbed then held in place by an elder African and bald vampire.

"If you value your life you will not touch her." The elder vampire threatened with a deep French accent.

A hand touched her shoulder, but she did not jump.

She recognized the touch.

"I agree." Eona stated having appeared from thin air, "Touching a member of my house is grounds for death."

The first vampire hesitated as he broke into a cold sweat, his pride and boasting, shriveled like a raisin. His eyes looked at the sigil on the collar. The red of his eyes paled, as he choked a response.

"L-lady Eona..." He bowed. "Surely such extremes are unnecessary. Over livestock —"

To the front, the older immortal stood at Kira's side.

"It does not matter what she is, she is the property of our Empress." He said, "If you were to touch her property, what would stop you from aiming for her throne next?"

It took a great deal of restraint for Kira not to smirk, but this was not an ideal situation. She was had attention drawn to her, and she needed to defuse the situation quickly.

While she kept her head down and her voice low, Kira spoke up.

"My lady, my lord...it was a misunderstanding. I have been tasked with delivering her majesty tea and if I am delayed..."

The noble vampire gestured toward the end of the hall, "Of course, we should not keep a servant from her master. Please express our apologies to her majesty for the delay."

With another bow she continued on, followed by Eona, who waited a few more turns before they spoke.

"You alright?"

Kira scoffed. "No thanks to you. You know your savior complex is getting old fast. I'm trying to keep a low profile and you jumping in like that makes it difficult to do my job."

"I won't apologize for protecting you." Eona stated without apology.

149

With a growl of irritation, they turned to the short hallways where the Empress's room was, "Eona." Kira stopped before she turned. "I'm serious, this... this needs to stop..."

For the last couple weeks, Eona had been very forward about her intent on winning Kira over and Carmilla had tolerated it for now. However, the Empress was very possessive of what was hers and does not give up anything. For now, Kira was one of those possessions, buy Eona was determined to take the human woman away. Carmilla had become more and more public with her affections, but for what? Just to paint a target on Kira's back? To win her over? What did they think would happen? Carmilla used Kira to satisfy her sexual appetite, but Eona wanted something more. She wanted to go back to how things were.

Chapter Eleven
Topics of Discussion

As she clenched the fabric over her chest, Kira slowly inhaled and exhaled and worked to slow her heartbeat. She sat on the side of the bed with Carmilla deep in slumber behind her. Moments ago, their limbs were tangled together, their morning occupied with the seemingly endless ecstasy and lust. It was vanilla compared to their recent adventures, but pleasurable and no doubt the entire hall was aware. Muffled or not. The sex was amazing. Carmilla's nearly infinite skill and talent never failed to unravel Kira.

Every touch sent a jolt of electricity through her, every brush over her skin, every slight graze of her fangs— heat and excitement swelled each time Carmilla so much gave an inkling glance. She had a way of making the woman come undone in any way possible and knew Kira's body better than Kira herself. Pleasure was never in question between the two of them, but what was in question was what happened outside the bedroom. The human's heart was not equipped to deal with emotions beyond the bedroom. She hardened her heart to ensure she could keep the two places separate. But now... what happened inside the bedroom had begun to leak out.

Kira looked at Carmilla, covered in the Egyptians cotton sheets of red and black. She was peacefully asleep. Strange how peaceful she looked, how docile compared two hours ago. Now the seductress was deep asleep, satisfied and content. She had wrapped herself around her partner and untangling took a minute. The human's eyes softened when she watched the other woman sleep. How did she get to this? How did she go from fleeing the vampire, from fighting through teeth and nail against them to being here? How did she go from hating vampires, hating the Empress to this... whatever this feeling is? Eona, Carmilla; these growing doubts conflicted her. This uncertainty and clarity was a rare occurrence.

Her throat was dry and itched to be quenched, but not by water. Slow to stand so as not to wake her, Kira had developed her own skills in the bedroom, she learned to tip-toe around without stirring Carmilla. It was quite a feat to avoid the detection of a vampire, especially given their enhanced abilities. As she walked around the room, Kira went to the couch where her luggage was left. She dug into her clothes and she grabbed out the jar of the medicinal, dissolvable cubes Emily had created. Kira filled a glass of rosewater then dropped two cubes; she watched them disintegrate and blend into the water. She drank the cup; it did little to relieve her; she dissolved two more and downed the next glass quicker. There was some relief.

It's getting worse. Kira thought when she remembered when she broke the chair on the train before. After she popped another two cubes, Kira watched Carmilla more then rubbed her neck. *If Carmilla was the base for the Stigma, why is she trying to override it? Does she want me to turn?* The woman sighed as she put the cool glass to her neck. *That defeats the purpose of keeping me human; is she having second thoughts?*

Though she to find reasoning behind Carmilla's actions, Kira knew she has lived her entire life never fully understanding the reasons behind the Empress's actions. She wondered if she should talk to Carmilla directly about it, but how to bring up such a topic?

Kira returned to the bed. *Does she want me to turn? Is that why she wants me to be with her all the time?* Another thought came to mind, but she did not dare speak it. She pushed it away and intended to bury it deep, no matter what. That thought could not be allowed to stay in her mind because if it did, she would not stop thinking about it. It would distract her again. It would make her forget she is a human living in the world of vampires. If she thought about it, she would forget she needed to survive and Kira knew if she did... she would not survive. Kira knew that, but while the thought was pushed away, the feeling did not fade.

When she returned to the side of the bed, Kira opened her phone and scrolled through news and emails. A rustle behind had two hands curl over her shoulders then lock over her breasts.

"Good morning." Sung, the risen immortal as she nuzzled her face into the curve of Kira's neck.

Her breath tickled.

Kira could not help but smile some. Her body relaxed. The vampire sensed this. She pulled her partner back and eased her until she rested her head in the immortal woman's lap. There could be no complaints. It was a decent view.

"You talked in your sleep last night." Carmilla admitted for the first time.

Kira was neutral to the statement, as though she had not fully grasped what Carmilla had said or her mind was elsewhere. She hoped she had said nothing embarrassing or something she did not want the vampire to know, which at this point was a great deal.

Carmilla rubbed Kira's temples. "You kept apologizing, it seemed you were quite upset."

153

"Probably had another nightmare from when I was a kid." Kira said truthfully.

There was a hint of curiosity in Carmilla's eyes, she wondered what event would spark a lingering trauma such as this. As a vampire born in a different era, war was an expectation. She fought in many battles and wars, mainly against other vampires who thought to challenge and defy Council rule or the Tepes. It was normal and expected of them to be accustomed to war so much it was more unusual to be outside of battle than within. Carmilla was a born warrior. She enjoyed the chaos of battle and excelled at it, nothing like her twin sister. She was the pacifist of the family it did not gain her any favors during a conflict. Eona's mother preferred to settle differences with words than wars. She had the right ideals in the wrong era and made an enemy out of most.

"I understand little about this era... nor how humans process trauma, but if you talk to me... I will do my best to listen."

Kira smiled lightly, "Don't worry about it, it's nothing an Empress should concern herself with."

"I'm not asking as the Empress..." Carmilla's tone softened, "I'm asking as a woman who cares about you."

The hesitation and shock left the human speechless and slightly frightened. That dangerous thought threatened to resurface already. Carmilla leaned down and kissed Kira on the lips as she smiled, her taste lingered on the bottom woman's lips. Kira thought about what she would say, how she would explain why she cried 'I'm sorry' in her sleep repeatedly. All the things she had to be sorry for, her life until now, how she has lived compared to what her father raised them to live as. The shame he would have felt if he had seen how she had survived until now and the lack of care Kira would have of his opinion. The conflict within herself was about the principles instilled by him to survive, to have pride as a human; the treatment she has seen of other humans against the life of luxury she has lived until now.

Kira sat up, her back to Carmilla as she leaned her elbows on her thighs, "My dad taught us it was better to die free than to live in chains." She breathed.

"And yet here you are." The vampire replied equally quietly, "But you are unbound. He could not dare fault you for that which is beyond your control or how you choose to live."

Unconsciously, Kira rubbed at the Stigma, "There are many kinds of chains. Ones that are unseen are the worst of them all: they give the illusion of freedom."

Her tone was aged and tired, as though she had lived a long life as a witness to many horrors. For one such as herself, perhaps it was true, she experienced the worst life offered, robbed of her innocence. Carmilla could not understand 'not' fulfilling expectations of her parents. She had done everything that was asked and more and yet that never won the eye of her parents. Her sister, the younger of the twins, was a pacifist, the opposite of the ideal vampire, future Empress.

When their parents chose the younger to become the next Empress, Carmilla could and could not understand. She was ruthless on the battlefield, valued the lives of the immortal over livestock, and her gift was one that allowed her a significant advantage in combat and compliance. Rule by fear was far more compelling than loving one's ruler. At least Carmilla thought so. She thought she had fulfilled her parents' wishes, but apparently they had a different ideal for leadership on and off the battlefield. That was certainly the older sister's shortcoming: she had no care for politics, especially the Game. She would have rather killed those who opposed them rather than the painstakingly long process of swaying another immortal's mind.

"Why fear the opinions of those long gone from this world? They have neither hold nor power over you." Carmilla asked, as she did not understand why Kira would care about the opinion of the dead.

With a small smile, "It's just how humans are. We don't get a lot of time on Earth, so things said and done have a much deeper impact on the person we live as or become." She explained, "It's a constant fight... between what we were raised to be and what we've lived as."

Carmilla tilted her head, "A fight for what?"

There was a long pause before Kira answered back, "Knowing whether feelings are my own, or a product of another unseen chain."

She kept her head down and her collar high, in order to avoid drawing unwanted attention to her neck. Apparently Kira was a delicacy, at least that is what Carmilla told her and Emily confirmed when analyzing the Empress's behavior. Given what she heard the servants whisper about earlier, Kira did not want to attract any more attention than she already had.

Human livestock had been brought in for entertainment and consumption. Last night there was more than Kira's cries that could be heard the hallways. *If I had known...* Kira shook her head when she set another plate down in the dining hall. *I wouldn't have done anything.* She admitted. Her own neck would not be stuck out for a stranger... even if it was a fellow human.

As they finished the dining room being set up, Kira found her chance to slip away, she had exactly thirty-seven minutes before the beginning of the next session of the Council's meeting. She needed to find the secret passage discovered on a side note left by one builder long before the humans lost control of the castle to the immortal.

A crawl space originally used as a servant path, changed for framework, then again for piping in the 1920s, eventually abandoned after many of the pipes proved too risky to update with the desire to keep the castle's authenticity in place. It ran around the Council's Chambers, its use as a servant's path walled up one way and forgotten, until now. There was supposed to be one entrance that still allowed access, but there was likely a bookcase or curtain in front of it.

From the pictures on her phone, she could enter a room, based on the amount of dust it had been a few days since someone had been in here. Of course, that was likely to change tonight based on her luck which meant she should prepare for the worst. First she undid her collar, then she removed her dark gray uniform top.

She recieved a matching uniform with the rest of the castle staff in order to make her more inconspicuous. After she removed the top Kira revealed the matching moisture-wicking long-sleeve shirt. She placed the shirt on an armchair near the corner of the room. If someone came in, she could create a story easily: she needed a place to rest, needed to adjust her make-up or take her medication.

Plan for the worst, expect nothing less.

Kira felt around the western walls and lookedbehind paintings, curtains. *A-ha!* She thought triumphant, as she pushed the bookshelf to the side. It was heavy, weighed down by dozens of books. Kira took a step back, she inhaled slowly, less than pleased that she was about to take this risk, but she avoided taking her medication most of the day for this While her emotional turmoil was seen in her weakness earlier in the evening when she spoke to Carmilla, she could hold back enough to avoid revealing her true feelings. Despite that internal conflict, there was something good that came out of these symptoms: her strength significantly increased.

This realization came when she broke the door frame at the Palace, though then she scurried to hide it. After she took the medication cubes Emily prescribed her, her strength returned to normal. For a while she could keep within the ranges of a human, but Kira has quickly developed a tolerance to the lower doses. Emily was the only one who knew about the increasing symptoms and theorized that the integrity of the Stigma is not to blame, but the effects of the consumption of Carmilla's blood. The blood of a Pureblood had enhancing effects on a human; extended lives and youth, temporarily increased strength and speed. Whatever the reason, it was useful this time.

After a moment of focus, the bookshelf moved with greater ease and revealed the hidden door she suspected to the passage that time and people forgot. She grabbed the metal handle, forced the lever up, but rust and immobility over decades proved minor challenge. A loud metallic *clank* sounded when it was lifted and the swelled wood squealed loudly when opened. *If they don't catch me in there, that door will certainly do the job of fucking me over*. Kira shook her head nervously. Thankfully, she still had twenty-three minutes before vampires began to fill the chamber, which was enough time to weave through the broken pipes.

The former servant's path was dark, the occasional beam of outside light from the outer wall. Centuries of weathering eroded the ancient block bindings and allowed the outside artificial light to peek through and provide some light of the broken pipes. *Good thing I got my tetanus shot*. Kira rolled her eyes as she shut the door behind her. She crept between the pipes and thought in hindsight to bring gloves next time as she tried her darndest to avoid being cut. If they did not sense her through the walls, an open wound not only rang the dinner bell, but practically broadcasted her location.

No one knew about this portion of her espionage. She did not tell anyone, not even Emily. There was no information Carmilla needed because she was in this meeting. This was purely for Kira herself. It was a colossal risk, single-handedly the most dangerous action she has ever taken, but it was necessary. After what happened in New York, the Last Stand would not blindside her again, and certainly not by Carmilla. Kira had to know what the vampires were planning. She did not know if there was something she could do, but she could no longer turn a blind eye.

Halfway down the passage, there was a thinner section of the wall next to the chambers, which Kira believed would be an ideal place. The piping was less here, probably for the lack of a need. She stood up in the carved section, seeing six holes, four occupied with nails and two in the center.

Must be a painting or something. Someone had the right idea when building this place. She crouched, pulled out her phone; there was a good service in here; she moved her phone closer to the wall inner wall which had her lose that signal. *Signal jammer; smart, but you didn't start doing this until recently.* Kira silenced her phone. *Something has you scared.* She heard the doors open. *Or someone.*

The Imperial Guards, clad in armor black as night, gothic and sinister, was the traditional attire donned by every guard during these meetings. A tradition unaltered even by the change times and entrance of the modern era, this was not by any means ceremonial. This was battle armor without shine, full of damage. It was a testament to the victories of the warrior. The guards opened the double doors, twelve vampires entered, people from all nationalities and origins, eras and beliefs, but all connected by their crimson-eyed immortality. Twelve small stone chairs organized in a crescent formation of the chamber, a large stone throne a top two stairs with the Imperial crest carved into the wall. Just behind that wall, Kira sat against the wall, silently and listened.

The Council members took their positions, each member the leader of their prospective Houses most Nobles who swore their loyalty to the Tepes. They turned around in unison and stared at the open doors as four more Imperial Guard filed in, the Empress Carmilla Tepes, donned in a long, silky black dress, her chest open and exposed; cut down to her the center of her flattened belly. It barely concealed her breasts. Fabric wrapped around her stomach and held back the flowing material, the v-cut reached up to her thigh. She donned a gold festoon necklace, golden forearm bracelets, and earrings.

As the Empress entered, the Council lowered their heads and bowed as they acknowledged their ruler, one of the strongest Purebloods in existance. She glided across the floor to her throne, turned and then sat which released the others to take their seats. They sat having concluded formalities and dove directly into business.

"There is concern the new recruiting regulations will incite further rebellion among the humans." Said the first to take the floor, identified as Isaac, a Romanian Noble born in the late 14th century.

Another vampire scoffed, "Perhaps a few brave ones may try to cause a ruckus, but humans are primitive, domesticated, sheep, fear is the perfect tool for their compliance."

Kira clenched her fist behind the wall.

"Even among sheep there are wolves." Isaac pointed out, "Those wolves are the Last Stand, and just two weeks ago they infiltrated the Empress's hotel and brought down half the building." He gestured to the Empress, "Not that they would have succeeded against her majesty, but the same cannot be said for immortals who lack her exceptional capability."

"Your majesty, is it true that there was a warning given just before the attack?" Another immortal man asked.

Carmilla sat upon her throne, unamused, "Instead of questioning the reason of the rebels' failed attack, it would be of better use of your time to discover the location of their leader." Her lips pursed a smile, "That which you have continued to cannot accomplish."

The council member became quiet and did not speak again.

"As for the new polices you agreed upon, humans will join the rebellion with or without their integration. There is no need to care for the humans. Our focus lies on a greater enemy." Carmilla began, Eona finished.

"The *Reich*."

She was less than traditional. The Pureblood Princess wore a white suit, her dress shirt black, accented by a red tie. Her short hair was styled back, kept subdued by a mixture of gel and hairspray, wearing no jewelry of any kind, but on her jacket lapel was a single pin bearing the Imperial Crest, just as those that hung on banners around the chamber and carved into the stone behind Carmilla and unknowingly Kira. Though she held a Council Seat, she did not care to have it. She would rather be elsewhere, be with other people. She despised politics and the Game more than anything else and attributed them as a leading cause of her mother's death. The room fell quiet with the mentioning of the name, a tar forming in the mouths of any who spoke it.

The *Reich* was not just a rival; they were a cataclysmic event. Any clash with their elite, but small forces devastated the Empire's armies. Though significantly fewer, they were trained and united under a single goal: eradication of every single vampire within the Empire. A secretive organization, they have been a knife in the side of the Empire for centuries, led by an unknown, masked immortal many believe to be a Pureblood.

His defining characteristic was his crimson and cat-like eyes, unseen in no other vampire, his gift as destructive as Mother Nature herself. A vampire of few words, if anyone knew his true name, they dared not speak it. The people often called him 'The Pureblood King'. No one has seen him in hundreds of years, though.

A woman immortal spoke carefully, "It has been centuries since we have detected any major activities and your predecessors—"

"Were betrayed by immortal conspirators, embers of discord that were not stomped out. A single ember can spark an entire forest fire." Carmilla cut off calmly, "Make no mistake, those who are responsible will be dealt with in due time. But the matter and reality we face now is the returned of the Pureblood King."

The chamber erupted in uproar.

Is that who he is? Kira typed into notes on her phone. *If the* Reich *wants to destroy the Empire, then that puts me back on the idea he may try to use me to get to Carmilla.* She turned her head to have an ear to the wall. *If he's as strong as they say, using me could mean when he disappears, he may have lost his power somehow. Going through me is a really round-about way with a lot of chances for failure.* The human typed notes down.

```
What's his endgame?
Why me?
How does he know my name?
```

"How can that be? None of our sources, our spies, have come up with anything hinting at his return."

Carmilla paused, "One of my own sources saw him in New York." She worded carefully.

Kira's expression softened. *She's protecting me.* She shook her head. *Don't get sidetracked.* The woman told herself, as she knew if she thought any deeper, then her turmoil would throw her mindset into chaos and she would miss something important. Despite that she told herself not be swayed and to not lose focus, she could not help... but feel warm inside...when she saw Carmilla protected her. *It's just possessiveness. Think nothing of it.* Her heartbeat increased. She shook her head again and listened back into the conversation with the hope it would distract her.

"Numbers mean nothing if they are not trained. Bodies to throw at the *Reich* are a waste of blood." Another Council member argued.

Carmilla agreed, "They will be trained, but it will not be as soldiers. No, I will oversee their training, we will implement methods similar to Nightcore."

Kira furrowed her brow. *What the hell is she talking about?*

"Lady Carmilla..." Many shook their heads or dropped it, "Using that method... even seasoned immortals have a low chance of survival. You are exceptional and even you were unconscious for a month. We disbanded Nightcore for that reason."

Eona looked to the Council members, then to her aunt. "Does anyone care to explain?"

Mablevi was one of the oldest of not only the Council, but of vampires. Born in the third century, he was a human given immortality to save his life when the Shaman of his village in the plains of southern Africa sought different means to save his life. Despite his long life, he remained compassionate towards humanity, having great respect for the late Empress, who shared the same. Her passing dealt a personal blow to him, his suspicions strongly aimed at the elder twin denied the throne. Still... she dots on her niece more than he expected for someone who should be a cold-blooded killer. He was equally interested in seeing the source of rumors swirling the Game: the Empress's Pet.

163

"Nightcore was the name of a group of elite vampires trained by the Empire to undertake dangerous and often deadly missions." Mablevi explained, "They were our Special Forces, trained in a method with techniques that killed eight out of ten who underwent the training."

Kira covered her mouth to silence a gasp. *Carmilla... did that?* She was in shock. *She could have died—did she even have a choice!* It was almost impossible to control her heartbeat now.

"I have no intention of re-introducing the ritual as it's far too dangerous; even against the *Reich*, the chances of another Demon appearing are not worth the risk." Carmilla raised her hand to quell the uproar, "Regardless if they are vampire or cattle, the Ritual is a waste of life, but the training to prepare one for it, is not."

With her back against the wall, Kira stopped typing on her phone for a moment. She leaned her head against the stone. *There was a reason then.* Somehow, that relieved the mortal woman.

"It would be wise for all to monitor your communication moving forward and to enhance individual security. Though the *Reich* is a priority, do not underestimate what they nor the rebels will do to accomplish their goals. Do not rule out any possibility, but do not allow fear clouding your judgement." Carmilla advised, crossing her legs, placing her hands in her lap, "If there are no other topics to be brought up in this session? Shall we wrap this up?"

I shouldn't move yet, they'll definitely hear me. Kira thought as she closed her notes and locked her phone. The meeting concluded. The immortals filed out slowly which made it difficult to find the chance to slip away. Eventually Kira navigated through the rusted, broken pipes, an insistent vibration in Kira's pocket had her stop mid-step. She took her phone out and saw Carmilla's name illuminate her screen.

`Controlling your heartbeat is the best way to hide.`

Chapter Twelve
Beneath a Mask

As she looked through the glass windows, she stared at the dresses of the boutiques. One mannequin wore a sleek ivory knee-length cocktail dress with side ruffle featuring a high neckline, closed back and sleeveless bodice. The next was a Burgundy off shoulder bodycon dress. A single ring on the left held the two fabrics that kept the dress snug to the mannequin's arms, connected to the main dress by the front corner above the heart. The last dress was in the center, a wedding gown different from a traditional one. With silky shoulders, the fabrics flowed downward to a V-neck, kept in place by a cumber-bun style wrap around its waist. It began its color in white, it was not until the end where the gown ended ombre, as though the fabrics themselves were ablaze in deep flame. It faded from white into yellow, into orange, red, purple and finished in blue.

Kira stared at the wedding gown she saw her reflection as if she wore it herself. It was beautiful, unique in its own way; it blended traditionalism and youthful flare to appeal to a younger generation. The designer succeeded in that regard. She never imagined herself to be the marrying type. Frankly, there was nothing that led her to believe not only that she would find someone, but live long enough to even consider. Being the property of the Empress of humanity's immortal overlords limited the dating pool; it was non-existent. Though, it did not help her in case that she was hell-bent on ensuring no one even had a chance. Kira did not want to make that mistake ever again.

"See something you like?" Eona asked curiously as she finished at the bakery next store, her arms full of a box of sweets and two bags from clothes shopping.

Kira shrugged. "Just window shopping." She said lazily.

"Oh, my fair lady! Do thoust wish'ith to go to the ball?" Eona sang in a goofy Romeo and Juliet diction.

Kira hid a giggle behind her hand and found she could not keep a straight face with the vampire's antics. It warmed Eona's heart to see the woman laugh and smile again. It had been such a long time as Kira's mood and temperament as of late made it difficult to have her crack so much as a smile. Always on guard, she seemed to keep her heart as stone and it was difficult to find a crack. Carmilla has spent years chipping away at that stone, but not Eona. She did not want to cause any more pain, to make the woman's heart raw. She wanted Kira to open herself willingly, to melt the stone and have her remember what they once had. Eona would not give up, not to Carmilla, not until Kira herself told her there is no chance. Seeing as Kira continued to wear the scarf Eona gifted her, she knew there was one.

"You're ridiculous." The human woman smirked, as she shook her head, "So what'd you get from the bakery?"

Eona smiled widely as she turned the box in her hand to face Kira. She opened the lid and revealed cinnamon apple puff pastry, cut and shaped to a rose. Light coated with powdered sugar, Kira stared at the desserts in a neutral surprise.

"They're..."

The vampire rose a brow, uncertain, but hopeful.

166

A genuine smile came across Kira's face. "You remembered."

Eona lifted one out and offered it to the other, "I never forgot."

Kira took it and bit into the pastry, her sweet tooth as it was back then. Many years have gone by since she had these. The bakery only made them during fall, and Kira never went with anyone other than Eona. Carmilla did not have a sweet tooth and Jake preferred sour treats, but she could not imagine coming here with no one else, even Emily. This, just as the cliff and secret entrance... was one of the few things only they did together. The bakery that created these was small, an in-the-wall business few people knew about. It was a hidden gem of the city and very LGBT friendly. It was there Kira and Eona often went on their secret dates. Back then, they kept their relationshiphidden from most people, but Jake and Emily, of course, knew. Carmilla, well... Kira had thought they had done a good enough job at not being obvious, but apparently not.

They walked down the street and browsed to the city to go clothes shopping. Kira had wanted to get more winter clothes, with the season change. She felt the chill when she practiced her bow outside, but in reality it was an excuse to leave the Palace. Kira wanted her individuality, wanted to have clothes of her choosing and to be able to not walk on eggshells. Carmilla had not let Kira out of her sight, especially since New York, not that she got a get-out-of-jail-free-card when she eavesdropped on the Council meeting.

She certainly paid for that indiscretion, or was about to: her punishment was to perform before all in attendance of the ball. One of the survival skills Kira gained over the years was learning how to properly dance; another type of entertainment and enticement, though she could not consider it wholeheartedly useless. It increased her flexibility and dexterity significantly, which adds to her overall physical capabilities. No matter, Kira could not say it thrilled her to display her skills this time: Carmilla was practically waved a steak in front of hungry lions. At least it was a Masquerade Ball.

"You decided what you're wearing'?" Kira asked with a mouth full of food.

Eona rolled her eyes with a frown, "Probably a tailcoat, nothing too flashy, I don't enjoy being the center of attention."

"Pfff." Kira sounded humored, "You're the Pureblood Princess, you don't have a choice, you were born important." She shrugged, "Perks of being human is I'm practically invisible." Kira stuck her tongue out, "Unless, of course, you're told to perform in front of hungry guests, then you're dinner on a silver platter—"

"I'd never let that happen!" Eona snapped firmly.

Kira spun around having meant it more as a joke, but clearly Eona did not take it as such.

"Carmilla wouldn't let anyone, *especially* you, anywhere near me. Hell, she'd probably lock me in a castle tower if she really wanted me all to herself."

"I wish you wouldn't do that... considering yourself as nothing more than an object..." Eona said somberly, "You're more than that, to me—"

Kira popped a pastry in Eona's mouth, "Don't." She warned, "We can't."

Eona leaned forward into the pastry Kira held, her gaze was steady and confident and challenged the woman's weakened resistance. Her reddened eyes were not violent and hungry, they were warm, soft. Many believe the red of a vampire's eyes are all the same, but Kira knew vampires sometimes better than they knew themselves and even herself. Even if just a small amount, every vampire has a slightly different shade of red. Jake's were focused, solid, like jam. Carmilla's were powerful, hungry, and trying, as though desiring to change like a true crimson red. Eona's... they looked deep into Kira's sky-blue eyes; warm, the same scarlet she wore around her neck; welcoming. *Oh, no*. Kira's resolve faltered, the warmth she felt in her chest, the comfort, the

168

familiarity, the safety. *I can't... not again. If I let my guard down again, it's over for me.* She averted her eyes and stepped back.

"Anything is possible, you just have to have hope." Eona softly spoke, quietly so no others would hear, "For you... I would give up everything."

The Great Hall was filled to the brim with vampires of significant class and families. Purebloods, Nobles, every Council member all gathered under a single roof, the amount of security the greatest that not even God himself could enter. The double-floor hall was second only to the Throne Room in size and magnificence, its walls decorated with hundreds of years of craftsmanship and artistry. In this hall, it had changed much since the previous Empress's reign. The wealth of the Imperial Tepes Family locked away in an attic, covered by white sheets, changed when the rulers before Eona's mother passed.

It was reverted relatively to what was originally in this hall, but what had changed was the era in which the architecture reflected. It was cleaner, simpler, but grander in this sense, as though entering the Palais Garnier in France, without the incredibly intricate carvings in each pillar. Black and red curtains hung between the pillars on the second floor, the crest of the Tepes family the centerpiece of the wall above the duel staircase entrance, mirrored by the same carving above where the Empress sat in wait.

Many people took this opportunity to gossip and speak rumor, even before the Empress herself. Others would request her hand in a dance if they were worthy or simply brave enough, but it had been many years since she agreed. Often a private joke, whoever's hand she accepted be the man, woman or fluid would be her consort for the rest of the evening. Many times she accepted only a handful of people and even before that she would not have over one consort at a time, moving onto the next when the previous either fell out of favor or she lost interest in. However, in these last few years she has not once accepted the hand of any, the latest rumor and gossip being the mysterious 'Empress's Pet' not a soul outside of the Palace knew of.

They were an enigma, entirely unknown to the outside world. Many came here with curiosity, a thirst to know one more juicy detail. Who or what has seized and held the attention of the Red Queen? It would be difficult to know for certain, a masquerade ball is such as because people can hide themselves behind the safety of a mask. A trick, in reality, a mask, is not to hide one's self, but to show the world who one really is.

She was in a pleasant mood tonight and looked forward to tonight's entertainment. Eona was not happy with her 'insistence' on Kira's performance, but refused to admit she also looked forward to seeing it. Dressed in a black and deep blue tailcoat, Eona donned a mask that covered her eyes; half black, half silver, accent details lined around her eyes and across the mask of the opposing side's color. Carmilla, as much of her habits are, had her wear an elegant mask of lacy gold. It covered much of her upper face, the mask decorated with medusa's likeness at the top and snakes lining the edges. Her dress was shorter and allowed for a greater range of motion than others, a tiered velvet gown with a trumpet end. She stood with her niece, away from the throne, mingling with fellow Purebloods. This was the event of the season.

From the stairs came the night's first entertainment. Beautiful women lined the sides of the stairwell, dressed as belly dancers, masked all in uniformity of blues and silvers. One stood separate from the rest: a single woman in the same uniform and mask was colored in the Empress's banner. Crimson and gold decorated her body, powered golden flakes sprinkled on her forearms and neck. The makeup artist did an amazing job to cover the Stigma and made it not only invisible but also drew attention to what was beneath the gold top. What distinguished her further was her additional fabrics held by rings on one finger of her hand, attached to her hips. As the backstage dancers carried on their choreography, their formations meant to emphasize the moments of the single dancer, the center of their dancing lotus.

Eona passed a glance to Carmilla, who hid a pleased smile behind her wineglass, but her eyes gave away her true intentions. She wanted Kira, wanted to devour every inch of her, to savor her, and Eona would be a hypocrite if similar thoughts were not swirling around her own mind. The difference: one wanted to dominate, the other wanted to deliver from this place.

"See. I am not quite the monster you paint me to be." Carmilla said quietly to Eona, "I know she is shy about performing, so I had others join her."

Eona hissed, "You're dangling her in front of a room full of vampires like she's a piece of meat."

"Perhaps." Carmilla chuckled some, "But when they learn of my protection of her, they will never dare lay a hand on her." She said more seriously, her smile lowered, "She cannot live shut away in the Palace forever, by making the Game aware of her place at my side—"

"It will protect her." Eona realized the length of Carmilla's genuinely thought-out plan, "But, if it had been up to me, I never would have exposed her to the Game."

Eona tilted her head in confused accusation, "Then why did you?"

"I didn't." She said as she watched the masked dancer closely, her focus had her ignore those around her. "She is not the type to sit down and let the world go by. You would know that if you stayed in contact."

"I..." Eona's expression became tormented and guilty, "I'm here now."

Carmilla grabbed another glass and passed it to Eona. "Yes, but you were not back then. Now, you have no right to complain when she moves on."

"If." The younger vampire expressed with a smirk.

The immortals of the room watched the dancers, some human, some not. They danved among them as a forbidden fruit they could not touch, the most tempting of all was the mysterious centerpiece. The dancer dressed in crimson and gold, no doubt bidding to be favored by the Empress, or is already in favor. They craved the sweet life currency of the mortal, her youth, her beauty, but they could not have it. The troupe completed their routine, their central lone dancer nearly presented to the Empress for her taking. Had the room not been full of slightly respectable company, Carmilla had no objection to taking the masked woman on this very floor.

All good things come to those who wait.

As she departed the Great Hall, Kira went light-speed to the troupe's changing area and practically leaped from her outfit; she had left her jeans and a t-shirt in a bag in the room's corner. It was gone. *Alright which one of you assholes.* Kira groaned in annoyance then saw a garment bag with a sticky note on where her backpack had been. She looked at the note; it was from Jake.

Knock them dead!

From the note she glanced at the hanging bag, then crumbled the note in her hand; she unzipped it and was left wide-eyed. *Oh. Wasn't expecting that.* With help from the troupe, her makeup, hair, and outfit were brought together. A standing mirror allowed her to see the finished product: A deep blue formal tuxedo, the jacket's lips were a step away from tradition, it flared upward with a gold accent which matched the color of her dress shirt. Held together by a chain of the same, she wore black gloves. She held her mask. Full-face, it took the eerie shape of a skeleton, though its sinister shape was lessened by a beautiful blend of black, blue and gold, decorated with gold vines. *That's ironic.* She chuckled. A lamb to slaughter, and I go as the incarnation of my fate. She put the mask to her face, then tied the bands to keep it secure and inspected at the final product. It was as though she was looking at another person.

Jake waited outside the door, excited to see his mother's creation on his best friend. It was one perk of having a fashion designer as a mother. Kira was happy to see he waited for her. She was nervous at the thought of having to enter the Great Hall alone. She had hoped Emily would be here, but she was away on business, apparently out of cell range too; she had answered none of Kira's messages. It made her sad whenever she could not talk to Emily. The woman was always an open ear for her. She never judged Kira, but always gave her opinion, even when it sometimes was nagging. It reminded her of her own mother.

"I had my mom treat the suit. No one will tell you're human...at least by scent." Jake bobbed his head, "Just don't cut yourself, yeah?"

Kira bumped shoulders with him, "Thank you."

"Hey, I'm just happy I got a say! Lady Carmilla wanted to make you eye candy in a dress, but I could convince her to leave you be." He explained triumphantly, "I think I'm quite the negotiator!"

They entered a side door on the second floor, less populated by the mass crowd.

"I'll go get us some drinks, and be right back." Jake said, responded by an acknowledging nod from Kira.

Left alone, Kira leaned over the railing and watched the people below. Vampires all mingled together, conspiring, gossiping; drinking their expensive wins, eating their finger foods without a care in the world. She let out an exhausted sigh, her posture slouching, tired from playing prim and proper. The rest of the night was supposed to be relaxation, supposed to be her alone time; being here was a significant risk, a danger to herself, with or without a mask. Still, Jake had gone through hoops and fire to make her as comfortable as possible, to make her as invisible as possible. The least she could do was enjoy herself. Free booze was free booze, no matter whose tab.

"Not for the life of the party?" A feminine voice asked from the stairs.

Kira shrugged. "Not all of us enjoy the party scene."

The woman chuckled, "Can't say I blame you, these aren't the people I associate with."

"I thought you were out of the country." Kira raised a brow at Emily, whose voice she recognized behind the cheap plastic mask.

With a shrug, "I was until this afternoon, frankly I had no intention of coming, but Eona insisted, if only to keep you company." She leaned over the railing and looked down at the floor below.

"These types of soiree are not my cup of tea. I prefer bars and clubs. Alcohol loosens truth from lies; a drunk man's words are a sober man's thoughts." Emily said as she set an empty glass on the railing, "Expensive wine still tastes like over-priced sparkling grape juice."

From her pocket, she pulled out a flask. Twisted the top off, took a sip, then held the container to Kira. The human did not hesitate to take her up on the offer and felt a cool, wet sensation travel down her throat and into her pit. It was smooth, did not burn as it went down. It surprised her to know it was whiskey. Most of the whiskey Eona drinks was dry and burned; it was a gained taste Kira avoided. The mortal herself preferred bourbon, rum, and vodka with mixers, though she enjoyed the taste of rum more than vodka, but vodka made her drunk quicker.

"Trust me when I say I wasn't planning on being here either, but Carmilla had a different idea." Kira said with agitation, "If it wasn't for Jake, Carmilla would probably have had me in some skimpy dress which showed a bit too much cleavage for comfort."

Emily took back the flask. "I thought you enjoyed wearing dresses?"

"I do, but I hate being paraded around like a piece of meat. For Carmilla it's one thing, but I'd rather be invisible to anyone else."

"Even Eona?" The vampire slipped into the conversation casually.

Kira rolled her eyes as she Eona in the company of two men and a woman. Obviously, the woman had an eye for Eona. Whether for her position, power, or gender was irrelevant, it was bothersome to watch her friend being hung on in such a way. Eona was kind and considerate, often polite when she turned down people despite the playboy persona she had at the club before. She was a bit of a pushover for beautiful women. In truth Eona found it hard to be stern and say no, she tried to redirect their advances and played off as oblivious or coy. Carmilla was very different.

She held neither shame nor restraint when she expressed her displeasure with others. Sometimes with a show of force, other times with her sharp tongue, she held no fear in shooting people down flat and did not care for the embarrassment of those people. She lived a life where 'no' was not a word in her dictionary and had almost always gotten what she wants without apology. Carmilla's habits had indeed changed over the years. With Kira, everything was more of a coercion than a demand, but even that the mortal felt was just an illusion of choice.

When they first met, everything was a command, an undisputed demand of obedience. She would force compliance if necessary and it made the beginning of their relationship one strongly built on hatred and resentment. Over time, Kira learned that resistance was futile and painful because no matter what, Carmilla would win. Avoiding punishments altogether, she obeyed because of the uselessness of resistance, but it took a great deal of time for it to fade. Eventually, the two simply ignored each other. Kira was always with Eona and Jake, out of the way, having learned the basics of edict and chores of a servant of the Palace. It has brought her to serve as Eona's friend, but she was a slave.

"She's stubborn, I'll give her that, she won't give up on me and Carmilla won't give me up." Kira quietly admitted.

Emily held the flask to Kira again. "Love triangles are often like that."

With a chuckle as she sipped, "That's a one-way street."

"Between?"

"Both of them." Kira's humor turned sour. "I'm not making that mistake again, it almost cost me my life."

The doctor sighed, "Telling yourself a lie enough times doesn't make it true, just as two wrongs don't make a right. You still like Eona."

With a soured frown, Kira shook her head.

"And you love Carmilla." Emily said outright.

"No, I don't." The human huffed in annoyance and shoved the flask in Emily's hands. "Whatever fantasy you're making—"

"Dreams can come true and reality can be defined by what you believe, but to deny that truth is to lie to yourself." Countered the ex-human, "You could have killed her years ago. You could have run in New York and yet you did not because *choose* not to."

For a moment she dropped her head to her arms on the railing then Kira shot back up and turned to the doctor.

"I made a deal with the devil, to survive, so what? Who the fuck is gonna judge me? The ones who died free rather than live in chains? Fuck that! Eona helped me to forget watching what vampires did to my family, what they did to me! Not my worthless father who drilled that bullshit into our heads then ran off to play rebel! And when she ran away when I almost died—Carmilla was the one who helped me; she made sure I ate, she made sure I got my schoolwork and went to all my appointments with you. That was *her*, not Eona, *her*."

She clenched her teeth. Kira lowered her voice, looking out to Eona, "How could I look my family in the eye... if I admitted I fell in love with the ones who tore us apart?"

Kira turned on her heels and walked back to where she came, running into Jake, who held two glasses.

"Hey what's—"

She walked past him, mutted and fumed at Emily before she stormed out of the Great Hall. Jake turned to the doctor, who stood cross-armed, joined by the fellow vampire who offered Kira's beer to her, seeing as she was no longer partaking.

"They still haven't told her." Emily sighed to herself, as she stared where Kira had left.

Jake tilted his head, frowning at her, "Would you want to be told?"

Emily turned to look at the party. "Humanity is unique in its ability to withstand hardship. However, the worst thing that can be done to a human, something that could break them, is taking away their choice."

Kira hid the rest of the ball in the kitchens. The Head Chief allowed her to assist in meal prep, which involved chopping vegetables, easily a mind-numbing task that had her pay attention enough just to ensure she did not cut herself. Hours went by. The kitchens were closed and emptied; the staff left for their homes, guests departed for their hotels in the city, and a handful of Council Members remained, offered rooms in the Palace in place of the time to travel down. Those who enjoyed and supported the Empress more often than not took her up on the offer. Not that Kira wanted anything to do with vampires for the rest of the night.

She removed the jacket of her tuxedo and held it under her arm. As she left the kitchen loosened the tie and unbuttoning the dress shirt then untucked until it was fully opened. She held the skull mask in the same hand as the jacket, as she swayed back and forth in the hallway. *Christ, that was a long night*. Kira thought when she blew out a huff when going down the ill-lite hallway. *I can't believe Em actually said that. She knows me better than anyone and she seriously said that.* Emily has been her sole confidant, the only person to have been human to have understood the pain inflicted by the vampire. Choice did not turn the doctor, she just ripped her choice as Kira's nearly was... or will be, it's hard to tell anymore.

She helped Kira to preserve her humanity. Her name, the name of a human, was a gift from their parents. The name of a human was sacred, holy to the owner, what separated them and made them individuals. It was not common for humans to give their immortal overlords their real names. For giving it to them meant being bound and chained in every part of their being. She held onto that name and kept, even if an acute amount, of a freedom that could not be taken. The vampire may take their mothers and fathers, sons and daughters, brothers and sisters; freedom, but there are things that cannot be taken: faith and one's name.

This is why Kira did not understand why Emily brought up the notion of 'love'. She has been her only staunch ally, able to resist 'Absolute Rule' from a Pureblood; she covered for Kira on over one occasion. Was she doubting Kira's conviction to survive? Did Emily believe Kira was losing too much of what made her 'human'? She did not understand why; to provoke her? To test her? Emily had never brought up relationships. It was a sore subject unofficially on the red list of things, not to mention in conversation.

Em is out of her mind if she seriously thinks I would even consider being in a relationship anything more than physical. Kira turned the corner to the familiar hallway. This corridor comprised of seven large bedrooms, each had a full bathroom and walk-in closet, patio access; in Kira's room, she had a queen-size bed as she was not comfortable with anything larger when she slept alone. In fact the queen was a bit too big for her liking too, but she knew it would not be changed. The room was spacious, there were very few personal effects that made it 'hers', since she owed nothing that was not given by the Empress. In her room she had a simple platform bed, no poles or canopies. She had a small couch that fronted a flat screen TV. There were three dressers, covered mainly with different plants. The space that was filled was green, different trees and bushes, plants of advanced and even master level of care needed. It was a quiet hobby, one that required great care and detail, but also forced her have patience. Many people had no interest in watching something grow. They cared about the end product, not the nurturing; not the time and effort.

This was Kira's second room, as she had 'graduated' from the first, which was more of a closet. Eona's room was the second on the right. Kira's was the first on the left; Carmilla's the master suite was the last at the end of the hall. As she turned the corner, Kira was in her hallway; her phone buzzed with a message from a friend of Jake's in a group chat of theirs. Pictures from the Ball of their gowns and masks. It made Kira smile, but not enough to distract her fully. She sighed and flipped through her phone to her messages with Emily. *I should just ask her outright* — A noise in another room, that room; the door open. She had not entered for years. On the way to Eona's room, who had a secret passage to the kitchens, was the room where she almost died.

She stopped as she reached for her own doorknob, but her hand hovered over. *Don't*. Her breathing staggered, her heart pulsed throughout her whole body as her hands shook. *Don't go*. She grabbed the doorknob.

A voice. A familiar voice, it silenced all rationality, any sense of self-preservation. Her body moved on its own she turned around and walked to the partly opened door; she did not think, only acted. She pushed the door open. Kira's first step was a stumble. She almost fell in; the door seemed lighter. It felt like it was going to fly off its hinges. She looked up, saw the owner of that voice; her crimson eyes closed. Carmilla was sitting on the couch. The other, unknown woman was a curly blonde, a model who wore a dress that bordered on lingerie and an appropriate ball gown.

179

The woman was kissing Carmilla, only to pull away and cast a disapproving eye to the rude interrupter.

"Oh? A mouse seems to have wandered into our nest." said the immortal woman, who smiled with a hunger to not devour in lust, but to consume, to quench her thirst.

Carmilla looked past the woman and saw Kira, surprised by the human's presence.

Kira looked at the Empress... and then she bowed her head low then broke eye contact. She rose, shut her eyes and gave the two immortals a small smile.

"My apologies to your majesty." She recited lightly and formally as she grabbed the doorknob and pulled it, "Forgive the interruption."

The door shut. Kira stood there for a moment; motionless, neutral in her face, empty in her thoughts. She walked away, down the hall, past her room. The Palace was silent, all but security was in their rooms either slept or otherwise. Her walk, step by step, increased. What started as a walk became faster, a jog turned into a sprint. Through the palace, past the throne room, the kitchen, the courtyard, the Great Hall. Kira ran as fast as she could into the garden and found the secret passage. She climbed dozens of stairs until she breeched the surface that overlooked the valley below.

She panted heavily, Kira's breath created clouds in front of her face quickly dissipated then renewed again with the next. She looked up into the blackened sky, the late fall chill crept into her heated body. Each breath brought cold air in, syabbed at her enflamed lungs, each exhale melted the icicles. Though she tried to calm her breathing, that sight could not escape her thoughts: Carmilla kissed that woman.

Who was she to feel this way? Who was she to think this way? There was no obligation between them, no vow; they were sex friends... Then why does it hurt like this? Why does this tight pain in her chest persist? This insecurity towards Carmilla; fear. It was not her safety, her sense of self-preservation of her life was not what was at stake; her heart, hardened to stone, now found a fracture in its surface. What is this? She was only human, insignificant, and mortal. She would grow old and die, but given her life, she would never make it that far. To them she was livestock, food for the taking; these were monsters in human form. How could she feel this way?

Eona ran from the passage entrance, her head snapped left, then right, before she saw Kira.

"Kira." Whispered the immortal quietly, she kept still as she stared at the other woman's back as she sat on the edge.

Kira glanced over her shoulder, her eyes betrayed her innermost thoughts to Eona. Cautiously, the immortal walked to Kira's side and sat down beside her. She held a hand to Kira, cautious not to touch her, not yet, not when she did not know what happened. Her eyes reflected a strange emotion she had never seen Kira express before. Was this caused by her symptoms or... Eona had come out of her room as Kira had turned the corner from their hallway, she sensed Kira and saw Carmilla leave the room, another woman in her company. It took little to draw a conclusion.

"I'm here." Eona reassured her soothingly.

Kira tried to hold back, but it was impossible. The emotion spilled out in front of Eona, who then pulled her into a hug, holding her against her immortal body. A selfish thought passed through the immortal's mind: this was her chance to discredit her aunt's affections for her, to convince her they should be together. But that was not for her to decide. It was not right to take advantage and right now Kira did not need a lover; she needed a friend.

The human woman finally put a name to the emotion that could no longer be hidden: jealousy.

Chapter Thirteen
Revelation of the Past

She leaned her head against the wall of the truck, the paved road ended miles ago, but the bumping did not bother her. Kira did not know where they were going. Eona refused to tell her, and she did not care. After the ball, the two women departed the Palace at first light, took a backpack full of clothes and little else. They hopped on the first public plane out of the closest international airport and were gone. After over twelve hours halfway across the world, they landed back in Germany. As German was not one language Kira spoke or read, she could not read signs that said where they were and she did not care to Google Translate.

"We'll go into town later and pick up groceries. Is there anything in particular you want to eat?" Eona asked as she the truck onto a bridge that stretched over a small creek.

Kira watched trees increase in number, the ground blanketed in decaying green, gold and browns. It was beautiful to see the transition of the seasons, if disheartening to see beauty in death. It was quiet. The noises of a busy industrial city did not travel up the valley walls and climb to a Palace high in the mountain.

"Hey." Eona gently squeezed Kira's hand.

The physical touch brought her back from staring off into the woods.

"You haven't eaten since yesterday." Said Eona with concern, "And you're no fun when you're hangry."

Kira cracked a small smile It made Eona smile too. Sure, the vampire's jokes and puns may lame, but even if it could distract Kira, even for a moment, it was worth it. No doubt their sudden departure would spark problems. Kira had turned her phone off while Eona left her on and it had blown up relentlessly. Eona put out the fires as Kira slept on the plane, but eventually she would have to deal with certain ones herself.

They would only be here a week, but it was a week away from everything. Friends, family, societal expectations; Kira was not a human and Eona was not a vampire, just two friends on vacation. Where they were going was special. No one but Eona and her father knew, a home away from home when they needed to disconnect and get away.

The truck rolled up a hill and came to a stop in the driveway beside a log cabin on a ridge that overlooked the rolling hill and woods below. On the back of the mountain, it was secluded, but only a half hour away from town by truck. Kira looked at the cabin, then at Eona in question.

"Go ahead and put your stuff inside, keys under the third rock on the left." Eona instructed as she got out of the truck and headed to the back of the cabin.

Kira grabbed her backpack at her feet and Eona's in the back seat, she left the truck and went to the front door. She retrieved the key and unlocked the door, the entered the naturally lit house. It was a cozy size, around seven-hundred square feet. The living room, kitchen and dining room were all together, two small bedrooms were to the right, a shared bathroom between the two connected with John and Jill's doors. She looked back to the living room and saw what she expected: a wood fireplace. Kira thought about her childhood, about her family alive and surviving in the woods, living in a cabin similar to this.

"This is my dad's cabin. We used to come here when I was a kid, when my mom needed a break." Eona said, her arms full of wood, when walking to the fireplace and set down the bundle

"He and I used to come every other weekend during breaks. He took me hiking, fishing. I was hoping to bring you out here under better circumstances..."

Kira walked up to Eona and hugged her from behind.

"Thank you." She mumbled into the taller woman's back.

Eona dropped her head some and cupped her hands over Kira's. She turned then kissed the top of the other woman's head. After they set their bags on their beds, they jumped back into the truck, made a quick run into town, and returned with their arms full of groceries.

"Mind starting the fire? I've never been good at it." Eona asked as she put the produce in the fridge.

With a nod, Kira took a box of matches. She threw a pile of tinder first, then formed a tent around with smaller kindling. Satisfied with the beginning of the fire, she kept smaller sticks to her side. An actual log would not be added till there was a decent fire and ember pile going. With a little patience and air in the right place, a stable and warming fire burned, and illuminated the room and heated the cabin. Eona was in the kitchen chopping vegetables. The stove was on behind her, water on the boil for whatever she intended for them to have for dinner.

Kira grabbed the throw blanket off the back of the couch and threw it over her shoulders. "Want some help?" She asked to come toward the bar.

"Nope." The vampire smirked, shooing her away, "Go sit down, before you fall down."

Doing as told, Kira found a comfortable place on the corner of the couch, she propped her head on her hand as she stared into the fire. Twenty minutes passed and Eona brought two plates of dinner: Schäufele. Pig shoulder, with gravy and potato dumplings. Savory and warming. Eona disappeared for

185

a moment, then returned with two German brews between her fingers. Grateful, Kira took one then curled her legs up to make room for Eona and began to eat.

"I'm thinking we can catch dinner while we're here. There's some good fishing up the stream. Maybe later this week we can try the spas? I've never been, but they're supposed to..." Eona noticed Kira stared at her with a small smile, "What?"

She shook her head, "I was just thinking about when I was a kid. Before I met you... I used to live in a cabin like this." Kira gave a pained smile.

Eona looked softly at Kira, "You never talk about what was before." She pointed out.

For a moment, Kira thought about what was said to her. It was true. She never mentioned her family, but it was not without reason.

Kira looked down at her half-eaten plate and her mouth dried. "Do you know why I've never told anyone my real name?"

Eona shook it in not knowing. She had always wondered what Kira's name had been before, but she attributed the lack of knowledge to memory loss, not a refusal to reveal it. After all these years, after all the years they had known one another, Eona had thought she would have told her if she had known it. Understanding that, Eona realized just how little she actually knew about Kira. Her real name, her actual birthday, her parents; it's like the person Eona knew the human as has been a mask to the person she was. If that were true, it would consider the person she is now truer than who she was.

"For humans, our names are sacred to us. The first thing we are given when we're brought into the world." She looked at the fireplace. "You really don't know how bad it was, after the Red Night."

"The first launch of the conquest..." Eona muttered, as she knew the name as a different, official historical event.

186

Kira did not learned it that way and continued, "My people hunted animals, they trapped us, threw us into cages; killing and draining us in front of our families. Our freedom was taken; our pride, our loved ones; our names were the only thing that couldn't be taken. They connect us to our parents, the history and memory of our ancestors."

Eona frowned shamefully.

"I didn't tell anyone because I was afraid that I would lose the last thing that connected me to my family." Kira said, her words seeped with sadness, "I'm forgetting them... the longer I live among you, the more I feel like I'm becoming someone my family wouldn't recognize, that I couldn't recognize and that terrifies me."

"Do you regret it..." Eona whispered quizzically, "Coming to the Palace...you and me...?"

A small smile cracked the side of her mouth, "My time with you all...as scared as I've been to lose who I was...I won't ever regret the time we've spent." She looked at Eona. "I don't think we can go back to how things were, but... I don't think I could be happy without you in my life."

Though she said that, Kira doubted there was a happy ending for them, not while she was the property of the Empress, not as a human in the vampires' world. Even if she were to be released from serving Carmilla, she would never be free. This mark, this Stigma was its own chain and the longer she was around them the more pieces of her former self would be chipped away. It did not matter; it took her choice away, and it made it impossible to know whether her feelings were genuine.

It would be a lie if she said she did not love Eona at one point, but whether those feelings were real did not change the fact they are not the same now. Kira would destroy herself as she fought her haunting past with the life she had lived until now. In order to avoid heartache, to preserve her own life, Kira shut her heart to everyone because she knew she needed to survive before earning the privilege of living. Such was the cruelty of this world. Even if Carmilla were to

187

somehow let her go, that she could get past the horrors she witnessed at the hands of the vampire, it does not change the rules of the Game. Eona may not care to play, but Kira has paid attention: they would ostracize Eona if she chose livestock as a lover, especially as a Pureblood of the House of Tepes. If something were to happen and she was named Empress, she would have no support from the Council and civil war would erupt, it would engulf humanity once again into a bloody conflict.

Something she never thought she would ever reveal, would ever talk about until the day she died, surfaced. Kira swore she would take this knowledge, this truth to her grave, that she would never give the vampire the satisfaction of knowing just how deep her pain was. But Eona was not just any vampire, she was not cruel or murderous; she was gentle and kind. This woman cared for Kira, not because she was human. She saw Kira for who she became. Eona was the beginning of her new life. She was the foundation of who the human is now. She helped give her stability, helped make her feel welcomed, feel safe, feel like the world was not full of only horrors.

"You know..." Kira set her plate on the coffee table behind her and opened her beer, "Emily is the only one I've talked about when my family and I were on the run, but there were things I never told her... I've already betrayed my people, but I didn't want to betray my family."

Eona shook her head as she leaned forward, she grabbed Kira's hands with her own. "You don't have to."

With a bite of her lip, Kira inhaled while she nodded her head, "I do... because I don't know how much longer I have until I forget them, until I can't recognize her anymore."

"Her?" Eona asked in confusion.

Kira breathed in deeply. "I'm the only one left in my family: my dad left and never came back. A year later our

cabin was found...my mom...and my sister... no one else made it out."

"Anna!" He shouted from the truck as he laid the horn repeatedly.

Kira and her sister were in the back seat of the 2011 Ford F-150. Their parents rapidly filled the bed of the truck. Usually they would be in their car seats, but they had been taken out to make room for supplies. Having been woken up in the middle of the night, Kira and their parents took her sister and put her into the truck in a haze.

"Daddy, I want my teddy bear—" Kira muttered in a sleepy haze and then coughed.

Her sister pulled the blanket up to keep the sickly Kira warm as their father twisted around in his seat, reaching out the bear to his daughter, "Here sweety, now try to get some sleep." He slammed on the horn again, "Anna, we need to go NOW!"

With three enormous books in her hands, Anna ran out and got into the truck as she shoved them in a backpack: photo albums. With no time to argue, Marcus quickly put the truck in gear just as Anna closed the passenger door. They turned from their street on the base, entered the main road that would have them out the front gate onto interstate 185 heading north. They had to get away from the cities, had to go as far north as possible, into the mountains, or forests, far from anywhere human or otherwise could access easily.

"Glove box." Marcus said. Anna did as instructed, she grabbed the holstered Glock and put it on her hip. "You still remember how to use that?" He asked as he turned again.

"Grew up country too, remember—now what's going on? Why are we leaving? Did something happen on your mission, you've been—"

"Daddy, where are we going?" Asked the older sister, as she rubbed her coughing sister's back.

Marcus and Anna exchanged a look.

"Something went wrong, *very* wrong." He explained, "War is coming and the world we know is gonna end."

Kira was tired, her frail body drained of her energy, and she fell asleep. She remembered being woken up much later, car horns and alarms blaring, her mother's voice in a panic. Her sister had woken her up. Though nearing five, Kira's other half was very mature for her age, she took care of Kira with her being in and out of the hospital much of their lives. Since she was born, she had a weak body. Her immune system was not as strong. She was slightly smaller than her other half. The elder sister had learned from an early age to be a support system, to help herself because in a way she had to feel what Kira was going through.

Suddenly someone hit the side of the truck which terrified the daughters. Blood smeared on the side as the person slid against the door and dropped to the ground. They had a massive gash on their neck...like an animal had torn it out.

"Shit!" Marcus cursed as he turned the wheel, the tires went over the street curb and onto the sidewalk.

The experienced soldier had tried to avoid the cities, but the rural areas were all out of gas and there was hope they had left and gotten ahead enough of it, but that was wrong. They were here, and they had already begun their attack. Marcus sped the truck up without care if anyone got hurt or injured. His priority was his family and no matter what... many people were going to die. They got around the traffic block, the off-raps to the city were bumper to bumper. It had already started and the people were in panic.

Despite their failure to avoid everything, they could get through many states before the rest of the country caught on to what was happening. They had to take many detours to avoid the interstates and the cities, all the way from Georgia to Virginia. Though they intended a straight shot to Canada,

Marcus was rethought his original plan. A few days' trip turned into many and his family was tired, they were not trained like him. He thought to connect with one of his former Commanding Officer in Washington DC would be his family's best change chance of survival. It was within an earshot of Norfolk and likely if the ships were not destroyed they would load persons of interest onto the carriers and make for the waters.

His friend had already contacted him and told him to rendezvous at the predetermined location where a chopper would meet them to take them the rest of the way. That was yesterday and his friend had not answered him today. Now he had to make a call, a choice that would protect his family. Richmond had no side-roads to exit the city and now that they had launched their attack at last, mass panic would fill the streets as people abandoned their vehicles to flee.

A dump truck ran through the streets, side-swiped the Ford, it spun, Kira slammed her head into the window, the tire of the truck hit the curb, it flipped once, then twice, hit a traffic pole and stopped it on its side. Everything went black. She awoke to her mother shouting for her daughters. Her sister helped her to her feet. They crawled through the center console to their mother, who lifted each girl into her arms and to their father out the front window, kicked out by him. Once a couple of quick bags were grabbed, Marcus snatched his pistol and rifle, slung the larger and swept one of his daughters into his arms while Anna grabbed the other.

"Mommy!" Kira cried, her face full of tears and blood. As she had hit her head and scraped her knees.

They ran through the streets, people screamed, cars blared their horns and gunshots down upon the people. Marcus jumped back as he avoided a falling human, attacked by a red-eyed and fanged monster. His warrior's instinct would have had him attack and kill the monster, but his knowledge and parental instinct taught him to stop and think before acting: to protect his family.

"Anna!" Marcus called as he held the elder sister and covered her eyes with her hood.

Anna did not have the time to do that. She had nothing to shield her daughter from the horror she was to witness. She held her daughter's head to her shoulder, "Honey, mommy needs you to close your eyes, okay—no matter what you hear—!"

But Kira could not hear her, not over the explosions, not over the cries of people who begged for someone to help them as red-eyed people ripped into their necks. She watched these people all wear the same uniform, as though they were like her father and a part of the military, but the military would not do something like this. They were good people; they protected them from bad people. Police and National Guardsmen organized, created blockades, despite the madness, they used their cruisers and trucks to stop larger vehicles from coming through. Armed with live ammunition, they unloaded their M-19s and M-1s on the red-eyed attackers. It did little to slow them.

They turned onto a larger street, Marcus shouted to Anna in the front that they needed to find a vehicle fast. He had seen a railroad system and active trains. If they could get on one, they could quickly escape the city to wherever it went and go from there. He needed to find his bearings, though. Marcus shouted screamed. He pulled out his pistol and unloaded half his magazine into the chest of a red eyed, but it did little more than make them smirk.

"Come here, sweetheart—" Smiled the monster at the child in Marcus's arms.

Anna set Kira down. She charged the attacker, shot him in the head then pushed him to the ground. Marcus scrambled and got on top of him as he drew his K-bar and stabbed him many times into the heart. It did the trick. Kira turned around and saw she was the only one in the mob motionless; her family was not in sight. She moved out of the way, afraid the people would crush her. Behind them, she turned to the sounds of marching boots.

She saw people cloaked in red and blacksThey were beautiful, like statues she saw in books at school, their crimson eyes mesmerizing; Kira remembered when she watched and listened to the vampire's words. No others seemed to listen, but she spoke anyway, her eyes locked onto the human child as though she looked at her and only her.

"Attention foolish humanity! We vampires take back our world and save it from you! Resistance is futile." Kira watched her without understanding her words, without understanding why.

Anna shouted for Kira. She sprinted and pulled her into her arms before she turned in the same motion. They ran down the street, but the daughter could not take her eyes off the silver-haired woman who marched in front of the army. Captivated by the deep red, she felt like she could get lost in a field of roses. The elegant, golden pauldrons she wore and her long, silver locks pulled up into a ponytail. Kira did not know who that woman was, but she was prettier than even her mom. The woman tilted her head slightly. Her eyes widened for a moment as though they were the only two people in the world. She said something, but Kira could not hear from that distance.

They were beautifully dangerous. Kira did not know what they were, who they were, but she could not stay here. She cried for her parents, but could neither hear nor see them. Her father, a very large, muscular soldier, broke through the crowd, grabbed his daughter, nearly threw her over his shoulder when he turned to run in the same motion.

"Marc, here!" Anna shouted as she cut through an alleyway and found a chain-link fence that bordered the railroad yard.

They found a break in the fence, the family slipped through as the train began its departure. First they loaded the girls then Marcus helped Anna into the slowly moving cargo car, then joined them. Together, the family watched the illuminated city grow smaller in the distance, but the fire that glowed in the night allowed for a second setting sun to be seen long after the city was out of sight. Kira's sister pulled from the backpack she brought, Kira's teddy bear and gave it to her to comfort when she coughed again. She rubbed her sister's back, as their parents talked then also watched the ground burn the sky.

"What was wrong with them?" Kira whispered. "Why were they hurting people?"

Her sister leaned in. "Daddy called them 'vampires'." She answered. "He said they're very bad, they're monsters."

They headed west on the train for as long as possible until they had not seen a city for dozens of miles. Once the train stopped, the family disembarked and kept on their feet away from the main roads. At one point, her father told them to stay put. He disappeared for an hour and appeared again with three backpacks full of supplies; canned foods, weapons, survival. Their parents argued about how and where, but Marcus would not apologize. This was how they would have to live if they were to survive.

A long time passed as they went from house to house they never stayed in a place for more than a night. Marcus taught his family how to survive, how to be unseen, how to scavenge, and above all, who their enemy was: the vampire. He taught them to read the signs of recent activity, how to hide their scents and how to slow their heartbeats. Many close calls came as the vampire began instigating hunting parties, weeding out any resistance to their rule, any renegade humans not tracked or registered. The first year after the Red Night was the most brutal. Millions of people died, drained of their blood, dying of starvation, exposure any attempt to fight back, if they were foolish enough. The military was the first to go, it gave little hope to Marcus that any of his Army friends had survived, let alone anyone from his unit. If he had to guess: his unit was most likely the first to be hunted down and killed.

Much to anyone's surprise especially without medication, Kira's health improved and allowed for her to be less of a burden, a worry that had formed in her mind because of their father's training. He had four very specific rules that would keep his family alive.

1. Never confront a vampire head-on.

2. Do not help someone in danger, it's a trap.

3. Always look out for each other, family are the ones you can trust.

4. Break none of the above rules or you will die.

There came a time in their year that they could not travel as effectively. Anna refused to allow her daughters to live in a world where survival was the only thing they knew. She reasoned with Marcus, together they made their journey into the wooded and mountainous region of Monongahela National Forest. There was a place hidden away from the public, full of ample resources and games. Here they were taught to hunt, to use a bow and arrow, silent and deadly. They learned to filter water, to create effective fires and use everything nature offered. Their mother was a nurse. She knew the medicinal properties of many plants and taught her children to avoid and to gather.

They built a log cabin together, within reasonable distance to a steady water source. They sheltered by a hanging cliff that would buffer the smoke from their fires and protect from heavy rains and snows. Further in, there was a small cave system that opened to the other side of the cliff. Their mother and father had taught them time and time again to use this emergency exit if they were ever found. On one of the last nights, Kira remembered when she woke to her father and mother in an argument in the other room. She crept to the door and listened to them.

Her mother sat in a chair.

"I can't believe you—we barely made it out the first time, now you want to go back?"

Marcus paced, a radio Kira had often seen him turn on once a day, in his hand. "He's my friend. I can't leave him. If I can bring him, we can gather others, we can fight back—"

"An-and what about if you bring them? Jesus Marc, you're not a Ranger anymore, you're a father!" She said as she wiped her face, "How will you protect us if you bring the hunters here!"

"I won't. I know how to stay hidden. It will only be for a few weeks. The girls know how to survive and they have you. Even if something were to happen to me—"

Anna shot up, "S-so you're willing to let your daughters grow up without a father? You're willing to throw them away—"

"Don't put words in my mouth Anna, you know that's not what this is."

"Then tell me what it is? They're hunting *us*, not just humans—*us*. What makes you think you can make it all the way to North Carolina and back without being caught?" She clasped a hand over her mouth, "I can't—I can't do this without you. I'm not you. I'm not a soldier, I'm a nurse. I don't know how to fight."

Marcus closed the distance and hugged his family. "Yes, you do, and so do the girls. You can survive and even if this place is discovered, I will find you again, I promise."

Their father left the next morning. He hugged his daughters and Anna.

"I'll come back." He said as he looked to his daughters and held the radio for the two of them to hold, "I'll turn mine on, every morning at dawn if I can. We can talk then, okay?"

The girls cried into their father's arms and hugged him tightly. Marcus left the cabin, Kira chased after him,

"Daddy!" She cried out, "I'll get better! I'll practice every day at the bow until you come back!"

They never saw him again.

A year went by, Anna accepted his death privately, but her daughters never did. Kira practiced her bow and arrow every single day, able to hunt medium sized game with precise accuracy. Her sister was one for a dagger and spear, her arm steady and focused when she threw and hit a raccoon fifteen feet away. They never had to worry about going hungry; they became predators themselves and learnedthe ways of the forest as though they had been born into it.

Yet nothing could have prepared them for what happened when the next winter came.

Kira and her sister trekked through the winterized white woods, having gathered a hide-bag full of bird game. Not that they were short on storage for the winter. Their mother had taught them how to preserve and smoke their food, but their father had taught them to never rely on storage. Accidents happen, things are burned, earthquakes break and shatter shelves; longer winters. The few animals they did hunt were active during the winter in regulated amounts helped keep fresh meat on the table, and their storage lessened a risk of running out. It was dark now, but the moonlight was high and bright, the skies clear after last night's snowfall.

The younger sister had won their challenge as she had gotten two birds, while the elder only downed one. Of course, that was because moving targets for a spear is harder to nail. They laughed, but then both stopped at the same time. Something was wrong. The winters here are usually quiet, but there was something in the air, something foul, something that smelled of blood and hunger.

They nodded to each other. That which hunted came out from behind the three. Camouflage. Though they may look human, their crimson eyes gave away their true nature.

"What are you doing out here all alone, little girl?"

The human held up her spear.

197

The vampire woman smirked, "Now, now, no need to be scared, I won't hurt you—" she disappeared, then appeared again behind the girl—a knife lodged into her chest, stabbed through her heart.

The vampire dropped and broke apart into ash. Another appeared and moved toward the girl with a mouth full of fangs. An arrow went through one cheek and the other, staggered him, to turn in the arrow's direction. The next sank into his chest, then another, and the vampire turned to ash before it reached the snow. Kira and her sister came together and exchanged looks before words.

"The cabin!" They said in unison as they dropped the game and sprinted for home.

Suddenly Kira snatched her sister's shirt and yanked her down beneath a bush just outside their cabin.

"What are you—"

"Shh!" Kira hushed as she pointed to the cabin. A vampire rounded the corner of the cabin.

They heard their mother scream, the elder sister tried to move in, Kira wrapped her arm around her and kept her in place. If she moved now, they were dead. The vampires did not know they were here. They could escape now and survive. Their father taught them to never confront vampires, but also to always look after family. What were they to do? Two children could take on a vampire by surprise one at a time, but there were at least two and if one died, it would make the other aware. Their mother screamed again.

"Come out, come out wherever you are." Sung, another vampire as he came out toward the front of the cabin, "We know you're here."

Kira squeezed her eyes shut, quietly she signed: **you, the cave. Me, distraction**. Her sister shook her head. **Bad idea. You Die**. She signed in return. In return. **Family. Together. Strong.** The elder sister conceded and nodded her head as she quietly snuck out from the bush and went into the hidden cave entrance. While Kira waited for her to enter, she then crawled out herself and climbed a nearby tree, changed in a way to be an outlook and a sniper's nest her father created and taught them to use. Usually they just climbed it for fun, but the tied down canopy cover was perfect and allowed an opening for an arrow, rifle, or spear to go through while it concealed the marksmen and gave an open view of the front of the cabin.

She drew an arrow and aimed the first one at the furthest vampire where the cave entrance was. Once she made a sound of an owl, it caught the attention of a vampire; she shot the first arrow and turned him to ash. It alerted immediately the others and spread out. She counted at least six of them now. It was a large group of Human Hunters. The packs they had come across before were only three... why were there so many and how did they find them? Kira drew another arrow, aimed at one whose back was to her. Waiting, waiting, she let the arrow fly—a vampire caught it mid-air, grinning at her.

"Gotcha."

Kira loaded and quickly shot another, but the vampires swarmed the tree. She jumped out and landed in the snow—she pulled out a knife given to her by her father and swung wildly at the first vampire. She nicked his arm and spilled his blood. Next she made a run to the innermost woods, hoping to distract them and pull enough of them away for her sister to get their mother. They may catch her, but if she could give them a chance to survive, then—a vampire fronted her, Kira drew her bow; they swung a sword and cut the bow in half. She did not stop; she bolted into them, stabbed her dagger into their stomach and knocked them onto the ground.

The vampire shouted in pain, but she had missed his core. She lifted the blade then aimed for his heart—the vampire kicked her and sent her into a tree. Kira staggered in the snow and struggled to stand with a sharp pain in her chest.

"Fuckin'—" The vampire hissed as he grabbed Kira by her hair and lifted her up. Kira thrusted the blade again, this time she hit his heart.

He turned to ash. Kira held her ribs as she scurried to her feet, she tripped and looked back to the cabin for a moment, her attention distracted at seeing a vampire's teeth in their mother's throat.

"Mom!" A vampire grabbed her from behind and pushed her into the ground then they pressed their weight on top of her to keep her still.

"This one's a fighter." He chuckled, "Maybe too much trouble keeping her around—" He reached for her neck, grabbed it, and kept her still.

"Let me—"

Another walked over and motioned for him to release her neck, "The more you struggle, the more it hurts." He said as he crouched down, "If you make this easy, we'll make your mother's pain stop."

Kira glared. She clenched her fist... then released her hold on the blade. The vampire smiled, as he took it away— suddenly another shouted. A spear stabbed through their chest and turned them into ash. The others appeared and grabbed the attacker and threw her out into the snow. The first vampire stood and looked at the second child.

"Two?" He was surprised. "There are two daughters?" He looked at the elder sister, then to Kira and smiled in realization, "What a lucky day."

Kira resisted again, "Leave her alone you fucking—!" She shouted and turned enough to punch him in the groin, which loosened the hold on her and allowed the small gap to escape.

She crawled into a run and sprinted to her sister. Another vampire snatched her by the arm and squeezed until the pain brought her to her knees.

"You're not helping anyone, little calf." Said their leader, as he brought out a short sword.

"The mother knew nothing, perhaps one of them will." He walked over to the Elder sister, his blade gleamed in the light, his eyes burned hot. He stopped at her side and hovered the sword's edge at her neck as he looked at Kira.

"Alright!" He clapped his hands together, "Time for a little pop quiz, girls: where's your daddy?"

Kira looked at her sister. While she cried, her elder half remained strong. She looked at the panicked other, scared without the knowledge of what to do. All the years their father trained them and there was nothing they learned that could have prepared them for this. This was the largest hunting party they had ever seen. They were deep in the woods, hidden, secluded; they had not seen another person in over a year. How were they found then?

"Come on, tell me where your daddy is."

"He's dead." The elder said calmly.

The vampire sighed, "Oh sweetie, didn't your mommy and daddy tell you it's bad to tell lies?" He shook his head, "Humans have no morals, but we do, we'll teach you right—"

Their mother hurled herself onto the vampire, "RUN!" She screamed, her voice gargled when she choked on her own blood.

The released daughter sprinted and charged at Kira's capture. The younger sister pulled a sharpened stone from her back pocket and swipted it across the vampire's arm which severed a tendon. They released her and she ran to her sister as they reached out for another—a sword opened the elder's back. She fell, missing Kira's hand she collapsed into her younger sister. Kira dropped them to the ground, her hand on the gash to her motionless sister's back. The warmth rapidly left the body, her blood soaked into the snow and changed it into the deep red of life's currency. They dragged her mother back into the cabin, her strength sapped away by the vampire, when he threw her to the ground and sank his fangs back into her neck.

"Mom!" Kira shouted as she pulled her other half into her arms.

Her sister barely spoke as she cried from the pain in her back, cooled by the snow pressed against it. She rapidly lost blood, and there was nothing Kira could do to stop it. The vampires pulled the two apart, they dragged the elder sister's limp body across the snow and left a trail of blood in the cabin. They tossed her beside her mother as Kira kicked, punched and screamed on top of her lungs. She screamed for her mother, for her sister, she clawed and scraped, against the pain inflicted on her. They threw her into the snow and kicked in her gut relentlessly. Still, she tried to crawl, to pull herself across the yard, in order to get to her family. Kira watched them in the doorway, their bodies bloody and broken, without movement.

Tears dried as Kira burned that image into her mind. She watched the vampires burn the cabin, as they lifted her. She fought every moment, every second to escape, to fight, and to kill them. Her sadness sharpened her teeth, her grief hardened her body and her hatred ignited her soul hotter than the fires that scorched what was once her home. Kira vowed her vengeance, vowed she would survive, no matter the cost; grow strong, stronger than these monsters. She would survive by any means necessary and achieve her revenge. She swore on the blood of her sister, her other half, that died that night. That was who she was, and that is who, deep down inside Kira Nightraven still was.

Chapter Fourteen
Time Apart Brings Us Together

"Have I mentioned I hate crossing water?" Kira mentioned as she stared at the creek waters Eona casually trekked through.

Eona stopped halfway across and turned to Kira with a disbelieving look. "You've attacked and killed people when you were seven years old and you don't like crossing a *shallow creek*?"

The human huffed as she crossed her arms, "Yeah and I don't like thunder either."

"*That*, I knew." Eona laughed as she came back to Kira's side.

She handed Kira the fishing rods, cradeled her arms as she jumped across, and showed off her superior abilities. Dramatically, Kira leaned back, her hand over her forehead.

"Oh, my hero!" exasperated the human. "You saved me from the cruel fate of a watery grave!"

Eona raised a brow, "You just don't enjoy getting your feet wet."

"That too." Kira smirked, she patted Eona's chest and hopped out of her arms.

"Good to see some things don't change." Rolled the eyes of Eona as she took the bait box from Kira and they continued down.

"Now you can't make fun of me. I haven't done this in *years*." Kira pointed her finger at the other woman as she began to set up their spot for the morning and afternoon.

"I can make fun of you all I want, you're the one who became all prim and proper." Eona laughed as she set her bait on the hook.

Kira shrugged, "And prim and proper here can still nail you between the eyes thirty yards away with an arrow."

"Now, now, don't tempt me with a good time." Eona winked in response.

"Won't it be so good if it's between the ass cheeks, hm?"

"Hey!" Eona straightened, her hand on her butt.

"That—that is a one-way ally missy, don't even think about it."

Innocently Kira swayed toward her chair to set up her hook, "Hey don't knock it till you try it."

For a second, Eona stopped what she was doing, but continued as she shook her head at the thought. After they cast their lines, a bobber attached to Kira's, it was not long before Eona got a bite. She reeled them in one after the next, she brought in half a dozen on her own, while Kira only caught something barely the size of a frog. Eona laughed so hard she fell over on the ground The other's pride was slightly hurt by her horrible fishing stills.

"Tell you what, we can go squirrel hunting tomorrow." Eona smirked over the pan of cooking fish, "Maybe you can recover some of your wounded pride."

She looked up to see the bird flipped in her direction, "Wounded pride my ass..." Kira grumbled as she curled into a blanket with coffee in her hands, "Hundred bucks says I could beat you in another way."

"You're *extremely* competitive today." Eona chuckled in amusement as she pushed the fish onto a plate, "And apparently confident enough to bet a hundred dollars." She set the pans in the sink and leaned on her elbows as she smirked at Kira, who peered over the couch with a devilish grin.

Kira turned back over to face the fire with a smug attitude. "I'd even make it two hundred..."

Weight pushed down on the back of the couch, which made Kira sink in a little. She looked up. Eona's face hovered over hers. The vampire's red eyes were soft, not as intense as crimson, but scarlet in tone. They were warm, welcoming, like a blanket to wrap around Kira's entire self in protection... but there was more than that. *You still like Eona.* Emily's voice echoed in the mortal woman's mind. She saw it in this woman's eyes, an unchanged, unwavering love directed at her present ever since they were young, now fully matured and yet the same. It was not a phase; it was not a crush; it was true; it was love, and it was real.

Years had passed since they had been alone like this. The only people in the world were the two of them. Now they were face to face, thousands of miles from the Game, from the weight and pressure of society. Here they were not human and vampire, slave and overlord. They were two womenwho cared deeply for another. Time or distance had made these feelings waiver, no matter what they did to suppress and deny their existence.

Kira's lips parted slightly, her resolve and confidence that led her to tease her friend turned against her. Her eyes wandered to Eona's hair, how those locks would feel tangled around her fingers. She thought of how soft her skin would feel, how electrifying it would be to touch, wondered if she would remember or if it would differ from before. Kira then thought of her lips, how sweet they would taste, pressed against her own.

Suddenly, the sitting woman realized she did not tease Eona as a friend and in this moment did not think of her as one, but how Carmilla would arouse her sexual desires before they slept with another. For a moment Kira hesitated, a moment enough for Eona to notice. Eona withdrew, and Kira became sheepishly ashamed. She went back to the kitchen, and grabbed their plates. Kira stood quickly as she realized where these thoughts led her, what she was about to do.

Outside, she felt her throat dry, desperate for a cool refreshment to quench it. She knew this thirst, knew what it desired. The wetness between her legs made her weak at her knees. When she came to this point, there was always a bed nearby. Her mouth and hands were always occupied and her need rapidly heated from below her waist until it consumed herself. She knew this feeling, but right now it differed from ardent passion, from the ecstasy she felt when being dominated by the alpha-personality that was Carmilla. With Eona, Kira was about to pull her over onto the couch and push her underneath. She has never had that initiative, that will to take the lead, but with Eona... she wanted to, she wanted to be in control; she had the confidence and will with Eona.

Carmilla had told Kira she became more outgoing and outspoken, an effect she believed to be from Eona's presence in her life again. She spoke about the masks they wear in the face of the Game, masks Eona refused to wear. Was the Princesses' presence having such an effect on them? The longer Kira was near Eona, the more of her mask seemed to be removed. But who was underneath now? Who was left to be exposed and unprotected to the world? The innocent child whose entire existence became ruled by hatred... or a stranger?

This confidence, this *aggression;* a need to *control.* Where did it come from? Never in a million years did she consider such actions to take rather than submit, but these thoughts persisted. Was being away from the Game, from the fear of death allowing her true self to come out? How was this happening? It was not the first time these feelings have appeared. Ever since Eona returned, Kira's emotional self-control has progressively deteriorated. She has attributed these flares and episodes as symptoms of the Stigma, but still there was no answer why this was occurring.

Outside, the crisp fall night air felt well, it helped clear her head and calm her. That was too close. She nearly acted without thinking, and she was about to undo years of training, of survival and what frightened her the most: she did not care. *What am I doing?* Kira asked herself as she wondere why? Not knowing was the hardest part, she felt she could tell Eona anything, that she could trust her with her life, her body, mind, even her very soul. *This is wrong.*

"Kira?" Eona asked softly from the back door.

Kira clenched her eyes shut. Was this acting out now because of jealousy? Was it the Stigma? Could it be their past she had been unable to fully let go? Her hands clenched the railing of the patio, wood stressed beneath her grip and threatened to snap if she squeezed any harder. *I don't know what to do.* She clenched the railing harder. *Survive. I have to survive, no matter what.*

Eona walked closer, "Hey."

She could not love them, either of them. To love them was to betray her people, her family. She could not love the very ones who murdered them, who slaughtered millions of innocent people. A slave was all she was to them, not a person, not a lover. She could not feel for them and they did not give a passing thought to food. *Why?* The railing snapped. *Why won't it go away?* She gritted her sharpened teeth. *Why do I have hope?* Eona touched the back of her arm. *That a happy future exists for me?* Kira spun around, grabbed the vampiress by her collar, and pulled her in.

Their lips crashed together. Kira went into Eona not caring how out of breath she had become. Eona broke contact first, but the mortal was left panting and conflicted.

"Sorry— " Kira apologized, but her regret did not lighten her grip. "I—" She did not think, "I just—"

Eona smiled kindly, "We'll worry about tomorrow when it comes, but right here, right now, it's just us." She said as she weaved her fingers with Kira's.

Gently, she cupped the side of Kira's face abd brought their lips together for a soft kiss. Kira firmly gripped Eona's sides and flexed her fingers as though she were a predator who held onto her prey. She did not care; she wanted to let go, to allow these feelings to take over and stop thinking of the end. With Eona, she felt free; she felt the possibilities were endless. Here, in this cabin, they would not be found. There were no witnesses, a secret only the two would know. Kira stepped into Eona, but the immortal was faster. She lifted the younger into her arms, cradling her like a bride on their honeymoon.

The wind picked up and shut the door gently behind as they entered. Into the master bedroom, Eona set Kira down, but that was the extent of her lead. Kira kissed her partner, her hands dragged Eona's shirt until it was untucked. She unbuttoned the flannel next and took her time as she savored every moment a button came undone. With each came the opening of Eona's shirt, revealing just a few more inches of the soft skin Kira yearned to touch. Her belly was toned and muscular the finished product of years of hard work. Kira traced the lines of Eona's abs and worked her way up to her bra. She snaked her hands beneath the liner of the sports bra until her finger touched a hardened nipple.

Eona inhaled sharply at the sensual graze of her breasts, then a moan escaped her mouth when Kira grabbed one with greater force. The smaller woman hooked her arm behind the other's back and dragged her nails down it, which sent electrifying pleasure throughout the immortal's body. With their bodies pressed together, Kira could feel Eona's excitement. It made her want more. She eased down the flannel shirt, allowing it to drop on the floor. Eona removed the sports bra, but not without distraction. Kira kissed her, on her lips, her neck, her collarbone, between her breasts; all the while grabbing her firmly on the ass.

"If you keep this up, I won't be able to keep my hands off you." Eona chuckled as she tugged on Kira's jeans.

Kira leaned in, whispering into Woman's ear, "Who says I don't want your hands on me?"

She found her back on the bed, Eona's speed impossible to follow in route, but not in bed. She took her her time, she moved on top of Kira. They kissed as she slipped her hands beneath Kira's shirt and pushed it until the fabric rested over her breasts. With the quick work of her bra, Kira's ice-cutting nipples were exposed for her pleasure. She took one into her mouth, a hand played with the other as she sucked and flicked with her tongue until the woman squirmed beneath her.

"Where's all the confidence, g—"

209

Eona felt Kira wrap her legs around her, she grabbed her waist and changed their positions. Below Kira now, Eona was straddled and watched as she removed her shirt and cast it aside, laying bare on her chest. Unable to bear the distance, Eona sat up. Kira met her halfway she cupped her face as the two locked lips. She held Kira close and her fingers traced over the aged scars on the lower of her back. She hesitated for a moment and drew back, though she remained still.

"That's right...you've never seen them." Kira said quietly as Eona silently nodded her head.

Kira moved her hair out to one side. The tattoo on the side of her neck was fully visible. "The ones on my back don't hurt."

Eona reached up and cupped over the tattoo, her fingers ran over the length of the artery the Stigma inked over. She stared at it for a long time. There was sadness in her eyes; grief; remorse. Kira had seen those eyes every time she looked at her neck, but it seemed to come and go just as quickly. The moment was enough, though.

"And this one?" Eona asked quietly, cautiously.

Kira held her hand over Eona's and smiled lightly. She leaned forward and kissed her again. Eona forgot the question she asked as Kira slipped a between her thighs, slipping to the wet place at the very top. Naturally, the vampire's fangs showed themselves. Her desire to have Kira, to mark her as her own, as her mate, a primal instinct within her immortal blood. The mortal knew this, knew that familiar grumble, though Eona did her best to hide and muffle it. She did not mind it; it was not something she was unused to, nor was it painful to her. In fact, she rather enjoyed it.

Eona refused. Not here, not right now. She did not want Kira for her blood; she wanted Kira for Kira. The mortal smiled as she unbuckled Eona's belt and pulled off her jeans off, which exposed her soaked boxers. She could not wait any longer. Once she discarded the boxers to the side, Kira lowered herself further and further until she was off Eona and on the side of the bed. She dropped to her knees and pulled the older woman until she sat on the edge. Kira dove between her legs and devoured her meal. She savored the taste, her tongue assaulted between Eona's lips and alternated between sucking her clit, and sending a finger inside.

Eona fidgeted, her body squeezed her finger the deeper she went and longer she allowed her tongue to work. Wet enough, Kira inserted a second finger and nearly Eona come in that instant. She stopped devouring her meal and slowly withdrew her fingers to postpone Eona's climax. Eona refused to allow that. She grabbed Kira's head, pulled her in and begged her not to stop. A small grin came across the mortal's face as she thrust her fingers harder, deeper, and faster. Eona's moans grew louder, her voice filled Kira's ears and made her own excitement wet her panties.

A few more thrusts, deeper, harder, and Eona was nearly there. Kira withdrew her fingers, she adjusted her tongue and penetrated inside. Eona gripped Kira's hair, her orgasm rocked through her body and shook her from her clit to her core. The mortal sat up, but she would not allow Eona to walk away. She kissed up the immortal's flawless body, inserting her fingers again. A gasp escaped. Kira silenced it with a wet kiss, which made Eona taste herself on her partner's lips. One thrust after the next, Eona's entire body clenched around Kira's fingers and threatened to devour them. She was tight and it made it difficult to wiggle her finger, but not impossible.

"Kira..." Eona moaned, as she gripped the dominating back, her fingers and traced the marks on the woman's lower back and upper shoulder.

Eona propped on her elbow and traced the scars on Kira's exposed back. It was the first time she had ever seen them healed and guilt ate at her for the pain she must have been. Like a lion gripping their prey before it tore into its jugular, these marks would likely stay with her for the rest of her life.

She hated that, for all this woman has suffered. It seems like it never ends in the Palace. Eona thought of what was to come after this, how to keep Kira beside her and away from Carmilla.

She would not leave her aunt because she was afraid, and a human had every reason to be. However, even after it seemed that there were still feelings between them why did it feel different than when they were younger? She thought this was the spark they needed, this was what would reigniate their love of eachother and yet Eona did not feel the same. Eona had at last gotten what she wanted and all she felt was…regret.

Still she wanted to be near Kira, wanted her in her life no matter how short a human's life is. Eona never regretted what they did when they were younger, but it seemed that she had grown out of those feelings…they both had. As Kira slept Eona sat up in the bed and let out a quiet sigh—she had been selfish, putting her feelings before Kira's and Kira was only here because of what Carmilla did. That should have been a sign…one Eona ignored.

She tried to tell me—shit she even said it out right.

Now their choice was about to have severe consequences. Carmilla would not take this well in fact there were already several threats given over the phone if Eona did not tell her where she meant to take Kira. The fact that they had now crossed a line, even if this was the last time would put Kira in danger.

Because of Eona's selfishness it was no wonder Kira tried to keep her at a distance—she was afraid how Carmilla would react. Given what she know knew about Kira's past everything, every action, every fear she never understood until know finally made sense. Eona wondered if Kira had thoughts like those humans who wanted to kill them; did she want to away and join the LSA to achieve revenge against those who murdered her family? She told Eona her past and yet didn't reveal her true name.

Regardless of these mixed emotions, one thing is certain: Carmilla's initial reaction to the two of them together again will not be received well. For as many years as Eona has been gone, she remains in the dark about just how attached to Kira her aunt is. As a child she had no recollection of her aunt having any long-term relationships ones that exceeded the physical domain. What she had with Kira was unlike anything she had seen before. If Carmilla really did care then they had made a mistake that made Eona wonder if they should return at all.

I just want her to be happy, I want us to got back to how the three of us were...but it can't be built on a lie. She clenched her fist. *How do I tell her the truth, though... I can't while we're here. She has enough on her mind.* Eona looked at the portion of the tattoo visible, it did not go unnoticed of how Kira ignored the question about her neck. The symptoms she experiences seem to follow with significant discomfort or pain in the neck. Eona frowned. *I should have protected her.* She thought with guilt.

Even if they did somehow leave the Palace, how long would things really be peaceful? How long before Kira would feel drawn to her people as conflicts grew? With the *Reich's* increase in power, it was only a matter of time before vampires engaged in a civil war and drew in humans either as soldiers, or simply as collateral damage. No doubt the LSA would take the chance in the conflict to secure humanity's freedom, alliances would be forged, bargains struck; war would reach the two of them in this cabin, just as it did her family.

Eona did not think she could fully abandon her aunt in such a way, not as a duty to her people, but love of family.

She stood still and looked up at the clear night sky, the moon's light gleamed on her. It was silent, such that not even a heartbeat of her own chest sounded. For a moment, she believed this to be what death was like. She knew better, though, knew this was not death, but a dream. For now, Kira could still tell the difference between reality and illusion. Kira looked around and saw there were ruins on the water's surface she stood on, as though a building had once stood here and had either been ripped off by some great unseen force or had sunk beneath the surface. Either way, she did not know where this was.

She walked to the foundation's edge and peered into the blackened waters. Her reflection was obscured, unrecognizable, though the water's surface was undisturbed. Her eyes dropped as sadness weighted them down. She knew this was a dream, but understood what the meaning behind this dream was: she was forgetting them and herself. The waters rippled from behind. Kira turned and saw a child on a floor, their knees brought to their chest as they wept. She was in another place now, a room decorated as though a cubicle game of chess. How ironic to her life this was: just as in the waking world, here she too was a part of a larger game, a pawn to be used and sacrificed.

Kira looked beyond the child, to the chess pieces behind them. Wolfgang stood as a knight, Emily was a rook, Jake a Bishop and the queen? Eona and Carmilla each sat on a throne of their own style, but it could not be told who was the 'King' or 'Queen'. They all stood and stared at the dreamer, yet did not speak, nor move. Who was their opponent, Kira wondered, looking behind her: the *Reich* or the Last Stand? Who was the greater threat? Who would make the first move and just which side... did Kira belong to?

The child was stood now. Their short raven hair covered their face as they lifted a finger and pointed at Kira. The dreamer looked to either side of her; the child was now on the opposite side as well and pointed their fingers at her. Every one of them pointed at Kira, their judgement onto her for her action and inaction.

A woman stood in front of the dreamer, with a smirk and had features unlike that of who she appeared as. Nearly a mirror image of the mortal, there was one distinct detail that separated them: that mirrored version had burning red eyes, seeped deep in hatred. They made a shiver run down Kira's spine. It was painful, suffocating, as though her throat had caught fire and scorched her from speaking. She dropped to her knees, clenched her neck and clawed at it before she dragged her nails into the Stigma until it bled.

215

"This pain has made you strong. Embrace it now as you did as a child." Instructed the ember-eyed twin as she walked to Kira and lowered herself to the other's level. Kira's eyes asked in the absence of words.

"You don't remember, but I do, for the both of us—they took our choice away. Made us playthings just to discard when they have drained us dry."

As though the words came from her own mouth, Kira was no longer in pain, but remained speechless. She had these thoughts often when she was younger, but buried them deep because they would have gotten her killed had they remained. Locking them deep within her, these thoughts, and the pain that caused it rooted them in the past she feared forgetting. Kira stood and gripped her neck, the blood on her hands not of her own, but of the bodies at her feet. She looked back, taken by surprise, the mangled bodies of Carmilla, Eona, Jake, Wolfgang and many other vampires in a sea of crimson flowers.

"Beautiful, isn't it?" The vampiric twin of Kira asked, her own body equally stained with the blood of her victims, "A world free of these beasts, a world where we humans can choose our own fates—"

"You're not human." Kira frowned, finally able to speak. "A human—*I* wouldn't do this—not to them!"

The bodies in the fields of red flowers blew away as ash in the wind.

The woman shook her head with a chuckle,
"*I* am *you*."

She appeared behind Kira and wrapped her arms around her which locked her in place.

"I am the one who loved my family more than life itself, I am the one who swore to slaughter every vampire until they were wiped off the face of the Earth." She shoved Kira forward then appeared again in front of her.

Kira swung and punched the woman in the face, but her hand hit nothing and the woman was gone.

"They're not our family. They murdered our family. That truth is not a dream." Said a young girl's voice.

Kira spun around to found a child behind her.

"Hey, do you remember?"

Kira froze mid-swing.

"When we were kids, when we had a family?"

Beside them, a broken image of four people who sat at a table together. They ate, laughed; they were happy. Kira could not recognize the faces of her mother and father. She knew it was them by their shapes, but it obscured their faces and voices; like a broken cassette tape. Their mother left and came back with a cake and wished the two sisters a happy birthday. They did everything together, ate, slept, and played; they even shared the same bed.

"We were happy, even in the cabin."

Kira clenched her jaw.

"We promised dad we would practice every day until he came home. We promised we wouldn't face the vampire, that we would only ever rely on family and never help others." The child tilted her head looking at Kira, "We broke every single rule— "

"Shut up."

"And they died because of it."

Kira wrapped her hand around the neck of the crimson-eyed child. "We're alive." She growled, "We're alive because we broke those rules."

The child smirked, "And so are the vampires."

Chapter Fifteen
Fear of Letting Go

Mablevi raised his hands to gesture the two women to stop. Whether at one or another, both or some other aggravation, the Empress was not someone that should be seen at the moment. She had been noticeably short-tempered this last week, but additional news from council members had drawn the last straw.

He had cleared out quickly to avoid her wrath from reaching beyond a few broken windows and cracked walls and ran into the niece and her human companion.

"It is good to see you—"

A small rumble of the Palace had Kira frown and tremble only slightly. Mablevi noticed this and was drawn in to know more—humans do not grow accustomed to such a terrifying display of power unless they are constantly with such power. Since Eona had been absent and likely seen along with her, it would explain the Empress's... temper this last week.

Kira sighed as she looked at Eona. "I should probably try to calm her down—"

"It is most unwise to further agitate our Empress's wrath." Mablevi warned, "Given her mood in your absence, seeing you now may only incur harm onto you."

Eona frowned and stepped forward protectively. "I'd never let her—"

"Lord Mablevi is right, probably not a good idea right now." Kira cut off quickly, Eona failed miserably at keeping a low profile.

Eona looked at her phone, "I'll go check in with my father, don't forget to text Jake we're back." Eona said as she threw her bag over her shoulder and headed down the hall.

Kira rubbed her neck and twisted it from side to side. It had been bothering her incessantly this last week. From intense desert dryness and pain to needle-like annoyance, no amount of suppressants was keeping it in check. This made the woman wonder if these symptoms were withdrawal; as Carmilla had given Kira vampire blood rather routinely, it could be her body has become reliant on it, like a drug. Emily has said nothing of the nature, did she not think of the possibility or did she believe it to be something else? Kira let out a heavy sigh. *Not to mention that bizarre dream I had the other night.*

"You seem to have a lot on your mind Ms. Nightraven." Mablevi stated his observation, his presence Kira actually forgot about for a moment.

She put on her polite, servant mask, "Please my'lord call me Kira."

"I would, but I trust that is not your true name."

Before she could think of what to say, he explained, "My ability allows me to detect lies." He smiled and it made her relieved.

"Do not fear. I will not ask you of your true name. Kira will suffice. Though I am very interested in knowing about the mysterious Empress's Pet, I assume that is you."

"It is not."

Mablevi tilted his head in contemplation as he narrowed his eyes when he tried to understand how she told a lie when he knew the truth. He understood it was the truth, simply not her truth. She did not believe herself to be the Empress's Pet and thus did not technically lie. Clever woman. This made the immortal even more interesting. While their Empress cooled her head, he asked for the two for the two of them to talk more. Kira agreed and remembered the kindness of the man during her time at the Council meetings.

"I have heard much about you, but I fear I do not yet know the woman behind the wonder." Mablevi began the two of them walked to the library.

"Where would you like me to begin?" Kira asked openly though she knew she would be very limited in what she could avoid obscuring the truth about.

Mablevi smiled, "How you could capture the heart of the Red Queen." He chuckled deeply, "I have been friends with and have known the Tepes family for thousands of years—Carmilla has never once had a serious relationship; it is not in her nature to settle down." The African man correctly said, "That is until now."

"I don't know what you mean..."

He clicked his tongue and waved his finger, "The worst lies one can tell is to themselves."

"Or one they wish were true." Kira muttered in response, "I consider myself just a body to warm her bed, but honestly... I don't know what she thinks of me."

Mablevi hummed with a smile, "In the centuries I have known Carmilla there are only four events where I have witnessed her change herself. One was when she undertook the ritual, the second was Eona's birth, and I daresay Carmilla was more excited than her own parents."

Somehow that image of an Aunt Carmilla made Kira smile. She has always doted on Eona. Kira being brought to the Palace was for Eona to have a playmate after all. With Kira, it's only because Eona is Carmilla's niece that she has been tolerant of the woman's advances. After this week, however... that tolerance may run out.

"Another was when her sister, Eona's mother, died." Mablevi grew quiet. "All vampire kind lost a great deal when she passed, but those two..."

"Were twins... I've heard." Kira nodded slowly,
"What was the fourth?"

The vampire's smile returned. "When the Council convened in Germany, during supper, I noticed her attention was fixated on someone in particular. It was not until you brought the tray over, that I saw how she looked at you; you are more to her than simply a body to warm the bed."

Kira's hand hovered over the massive doors. After a moment or two more of self-reflection that this was quite the bad idea, she knocked three times. For a moment, there was silence, then one of the two massive doors flew open. Carmilla, already on her way back to her wine, sat beside her chair. Papers were scattered on the table in front of her, reports from her spies planted throughout the world, all searching for a single man. A man, if you were to call him that, alluded to every single spy.

With the knowledge this was going to be silent or short, Kira lessened her tension as she closed the door. Carmilla has never once hurt her, has never attacked her whether mentally or physically; she trusted Kira and despite their differences and disagreements... Kira trusted her. Her hand left the door handle and dropped to her side, but it was another few moments before she turned around and not before Carmilla spoke first.

"I see you enjoyed your little get away with Eona."
She said with a knowing tone.

With a nod, "I did, we went back to Germany since
we didn't get the chance to during the Council Meetings."

Kira continued, she manipulated her tone and words
to ensure she did not appear to hold guilt.

She did not feel guilty about what she and Eona
shared, only the consequences of after.

"We went fishing and hiking. I haven't done that
since I was a kid..."

Carmilla ran her fingers through her hair, grabbed a
cigarette from the carton on the table and lit it she sat back in
her chair.

Kira was confused she had never seen Carmilla
smoke before and she appeared...stressed. Was it over
the *Reich*? Was the Last Stand Army causing more problems
than was publicly revealed... or was Kira's sudden departure
to blame? Emily had openly revealed the mortal's—
affection—of Carmilla, though Kira believed such a
conclusion was wildly exaggerated from 'gratitude' and
'survival', but Mablevi had also pointed out Carmilla's own
change in personality.

It would be a lie to say she had not noticed the subtle
changes. Before the two of them could not stand, another one
was a human slave who burned bright with hatred of the
vampire. The other was the master, the Empress of all
immortals who regarded humanity as expendable livestock.
Kira often butted heads with the Empress, openly defied her,
no matter the amount of trouble she would get in. Eventually,
the two simply ignored each other for many years. Kira
quelled her hatred, nearly forgot it completely in Eona's
company. She never regarded Carmilla as her master in the
beginning, but with time she obeyed the vampire's
commands, not without attitude.

It was an unspoken truce to stay out of the other's way in order to avoid a plethora of public humiliation. When guests arrived at the Palace Kira would keep to and hide in her room, not coming out which originally was to avoid Carmilla, but over time became a normal routine to avoid the hungry eyes of her guests instead. The Empress rarely gave the mortal a passing glance and for a while, that was the extent of their relationship. All that changed when Kira was attacked and nearly killed.

"I'm sorry..." Kira muttered quietly.

Carmilla exhaled a puff of smoke as she raised a curious brow at the mortal.

"And what have you done to be apologetic towards me?" She asked as she took a sip of her wine without breaking eye contact.

The intensity of her gaze made Kira unconsciously avoid her eyes. "I never responded to your calls or messages..." she answered as she stared at the ground.

A shadow loomed over her. Kira jumped. It was easy to forget how fast Carmilla was. Even among the immortals, it was exceptional.

"Is that all?" The immortal asked in a manner that made Kira uncertain if she wanted to be left alone or if there was something else she expected her to apologize for.

She knew she was wrong, Eona and her had talked about it and agreed it would never happen again. That did not change the fact that it did happen. It had been over a week since she had been this close to Carmilla and there was a eurphoric feeling. The smell of cigarettes irritated her eyes, just as they did whenever Emily smoked them. Unlike the doctor, this woman did not smoke often, and the stench had not quite set in her clothes which seemed to mean this was a recent habit. Most likely the last week, which meant the latter of what upset her was being proven true. Carmilla was, without a doubt, pissed at Kira not only for disappearing *with Eona*, but what she did. *I'm fucked.*

Carmilla's breath smelled heavily of alcohol, of the many glasses of wine she partook in to numb her, no doubt to the aggravations of the last few days. She was angry, but there was something else, something she was fighting against, fighting to hold back. Kira has seen many faces of Carmilla, some fewer than others, but this face she had only seen in the last few months... anytime she was alone with Eona. She looked into Carmilla's eyes and felt something make the hairs on the back of her neck rise.

Oh fuck! Fuck, fuck, fuck! She's jealous! The mortal stubled back and her back fell against the door as Carmilla slammed her hand to the side and broke the wood.

She expected the Empress to be angry, but jealousy was never something Kira would have thought of. It would mean that towards the mortal, Carmilla's feelings were without question beyond that of sex friends. Kira knew. She knew there was something more the Empress wanted, but she had ignored it, denied it every step of the way in an unconscious hope that Carmilla would just keep their relationship as it had been. Kira was a selfish fool in believing she could ignore it long enough and it would go away, that it would not surface. If Eona had not come back... things would have been much simpler. It was far too late now.

Carmilla downed the last of the wine as she set the glass on the table beside the door

"If you have no other guilt, why do you cower before me?" She asked with a hiss, "Why do you fear retribution from me for something as meager as a lapse in communication?" She backed Kira into the wall.

She's pissed! Kira panicked internally. She had never seen this side of Carmilla, she had no plan. She expected to have something thrown at her, to even be cast from the bed, but this was out of character. When all thought ceased planning rational thought, Kira remembered: she saw Carmilla kissing another woman.

Who the hell was she to judge the mortal? The fear, the uncertainty, vanished from Kira's demeanor and instantly turned into indifference. It was just like a vampire to shove off responsibility to someone else, to think they could do no wrong—Kira would not stand for it.

She shut her eyes, neutralized her facial expressions and prepared herself to accept whatever punishment was about to come, but she would not except sole responsibility. They were not in an exclusive relationship; they were not dating. If Carmilla could go off and sleep with whoever she wanted, then Kira was under no such obligation of elusiveness.

Carmilla reached her hand—and grabbed the door handle beside the mortal and opened it.

"Get out."

"Carm--"

"**Now**!" Carmilla snarled as she extended her fangs out viciously which made Kira jump and bolt without a second thought.

The door slammed behind her. Carmilla swung her hand and sent the table and glass flying, the impact shattered both. The shards cut into her palm and caused her thick blood to ooze from her hand, before it rapidly healed. With her ability, she could easily make it heal instantaneously, but she did not want to. This pain was retribution for lashing out at Kira, for being the cause of all of this because she did something stupid she did not expect Kira to react so poorly.

You're losing her. Said her voice within her mind, a phantom beast in human form appeared over her shoulder. A phantom figure of Carmilla smirked and leaned her head over the Empress's shoulder. She whispered into her ear. *Eona will take her from you. Wouldn't it be easier just to take everything she is into you? To keep her with you always?*

"You're noisy." Carmilla waved her hand in the phantom's face. It had been quite some time since her instinct had emerged, which could only mean her control had temporarily slipped.

226

Only as noisy as you. Did you see how she looked at us? How sweet that fear was, how it hardened like a sharp bite of spice into that anger? The phantom chuckled. *She's delicious, you want to eat her. I know you do because I am you.*

Carmilla huffed as she grabbed another glass and poured the a glass of whiskey.

It's not too late. The phantom whispered as she wrapped her arms around Carmilla as she drank. *She can be ours forever, just as she should have been all those years ago.*

"Shut your filthy mouth!" The Empress hissed, as she slammed the glass down.

The phantom giggled as she sensed her time was nearly up with the Empress, who forced her back into the depths of her own mind. *You think that by giving her our blood she will understand our Bond? So long as she remains human, she will never understand, and so long as she loves Eona, she will never be ours.*

The hot waters of the shower brought her no further ease. Kira had stood in it, hoping everything that happened in the last few hours would wash away and she would no longer be burdened. A useless wish, which would never see fruition. She clenched the wet tile to the side of the shower, cursing herself for the situation she placed herself in. She could not regret her choice to acknowledge that she still loved Eona, but her feelings towards Carmilla were overwhelming everything in her mind. *God-damnit.* Kira flexed her fingers. *How the fuck am I supposed to handle this?* She rubbed her face and cleaned the last of her body. Her neck bothered her increasingly since she left Carmilla's room, as though she had not taken her medication in days. Aggressively she scrubbed her tattoo and hoped somehow that would distract her and was disappointed when it did not, therefore she ended her time in the shower.

After she grabbed a towel, she dried herself off, when a sudden surge of needles in her neck nearly had her slip. *What the fuck?* She nearly slipped when she went to her sink and grabbed the edges to keep her stable. She stared at her reflection. Her heart sank. The blackened ink of the Stigma now glowed a furious red and vine-like extension had spread from the initial seal. She had never seen it change like this before and for a moment Kira thought she was hallucinating until a quick slap to her face had her seeing the reality of the situation. *Has it done this before?*

Quickly she snatched the medication and poured half the bottle in her hand then threw them into her mouth. She turned on the water and drank from the faucet. A cool rush came through her body as the medication went down her throat, but not everything was well. *What the fuck is going on!* She saw the shadow of the vampire in the mirror, the immortal whose scarlet-eyes had haunted her dreams for years. They reached for her, Kira growled at them. *Go to hell!* She gripped her neck, squeezed then choked herself until air would not pass through. She looked at her reflection. A embered-eyed child stood in her place and frowned in sadness and pity. It cast the shadowed attacker away. *Don't forget.* She said as she touched her own neck and disappeared. The mortal watched the vines retract into the Stigma, their glow darkened, her pain subsided for now.

A knock on the door caught her attention. She looked out, then back at the mirror, saw nothing aside from herself. Calling out to give her a minute, she threw on a quick set of clothes, going to the door as she pulled down her t-shirt. She reached for the handle, her hand stopped. She felt something, a presence, a smell distinct and strong, like an Iris. The Bearded Iris in particular she remembered Eona describing when they were in Germany.

It was a smell she thought would have led her to Eona, but when she opened the door, it surprised her to find Carmilla stood at her door. After earlier in the night, one would expect her heart to race, that it would throw her into a panic and cannot meet the Empress's eyes. Ordinarily she would submit to the presence, the domination of the immortal, but this time was different. Kira did not care about what would happen to her. She was too worn, too weak to fight back, anyway.

Kira moved out of the doorway and left Carmilla in. The door shut behind her, closed by Kira's back. She stayed at the heavy wooden door and knew that she had condemned herself by shutting her last chance of escape. Not that she would be able to even if she tried, Carmilla would never have let her go. If the Empress was here, then it would mean she had sobered up and calmed down, but whatever she was going to talk about, Kira did not bother to speculate.

She knew this would be about her and Eona, a conversation that was inevitable to happen, that would once and for all give Kira and Carmilla true clarification of what they were. The mortal needed this. She could no longer stand the unknown, the uncertain; tired of playing these games. She needed to know which feelings were real, which were of a sire and which she would follow, if any at all. This was not for the sake of survival. Her life was giving up the moment she shut the door. Now it was up to chance and fate.

"You and I tell lies in order to protect ourselves. I tell them to protect others, you to protect yourself." Carmilla began as she looked out the window, her back to Kira.

Kira stood silent in the room's darkness, but Carmilla was in the last light of the night's moon they set over the horizon.

"Eona, on the other hand, is honest to a fault. She is a terrible liar." Carmilla smiled some as she remembered how much like her mother she is, "Her entire life she has never been very good at it and it has reached the point where she does not bother with the effort." She turned to Kira, calmly, "The moment you returned, I could smell Eona's scent all over you and you on her. That kind of crossing does not occur simply by being in the same room." Carmilla looked into the mortal's eyes, "Tell me the truth."

Kira's exhaustion was apparent. For a moment she refused to speak, the limit of Carmilla's patience quickly running out. What did she expect her to say? She slept with Eona just to get back at her? After seeing Carmilla with another woman, she was distraught and Eona took her on a trip as a friend, not using the chance to get back with her. It was not the vampire's fault; it was Kira's, just like everything else; all of it was her fault.

"It doesn't matter—"

Carmilla instantly moved in front of Kira she slammed her hands onto both sides of the door with the mortal in the middle.

"It matters to *me!*" She bared her fangs, her intense eyes in fury; Her nails dug into the door which marked them with her presence, "I do not tolerate people touching what is mine, or what is mine touching someone else."

Without restraint, a resentful growl escaped Kira's throat.

Carmilla hissed, "Making me jealous, is not wise—"

A surge sent a jolt from Kira's neck and snapped out, "You think you're the only one who can get jealous!" The mortal got in the immortal's face that instantly made her jerk back in surprise, "Do you have any idea how I felt watching you kiss that woman!"

Kira had no control, no tact in her words; her sense of self-preservation, of survival, was replaced by raw, unfiltered emotion held back and suppressed by years of being a human in a vampire's world. This could be her death sentence, but she did not care. She did not care about anything except the fact she had ignored and resented her emotions for years, all for what? To survive, existing instead of living? Suffering in a world she had no fault in making? She needed to get it all off her chest, this confusion, this fear, she could no longer exist with it. If Carmilla wanted to get rid of her, then she could do so. Kira refused to be led on and refused to be treated like her feelings were not valid. It was not fair, and she has felt more pain than anyone else here and more than enough to have earned at least that fairness.

"I've spent *years* walking on glass around you!" She pushed Carmilla back and freed herself from being pinned.

"I've done everything to survive, trying so hard to keep myself alive, terrified if I so much as breathed wrong, I'd be killed! And you know what?" Kira shoved, bared sharpened fangs. "I'm sick of living like a scared lamb waiting for lions to tear me apart! I'm sick of being toyed with like a fucking puppet with no feelings!"

Carmilla did not retreat.

"I'm sick of having no fucking clue what the hell this is! Three years! Three years you and I have been in this... relationship—arrangement, I don't even know what it is! It has terrified me to think what it is or isn't—how long until you throw me away! Then Eona comes back and—!" Kira paced back and forth. "I don't even know if these feelings are real! If it's something that was put in me because of this fucking thing on my neck or whatever, the reason you've been giving me your blood!"

231

Carmilla waited for Kira to catch her breath before she spoke. She did not defend herself, there was no defense, and she wanted this, wanted Kira to express herself, her emotions: she wanted the truth. Good, bad, it did not matter; she trusted Kira, and she wanted Kira to trust her enough without fearing what might happen.

"That woman is a vixen who thought she could seduce her way back into my bed. She is nothing, but a body who fulfilled my physical desires in the past. You differ from her."

For an Empress, she needs no justification in her actions. An Empress owed no one nothing, especially a human, but she was not here, in this room, as a ruler, as a master, but a woman. Kira had left after she saw a questionable sight and refused to answer any phone calls or text messages. It drove Carmilla mad, that she was being denied what was hers, what she wanted; Kira. Her body, her mind, her heart, her very soul, Carmilla wanted it all and while she fought the vampire within to devour her whole, she wanted Kira not just in her bed, but by her side.

Somehow even when she heard Carmilla say that it did not make Kira feel any better, it did not calm her down, it only enraged her further. Why did she even entertain that vampiress in the first place? If things were over, then she should never have been alone with her, allowed her to kiss her. If Carmilla was telling the truth, it could always be a trick, a manipulation to get her to submit to her once again. Her previous partners were always there to satisfy a physical need. What would make Kira different it would consider her a downgrade, being that she is an ordinary human.

She gritted her teeth, her hands shook from her anger. It was all out in the open now, her fears and anxiety of the uncertain; the doubt she felt in herself and those around her. Friend or foe, she did not know how she could feel this way, towards vampires, towards the very woman who literally started the apocalypse of humanity. Her people would lynch her if they discovered her betrayal. Vampires would ostracize her because she was not one of them, and now she did not know where she could belong.

Carmilla walked to Kira, the mortal was on the verge of tears, whether in anger, sadness or confusion did not matter.

The immortal hesitated a first, but then she wrapped a hand around the younger woman's waist and pulled her closer when she wiped a tear from her cheek, "She is nothing compared to you, you are more than human, you are not a slave, you are precious to me. I...do not quite understand how humans express affection and I apologize that my actions have hurt you."

The tension in Kira eased, the pain she felt in her neck subsided as her body contoured naturally to fit into Carmilla's.

The woman called softly, "I want you to stand beside me, to support me, love me, now and always. Be mine alone; your mind, your body, your heart, your very soul." Carmilla pulled her closer, resting her forehead on Kira's, her eyes softening, "You are the one I want to spend eternity with, my Mate." She kissed her sweet and gentle, "Marry me."

Chapter Sixteen
Orchestrated Doubt

Kira was speechless, her mind completely blank. For a moment she thought she had misheard Carmilla or that her mind had played a trick. It would not be the first time, and with the reality of what was asked of her, it would not be the last. Carmilla kissed her softly, sweetly as a goodnight before she left her in her room to her thoughts and awaited her answer. Her heart raced, confusion, dumbfounded she had no idea how to process what just happened. She had no ability to plan an answer and could not to comprehend what Carmilla had asked her.

She told Kira she was her Mate that she wanted to spend eternity with the human. The shot had been shot, and the ball was now in Kira's court, but she did not know how to play. She had spent years working to survive and while recently Kira imagined that a future for her might be possible, this was never in the cards. Nevertheless, it was imagined by Carmilla. It was not for a lack of imagination, but a lack of understanding how: how this would work; Carmilla is the Empress, a Pureblood Vampire of the Tepes Bloodline. How could this possibly end well?

A human woman, a slave in the eyes of the Game, suddenly made a debut in their world as the chosen lover of the leader of all immortals. What would humanity say? Was this a play to make them compliant? Was what she said and asked even true, or was it playing politics? Kira held her head between her hands as she sat on the roof and looked over the valley to the rising sunset. What would happen if she rejected the offer? What does she even feel for Carmilla?

Was it real? Was it true, or was it the Stigma? The blood? No, Carmilla was not the one who attacked Kira that she was certain of. There was no reason to almost kill her. The two of them despised each other for almost ten years, Carmilla ordered Emily to save her; kept her human. Why? She never looked at her sexually or romantically until she was an adult. If she wanted to manipulate Kira into falling in love with her, to use her as a puppet, she should have started when she was young. Stockholm syndrome is far more powerful the younger a child is. The fact she waited until the last three years... years after Eona had gone, it made little sense. Nothing made sense.

Marriage. Kira looked out at the sunrise with a twist in her gut. *She called me her Mate.* She has had little experience in understanding the romantic affairs of the Immortal. Outside of learning about how Carmilla ticked, her likes and dislikes both in and out of the bed she never cared to learn. What she did know is that the use that term was significant to the vampire. It held a different meaning than being a girlfriend or fiancée as a human couple. Carmilla used that word specifically and avoided a misleading term such as 'lover'. What does that mean, then?

She leaned on her elbows as the light of the sun slowly traveled over the mountain, its beams rose gradually as it peaked the top. She did not move. Hours passed, and the light covered her completely and warmed her from the winter weather. Kira stood, recharged, refreshed, but she did not feel ready to face the immortal. If Carmilla wanted to marry to make her a Mate, Kira needed to know what that would mean. Not only to stay alive, but what she meant by eternity.

She gribbed the Stigma and exhaled, her breath visible in the chilled air.

Carmilla knew something more about the Stigma, something that Emily too concealed.

After a long pause before she knocked, Kira opened the door to the office and saw Carmilla sat behind her desk. She had woken up early in order to get a head start on the tasks at hand. She hoped to finish early which would empty her schedule for Kira under the assumption she would not get an answer for much longer. The mortal entered the room and shut the door behind her. Carmilla looked up from her work and was surprised to see Kira so soon, but nevertheless was pleased

"You said that you don't understand how humans show affection, well the same is for me with vampires."

Carmilla quickly stood and came around her desk then leaned against it. "What would you like to know?"

"You called me your Mate... what does that mean?"

The vampire smiled, "You noticed." She ran her fingers across the desk. "To an immortal... a Mate is one we are bound to for all our immortal lives. While we can have many partners, vampires can go thousands of years before meeting what you would call a 'soulmate'. An invisible link called 'Bond', I suppose a term humans would call it..." she pondered for a moment.

"Destiny." Kira answered sheepishly, having read one too many romance novels, "But you and I hated each other. We barely spoke more than a couple words a year to each other before..."

"You were almost killed, I know. If we are to be honest I've always suspected something between us, but I could never put my finger on it until that night." Carmilla explained as she crossed her arms, "I was leery at first, a Bond with a human usually only happens with ex-humans,

237

but eventually I accepted the truth, that you are my one true Mate."

Kira sat down on the couch. "Okay, I get the Mate part, but what about the bond?"

Carmilla hummed to herself in contemplation. To describe Imprinting to a human: consider an invisible string attaching the two of them, syncing their hearts, their minds, and their souls together. A force that pulls them together. They can sense whenever that mate is, there are even reports they can feel the emotions of one another. Kira's eyes grew wide. Wait, if she's the base of the Stigma, then are my symptoms because of her?

"You look as though you are uncertain to ask me something." Carmilla gestured, "There is nothing off limits between us."

"Okay... then why have you been giving me your blood? If you have a bond with me, if you want to marry me, why didn't you just let me turn?"

The door flung open, Eona came in with a face of anger, "You're getting married?" She questioned loudly.

Carmilla stood calm, Kira shot up, "You knew she was there..."

"She deserves to know." replied the eldest with the same demeanor, "If you decide that is." Carmilla added at last glancing at Eona, "It is your choice, this family owes you that much."

Eona hissed, "Kira deserves to be given an actual choice, not being given the illusion of one! You've been ostracizing her from everyone else, so she thinks she loves you!"

Carmilla did not speak.

"I know you're the one who cut off our conversations. You gave the order to intercept our letters! You made her think I abandoned her!" Eona accused angrily.

The Empress rose and Kira kept on her toes.

"Be very careful how you go about the truth, my niece. Lies have the tendency of revealing themselves on their own." Carmilla said as a warning, not a threat.

"Guys please..." Kira intervened, "Don't fight, not because of me—"

"You knew Kira, and I were together! You knew the entire time and you've done everything to keep us apart!" Eona ignored the tiny whisper and continued to argue with her aunt.

Carmilla had enough, "Do not twist my actions to feed your narrative, you know exactly why you were separated." She glanced at Kira and refused to say anything else.

"Will someone tell me what the fuck is going on!" Kira snapped at them, "You told me you left to protect me, now she's saying she separated us for a reason—one of you better tell the fucking truth right now!"

Carmilla and Eona became quiet. Eona wore a face of guilt; Carmilla pity. Kira demanded an answer immediately and had enough of lies, enough of omission of truth and if she was to live among them, if she was to give herself to either of them, there could be no more lies between them. She trusted Carmilla to tell the truth of any knowledge that was hers to give, but what she knew of others, of Eona, she showed reluctance; refusal. Instead, the mortal turned to Eona, who has long since hidden the truth behind why she left, what she was protecting Kira from, that she needed to leave without a single explanation.

"Tell me." Kira said quietly.

Eona did not speak.

"Tell me!" The youngest woman repeated with a loud snap.

Eona choked on her words, a lump forward in her throat, and it was difficult to say even a single word.

"The truth is—"

"Eona, wait, you don't have to—" Carmilla quickly came to her defense, "I will explain—"

239

Eona shook her head, "No...no she needs to hear it from me." Tormented, the Pureblood Princess, looked at Kira, but could not meet her eye.

"I left because you almost died because of me." Eona said in a single breath.

Kira looked at Carmilla for an explanation, but the Empress shook her head and dropped it with her own sadness.

"What—what do you mean by that, I almost died because some vampire attacked me—!" The mortal's heart beat rapidly, her eyes widened in realization. "You...?" she asked, the quizzical word shaking in her voice.

"...no..." Kira shook her head, "No, no, you wouldn't..."

Eona clenched her fists. "I was a kid. I thought I could control it, that I could stop myself in time, but..."

"In time?" Kira looked at Eona as she repeated, "You—you wanted to turn me..."

"Kira, I wasn't thinking, my instinct took over, I wanted us to always be together—"

Desperately the vampire tried to explain, to justify what she did, that it was not entirely what she wanted and it was a complete accident that she was hurt as she was.

Carmilla pushed off the desk. "It's difficult for young vampires to control their urges. Eona's intentions were not malicious. She wanted you to be with her forever... just as I do now."

Eona reached out to the motionless and silent Kira, "Please, Kira, I'm so, so sorry. I never wanted to hurt you! After I bit you, my instinct went wild. I couldn't control myself—"

A hand slapped away Eona's hand and threw it back with enough force to make the immortal stagger back. Carmilla hesitated as she the Stigma on Kira's neck burn furious red, vines rapidly spread and worked to suppress what was within. She almost killed her. She could forgive Eona if it was truly an accident, but those thoughts were hers alone. She

240

wanted to turn Kira, to make her into a vampire just like them, so they could be together.

"You took my choice from me." Kira growled, clenching her jaw.

Eona tried to get closer, Carmilla saw the look in Kira's eyes, and she quickly grabbed the human's fist, and stopped the lightning fast fist from hitting her niece. She was surprised by how strong the mortal was, that she wielded a strength the Empress knew was not mortal.

"You knew!" Kira turned her aggression to Carmilla and pushed her back which made her slide a couple feet back from the force.

Kira bellowed, "Did everyone know?"

Carmilla shook her head, "Only a handful of people. We kept it quiet. I was trying to keep you both safe. Be angry with me if you wish, hit me, scream at me I will take it all."

"YOU'RE NOT THE ONE WHO ALMOST KILLED ME!" Kira roared as she turned to Eona, "I TRUSTED YOU! I LOVED YOU!"

Eona grew small.

Carmilla came between them, "Kira please, Eona made a mistake, she never meant to hurt you, a vampire's instinct is overwhelming—"

"MY ENTIRE FAMILY WAS SLAUGHTERED BECAUSE OF YOU VAMPIRES, DON'T YOU DARE TALK ABOUT WHAT'S OVERWHELMING!" Howled the woman, the floor beneath her broke, the glass in the room cracked and then shattered completely.

The Stigma burned bright, its vines stretched across her neck, down her shoulder and over her heart. Without restraint, without suppression, her rage, built of fifteen years of pain and suffering, broke free. It empowered her, broke her limits and called out the vampire within her, held back only the Stigma that acted as its cage. Now, the cage rattled hard and loud and threatened to be broken.

Kira's head pounded. Flashes of thoughts and memories she had long locked away began to slip through the

241

cage. Its murderous aura leaked into her rational mind, infecting it, corrupting it. She saw the room lose its light and color and felt a hand on her shoulder. *They took away your memory, but I remember for us*. The young phantom that was a vampire-like Kira whispered an engraved hatred back to the surface.

The scars on Kira's back dug into her back, the pain she felt the night those nails were engraved on her flesh as fresh as their making. That pain pulsed throughout her body, intensified by the glowing Stigma, the more she felt, and the stronger her hatred grew, further overwhelming her rational mind. There was no happiness in the last thirteen years. They all seemed to be overwritten by the anguish, the fear, the sorrow; guilt of losing her family and loving the ones responsible.

As she gripped her throat, Kira's rational self began to lose the battle.

Eona mistakenly tried to reach the mortal woman, to calm her down, but she would not listen. Instead, Kira grabbed Eona and threw her across the room. *Kill her*. Whispered the phantom child. *Kill them all.*

Carmilla moved in front of Kira, not to attack her, but to stop her and protect her niece. This was all their faults, but this was not what she thought would happen. Kira's sudden display of vampire-like strength; the doctor did not say that adaptation was to this degree. The 'symptoms' Sanders mentioned, she described as lingering phantom pain of the attack.

She had warned Carmilla privately that Kira's turn was stopped, but not reversed, that while the Stigma suppressed further change, it did not stop what it already did. This was not phantom, this was very real and given the appearance of the Stigma... Carmilla's efforts at suppressing the vampire proved a failure.

Kira growled with bared fangs, but when her eyes went from a recovering Eona to Carmilla something pulled at the mortal's heart. An instinct, not an emotion, that had pushed back her hatred and filled her mind with only the sight of this vampire. The mortal looked to Eona, then to the damage and realized she had done all of this. Horrified by what she had done, that she was becoming no better than the monsters that stalk the night, she ran. Out of the office, through the Palace she sprinted as fast as she could. She made for the woods and escaped the gilded cage before being lost deep in the forest.

She did not know how far she ran, nor how long her legs could go further, but her heart had reached its limit. However long it had been Kira eventually slowed then propped herself against a tree as she gasped for air while tears fell uncontrollably. She slid onto the ground and sobbed.

It hurt, everything; her legs were lead, her lungs were on fire; her arms shook as her mind was slammed with clashing emotions. This anger, this rage, this hatred she had known all her life, though it had faded with time, it never disappeared. Now, as though gasoline had been thrown onto an already burning log, that hatred was all she could feel. Her memories ran wild, unwanted, painful collisions of who she was and who she was. She did not know which was which anymore. Kira watched the shadowed vampire loom over her, their embered eyes glowed in the darkness. In her mind, memories crossed, her neck burned; Kira turned over and slammed her fist into the ground.

Stop. She begged her betraying mind. In that room; her memories bled into another. Eona, bloody, horrified, stood at the side of her bed; Carmilla was next to her and held and comforted her. Kira was on the floor, her blood pooled on the ground as she held her neck. Emily was in the room, beside the shadow that was now Eona; she ran away. Carmilla and Wolfgang were in the room and held Kira down. In that room she screamed until her throat was raw; it burned; Emily pressed her hand hard into the turning human's neck. The Empress held out her arm; she opened her flesh with a flip knife. *Please.* Her tears fell harder. *Please stop.* She saw Carmilla at her bedside as she fed Kira her blood and helped to change her bandages. Then she saw Camilla stand in the ashes of the city and order for the slaughter of Kira's people. The Empress stopped Kira when she clawed into her own flesh and dragged her nails across the Stigma. When Kira wanted to cry and scream, Carmilla, the Red Queen, hugged her. Jake and Eona laughed with her. Their laughter persisted as Kira watched her sister be opened from the back, their mother bleed from the throat a hungry monster had torn that out.

I don't want to remember this... I don't want to feel this... Kira's finger dug into the tree root as she dragged them down to her side. *They killed my family! Tried to turn me!* It was unforgivable. Eona had wanted to make her a vampire, and she took her choice away, the only thing more sacred to a human than their name. She roared angrily into the sky, her voice echoing for miles.

The rustle of dead leaves caught her attention, but whether animal or vampire did not matter because she did not care. She opened her eyes and saw between her fingers the blurred image of a man made clearer as he drew closer. A vampire with cat-like reddened eyes: the Pureblood King.

He looked at her silently, eyes that told her he did not want to pity her, but did anyway. He walked closer until he was beside her. He knelt down and placed his hand on her neck. The Stigma submitted to his strength and dimmed as its appearance and color returned to normalcy.

Kira stared at him for a moment. This man Carmilla feared, the entire Empire feared. He came to her, helped her, just as Emily had said. When she was at her most vulnerable, he would be there.

The King offered his hand, "Come, I'll take you home."

The King had pulled Kira close and was carried in his arm while the world around them shifted and flew past them. Browns, golds, reds and yellows eventually bled into white and when they stopped, their feet were in snow. Looking around, she knew they were in the woods, but not the ones in the valley. They were further than that, deeper into the mountains north of the Tennessee Valley where the Palace lived.

They stood in a light layer of snow. Winter had not quite gripped the area, but it was a sign of the weather to come. Kira knew this because she had lived here, had bared through the summers, falls, winters, and springs in the cabin through the trees. Her home, where her family had lived at the war's peak, and where she lost everything.

Kira looked at the King, who nodded silently, but allowed her to take the first steps. These grounds were cursed, barren. Nothing had grown in the clearing between the woodbine and the house beneath the ridge. Only decay was here. She walked in the snow. Despite the little clothing, she felt no chill from the cold fangs of the season. She walked to a tree, logs nailed into the trunk where some had fallen off due to time.

Her old perch, built by her father for her to protect her family. She touched the bark, its rough, cold and wet exterior covered in snow on one side. Her memories played in front of her and reminded her of the arrows she shot which killed a vampire and drew attention so her sister could enter the tunnel. She remembered when she jumped from the perch as she tried to fire another arrow, but was attacked from behind.

Kira looked at the cabin, then walked into the camp limits. She stood in the place where the vampire had her on the ground just before her sister attacked with a spear. Kira picked up the rotted shaft and lifted it from the ground and it nearly fell apart in her hand. She held the spear and crushed it when she gripped it tightly before she dropped it then walked to where her sister had been cut down.

She heard her mother's screams which drew her to the broken door of the cabin. They had dragged her sister's body in there and threw her with their mother like someone's trash. Kira looked at the state of the cabin. Years of neglect did little to it, even with the fire the vampire attempted to use to burn it down. The door and outer exterior were hard, parts of the foundation were burned to ashes, and a hole in the roof had caused it to collapse inward. The windows were broken, the panels that closed them having fallen and decayed on the ground. The porch sank into the dirt, the pillar in the front left furthest from the door had a broken support which cause half of it to drop.

She remembered the smell of burning the logs; blood filled her nose of her own and her family's. They stabbed Kira with a needle and made her unconscious with her last waking sight of the cabin in flames and her mother and sister motionless in the doorway. Now, as an adult, Kira looked at the doorway, but there was nothing. She walked to the cabin, she entered, face to face with a blackened skeleton, face down in the center of the room, on top of a destroyed pelt.

Kira dropped hard onto her knees.

"Mom..." she whispered weakly.

She finished digging with makeshift tools and then her hands when they broke until a proper grave had been created. With each piece of bone, she carefully arranged them in their proper place, and set them with her mother's remains. Kira gripped a carving she and her sister had done for their mother that survived all these years. The class ring their father had from Ranger school hid in a box, unfound and left eternally with her for the afterlife.

Her hands were raw in front of the partly frozen ground, cut and blistered, but despite this she refused the King's help. She was not there for her mother in this life. The least she could do was give her a proper burial. Kira stabbed a rough wooden cross into the head of the grave. She carved her mother's name into it and felt guilty she could not remember when her birthday was, but she certainly knew when she died. In time, the daughter would want to give her mother a real headstone, made with her own hands if she must, but this was all she could do. It was not enough, not for her, not by a long shot.

"It is a sorrow to lose a mother." The King finally spoke as he stood behind Kira, "Yours is very fortunate to have children who care for her as much as you do. Even after all this time, living among the enemy. Many would lose sight of who they are, who they were, becoming someone—something else entirely."

The woman said nothing to him, but she listened.

"The Tepes stripped you of everything you were. Your name, your body, the memories of your family—how much longer until they fade away completely?" Asked the King.

Met with silence again, he continued and watchedher body tense at his words.

"You were the lucky one. Most taken as slaves suffered far worse than you. They fought like animals for scraps their masters tossed them. You ate as a king every day. Your fellow slaves froze without a fire to keep them warm, their clothes torn and shredded while you received a new wardrobe whenever a single string came loose. They slept in the dirt, while you were in a comfy pillow top bed." The more he spoke of her good fortune, the more Kira's anger swelled.

He was right. Kira was fortunate with her mistress that she was still breathing, still human. The atrocities committed against her fellow man, however, most were not so fortunate. She knew what the Nobles did to their slaves, knew what happened in labor camps, but ignored their pleas. What could she do to help them? She was not Moses who would deliver them all to freedom, to a home free from oppression.

Kira knew she was powerless to help them. She saved herself to protect herself rather than waste time and energy on those she could do nothing for. If one lesson from her father's teachings persevered through the years, it was self-preservation.

The King judged her for the act of inaction. She chooses ignorance, which is expected of a child, but she is no longer one. What Kira did not know was that she was no longer a powerless child. She had the strength to change the world. She needs only the proper teacher to show her the way.

"The dead will not return, but we cannot let their deaths, their sacrifices mean nothing." The King said softly, "That is why the *Reich*, the Last Stand exist, to fight in the place of those who cannot. We have a duty, as citizens of the world, to fight for a future where generations will not bear this pain."

The mortal clenched the stone in her hand.

"Now I ask you, as one of the fortunate ones to have survived this long, will you continue to live in the fantasy of the Tepes? Or do you seek to open your eyes and choose a future of your own making?"

Kira who had kneeled at her mother's grave, set another stone on top, "Where is she?"

The King knew she had realized that in that building, there was only one skeleton.

"Alive." He answered.

Kira realized immediately that her mother was face down because she was using her body to hide and protect the secret door. Their mother would have given the world to protect her daughters. Her fate was sealed, but she fought to the last breath to ensure at least one of them would not share her fate. She loved them, with everything she had and a love like that can give one the strength to overcome even death, if for a short time.

He continued though he knew Kira would likely not respond, she still heard them. Her mind, however, was focused on only one thing.

"I searched everywhere for you, but there was nothing, as though all traces of you had been destroyed, both human and vampire. Even the original Hunters who caught you, all had mysteriously met their end not too long after they captured you. Who would have thought you were at the heart of our enemy—"

"Where is she?" Kira asked again as she clenched the disturbed dirt and stone in her palms, her eyes never left the name of her mother upon the cross.

The King's answer was as obscure as the first time. "Eager to be united, would you even recognize another? You have spent more of your lives believing the other to be dead than living together. I wonder... will you bring her back to them, to the vampires you have warmed the bed of—"

A blur of black had him pinned against a tree. Kira's strength intensified by rage.

"Leave her out of this!" she snarled like a rapid animal, fangs sharpened and protruded from her mouth as she pressed him into the tree until it creaked and snapped under the strain.

He did nothing to defend himself.

"So quick to protect the ones who have cast the shroud of a fantasy life. Who would have you become one of them? A true slave to the whims of the immortal Pureblood; I wonder, is it loyalty or the Sire that commands your actions?"

Kira clenched his clothes tightly, a deep growl came from her throat, her sky-blue eyes darkened to the storm within. Her Stigma slowly glowed, but it was not wild and untamed. It was gradual, her anger responded to a focusing mind.

"You think you know me—think you know what kind of life I've lived. I've survived—!" Her strength increased as she held the King higher until he was off the ground, "But you have no idea who I am!"

The king raised a brow. "Do you?"

The woman frowned.

"Do you remember who you were, before you allowed the Tepes to tell you who you should be?" He asked, placing his hand on Kira's fists, "Do you remember your father? Your mother? Would you even recognize your own face? Or have you lost sight of yourself you cannot even recognize in a mirror?"

249

Kira gritted her fangs as she pressed him harder into the tree's trunk. The Stigma glowed brighter.

"Remember: the free to choose, a slave obeys."

Her eyes dropped, an easy tell of her consideration of his words. She eased him down slowly and released him before she stepped back. Without the medication to satisfy her inner beast and the Empress's blood to contain it to its cage, her hatred alone was all that could give her the focus to control it.

He adjusted his suit jacket. "How does it feel?" He asked, "To choose of your own free will. That is what I want for all of humanity: the inherited right denied to you by the vampire, stripped from you by becoming one of them."

Kira stared at her mother's grave again. The Stigma darkened and the vampiric features she lightly adopted returned to their human origins. *This whole time.* She thought, clenching her fist. *They all knew and lied to me.* The mortal shut her eyes, quelling the fire within her. She could not lose it now, and she could not give into her emotions. No, that was not right. She locked her emotions away to survive in their world and yet just when she was living... No more.

She grabbed the bag of the last possessions that survived the fire and the test of time. An old, rusted knife, given to her by her father, her mother's journal, dusty, water-damaged and flame-kissed, but miraculously intact otherwise. The last was an aged walkie-talkie, its battery corroded; the antenna was burnt and melted. It would not work now, but this was the walkie-talkie their father left them he promised to call every sunrise if it was safe. They never heard from him again.

Their parents were gone. Nothing would change that, but there was hope. Kira was not alone and she would not remain in a cage while she was alive and outside in the world. Kira turned to the King and asked that she be brought back to the Palace. There was unfinished business that she could not leave. He agreed, the two of them arriving near where he had met Kira initially. Night had fallen, the bustling city in the

250

valley below had its weekend noise reached high into the mountains, reaching them faintly.

The King removed a mask from his cloak and fixed it onto his face: "When you are ready, seek the child of Hippocrates."

Chapter Seventeen
Key to Evolution

Carmilla called Jake and asked him to come to keep Eona company. Someone needed to watch over her. Kira had not returned for hours in fact, when they tracked her phone, it appeared as though she went into the woods and vanished. Her trail stopped a mile in and then nothing. They made Wolfgang aware, but no others were informed—of the original five, they kept only one in the dark for questioning of motivations.

The Empress was never fond of the doctor, an ex-human with questionable origins. She had in-depth expertise in human and immortal anatomy that exceeds that of an average doctor. Her knowledge related closer to that of scientific theory and experimentation than treatment. Doctor Sander's possession of an archaic technique used by Purebloods in ancient bygone eras, altered to halt the turning into a vampire, yet removed its initial control properties.

Many would see a technique such as this as the benevolence of a woman trying to help humanity, the work towards the pipe-dream of developing a cure. Carmilla considered this angle, but she was not Empress simply because of inherent right. She had lived centuries fighting her way through the Council and emerged with one victory after the next in the Game.

She had more than a few people, vampire and human, come for her life and they would not be the last. A Stigma to help humans keep or regain their mortality, or to raise an army of immortals, protected against Absolute Rule. Regardless of her reasons, the doctor failed to help her patient and now she would no longer be her physician.

Carmilla could no longer stand waiting. She opened the window and vanished from the Palace as she reappeared in the courtyard dozens of feet below. She cleared the walls, and was outside the limits of her home, then proceeded to follow the trail of Kira's scent. The others may have come to a dead end, but she was different: Kira's and her blood were intertwined, blended together; with her ability and her Bond, meant finding the woman was easier. However, if Kira rejected her, it would prove significantly more difficult and quite painful. *That does not seem to be entirely the case, at least not yet.*

She's near. Carmilla sprinted off the road into the woods. The fresh scent of Cherry Blossom was stronger, as though once again she had appeared. *Someone else is near.* The immortal sensed a strong, overwhelming scent of Sage that grew stronger the closer she came to Kira's location. Through the trees, despite the night she saw clearly Kira stood in the woods, but she was not alone. A Pureblood of immense, but unrecognizable power, the Empress demeanor changed immediately. She too came to be sensed, and the masked immortal grabbed Kira and pulled her behind him.

Carmilla did not take kindly to Kira being touched. She hissed and opened her wrist. Blood sharpened and dagger-ed out in zig-zags and aimed at the unknown immortal. He countered the blood whose strength rivaled that of steel, but the Empress's purpose was not to defeat this man. Behind Kira, Carmilla wrapped her arms around the younger woman's waist and moved again to in front of the other Pureblood many feet away.

"Are you alright?" Carmilla asked protectively as she kept a hand on Kira.

The masked vampire raised his hands. The earth shivered and cracked at his command and raised, then shaped into spikes that hovered at his sides. *How interesting*. He knew the Tepes took a special interest in Kira, but this level of protectiveness.

"Carm wait! He's—"

"The Pureblood King." She answered with anger, "He will not touch you again."

The King chuckled, "The harder you hold on to her, the quicker you will suffocate and kill her." The spikes of rock hurled forward.

Kira grabbed Carmilla from behind and made her fall into the ground. She used her body to cover the Empress, as the rocks flew past her, one grazed and cut her cheek. The King looked into the mortal's eyes; she need not say a word. Her message was obvious and he would adhere to it for now. She was in a state of turmoil, hesitation and clouded judgement created out of years of grooming and survival. She was not a lost cause and she had not completely forgotten who she was or where she came from.

"Until next time." Said the King as he vanished in the next moment.

With the King gone, Kira removed herself from Carmilla and sat on the dirt at her side as the vampire sat up the looked to Kira for an explanation. She refused to look at her, not for shame, nor shyness, but out of spite. The mortal got up and grabbed the bag she dropped.

"What are you doing here?" Kira asked, annoyed, but offered her hand to the woman on the ground.

Carmilla frowned as she stood quickly on her own, "You already know the answer."

Kira huffed with a scowl, "Do I? There's a lot of things I thought I knew—like how I might trust you."

Her words stabbed at Carmilla's heart deeply. It hurt her to hear her Mate say that, to feel her sadness, her grief. The shell that was around the mortal's heart began to crack. The stone chipped away and revealed the raw softness beneath. For Kira, who spent years hiding her emotions, it was painful to have them come through like a scar torn open as fresh as the night it made them.

Carmilla felt that pain. She walked to her destined mate, "Did he hurt you...?" She asked as she looked at the blisters and cuts on her hands, "When I saw him with you I feared—"

"That I went to play for the other team?" Kira cut off snarky, "Because I'm that *easy*." She sarcastically ended.

The immortal tore a piece of her own shirt and gently took Kira's hand then wrapped the fabric around her palm.

"I feared... he was going to hurt the woman I love." Carmilla corrected quietly, "He has earned more than fear, but hatred not only from the Empire, but me personally."

Kira stared at her quizzically.

The vampire frowned darkly, "He was involved in the murder of my sister, Eona's mother."

The proud, confidante Empress of the House of Tepes was not to be found. Instead, a worried, soft woman was in her place, fearful to lose what she loves, even if that love was to reject her. Carmilla smiled lightly and chuckled weakly when she finished the tie of the wrap around Kira's palm. Who would have thought that they would wrap her around the finger of a human, all these years people thought she was in control of Kira that she was the master, but it was the opposite.

She wanted to please Kira, to serve her in every capacity, but now Carmilla has grown tired of obscuring her feelings in a cloak of sexual ambiguity. For Kira's safety and no other reason would she not reveal to the Council publicly of the finding of her mate. In the short run it would... *complicate* her relationship with the Council and with the Pureblood King being bold enough to approach Kira right at their front door she needed all the allies she can get to protect not only her people, but her family.

Kira opened her mouth to say something, to tell her the truth, but her lips closed. She could not tell Carmilla, she could tell no one because no one in this place could be trusted. A woman she loved, her best friend, betrayed her, nearly killed her, Carmilla knew the truth and kept it from her and still she has more questions than answers. No, she would not tell Carmilla anything, would tell no one, not even Jake.

Her body moved on its own. Kira went into Carmilla and pulled her into a tight hug. For whatever reason, she felt guilty for running away, even if they brought her back home, even when she could bury her mother. Kira regretted hurting Carmilla despite her anger. The vampire seemed genuine in every action she made towards the human now. Before, she was possessive, wanting Kira all to herself, but now she believes it was not for the sake of defending property... but a way of showing affection.

"I'm sorry." Kira squeezed tighter. Carmilla gently wrapped her arms around the mortal in response.

The immortal rocked Kira and her gently. "I have said it before, as I will say it now: you have my complete confidence and trust. Whatever the King wants from you, I will believe you will not betray me and I will never betray you."

Kira wanted to cry. She wanted to fall asleep and never wake up. It was easier to sleep than to be awake, like a reverse nightmare where peace was found during sleep and one wakes to a nightmare. Being awake was painful now. Her heart was cracking, and pieces fell off, revealing the raw emotion beneath. Emotionally, she was not prepared to deal with and never expected she would have to deal with, never like this. Carmilla's confession to Kira, the truth behind her near death and eternally changed body and the revelation of a truth of the past...it was too much. She wanted to forget everything in the last forty-eight hours, to go back to before all this madness, all this confusion. All of this began because of an unnecessary jealousy.

"Come, my love, let us go home."

Over the next several weeks, Kira became unable to ignore the state of humanity any longer. Many trips had her out of the Palace often. Ever since the King's appearance, Carmilla has not allowed Kira out of her sight. Her sexual advances have significantly decreased, freeing the mortal to partake in other activities. Most of these involved the gathering of information; eavesdropping on nobles, talking to servants, and enslaved humans. From the shadows she watched the Council and began to understand despite Carmilla being Empress, she tip-toed around them. Most of the policies that oppressed humanity, were not hers.

On the television, she watched reporters on battlefields, show the devastation, areas once green in forestry and blue with life now as barren and deserted as the desert. They disintegrated entire mountains by weapons of mass destruction, fighter jets on both sides leveling what were once bustling cities, now a war-zone. Millions became refugees, thousands died or were taken prisoner, forced into slavery or worse.

The Last Stand fought with a mix of standard American military and guerrilla warfare, while the *Reich* worked and lived in the shadows. They cared little of publicity, the King avoided showing himself to the world. Even those who followed him all wore masks of original designs and materials. Each reflected the personality of its wearer. Whether it hid the person's identity or for the simple act of unity under the King's cause, both would fight and die in order to overthrow the Empire.

She watched the people, these humans, of the Last Stand fight, suffer, and die before her eyes, all for the sake of freedom. They did not want equality; they wanted an end to tyranny, even if coexistence, if abolition of oppression was they could achieve all that. To live in a world where they could live as they wanted, to govern as they wanted, to raise their children without fear of them being taken in the night by bloodthirsty monsters. To Kira, however, that was only a dream: there would be no peace between them, no equality—. Someone was going to lose, and she wanted to be as far away from that death-match as possible.

As time passed, Kira's indecisiveness lessened and she focused on the conclusion she had drawn, but her turmoil grew. She had not spoken to Eona ever since the night she learned the truth and with the resentment received from the mortal, the immortal's regret matched. The both of them had changed from when they were children, but that did not erase the actions of the past.

Neither woman would be in the same room for long. If Eona was already in the room, Kira would ignore her completely and carried out her business before she quickly left. The human would not allow her even two words and the vampire could not bring herself to force the other to listen to her.

Jake's words would not reach Kira, her anger also glanced off of him as he too had known the truth. The only difference was they silenced him under the effects of Absolute Rule; this Kira forgave him and would at least talk to him. The moment he tried to bring Eona into their conversations and Kira's glare was enough to cut his attempt incredibly short. Both tiptoed around the third of their trio, the group splintered and broken by the vampire's own doing. Now, more than ever, Kira kept her true thoughts and feelings to herself. Much of the time at the Palace she would be one of two places: her room or in the gardens practicing archery.

Her self-isolation was not at her disgust with the vampires of the house, but her disappearances to Emily's personal residence. Carmilla dismissed the doctor as Kira's physician, but neither Kira nor Emily were inclined to obey. Kira sat in the condo in one of the city's few skyscrapers as Emily cleaned the wound.

"Must you be so reckless?" The doctor scolded, when she placed a bandage over the gaze, then tapped it on all four corners, "I swear every time you see me you're bleeding or bruised."

Kira chuckled, "You expect any less?"

"I *expect*, you not to get into a bar fight, especially with a vampire." The doctor shook her head as she came to the side and lightly on the woman's rib cage.

Thankfully, nothing was broken.

The injured woman scoffed, "Not like I started it, sure as hell finished it though—" she hissed at the ointment applied to her knuckles.

"Just in the nick of time, do you have any idea how much trouble you would be in if you had gotten caught? You could have been arrested or worse." Emily's words felt more like badgering than that of a concerned friend, not that she has many friends she feels she can even trust to be concerned about.

While she frowned Emily looked at the bruising and cuts on Kira's body. Some of these were older, but it was difficult to tell. Her body was changing. It healed faster than it should. The doctor kept quiet about her earlier suspicions and theories and is now convinced more than a few are coming to fruition. Kira is no longer sought the medication to suppress the effects, which meant she had either accepted the changes... or stopped caring.

"You've changed." Emily pointed out as she looked at the Stigma, "You used to do everything and anything to survive now..."

"Now I'm seeing how much of a bastard I am." Kira flexed her hands, "How I've ignored the state of my people, using my need for self-preservation as an excuse; I knew what was happening and pretended I didn't see it."

Emily shook her head, "Self-preservation isn't an excuse Kira, it's an instinct. It's natural for anyone to want to protect their own life. It isn't selfish to want to live, especially surrounded by those stronger than you--"

"I'm sick of it." Kira hissed at the sting, "Sick of watching my people suffer, of watching them die, I'm sick of doing nothing—I can't stand it anymore!"

Emily finished cleaning one hand, but drew back the cotton swab, wet with antibiotic ointment. This was a huge alteration of mindset, especially in a few short weeks. While Kira had told Emily that she met with the King and of her learning the truth of who attacked her, a few hours could not possibly be enough to alter years of a single way of living. It had been weeks since they saw another and Kira had kept their conversations over the phone limited and unrevealing. That meant there was more to that meeting than she let on. She had not spoken particularly about Carmilla, their relationship, nor of what Emily said to her during the ball.

"Have you considered what the King said? It sounded like he wanted you to join him and apparently had a tempting enough offer to sway you like this. What could he possibly have to give you?" Emily rose a brow and she leaned back.

Kira kept quiet for a moment. "It doesn't matter now." She said as she avoided the subject.

The fewer people that knew, the better.

There was no telling who she could completely trust now.

"I'm leaving." The mortal said firmly, finally, "I can't stay here anymore, not after everything, not with the state of the world."

Emily smiled lightly. "So you've finally joined the fight?" She asked with crossed her arms.

After a few more moments, she nodded in confirmation, "I don't know if I can make a difference, but..." *But if I can find her, then everything will be worth it in the end.*

"Maybe there's something I can do to help... maybe one day... convince Carmilla to make a truce with humanity." Kira said softly, shallow of hope.

Emily gestured, "You have the Empress's ear, but you have the King's attention. This you can use to your advantage. Rumor has it the King is an Ancestor, having been on this Crusade of his since before even the Empire."

An Ancestor is considered being the eldest of all vampires, the first and second generation of the original vampires. It is said the immortals have existed since the end of the Ice Age, the earliest records being of the Sumerian civilization. Some stories of the origins say immortals came from two gods, others say it was a from the fruit of a tree, but no records exist. What does is the knowledge that those who were the first of the vampires were Ancestors, the first Purebloods, born from human parents. They could survive the harsh environment and their families well beyond the lives of those around them.

"Having him as an ally would be a good card to have." Emily pointed out as she started treating Kira's other hand.

Kira huffed in amusement. *Oh sure, be friends with the Genocidal Crusader because that ended soooo well the first eight times.*

She did not know what to think of the King. She knew nothing of him, nothing of his motivations: he told her he sought to eradicate vampires, to free humanity and that their existence was a mistake. What drives a man to turn against his own people like this? What drives him to undertake a single mission for thousands of years? What drives him to believe a woman vampire destroyed and gave whose life would be of any help or use to him?

"Whether the *Reich* or LSA, you'll meet him again, either he'll find you, or you'll find him." She finished working on Kira's hands and closed her medical kit. She paused for a moment, Emily rested her palms on the kit.

"If only you hadn't been born as you had...you could have had a normal, happy life."

She disappeared and returned moments later, a book in hand.

Kira's brows rose, "Ah... Em?"

"Do you remember how I explained how your Stigma worked? It blocked you from turning completely, but you were indeed turned if only partly." The vampire reminded, "Between the Stigma, Carmilla's blood and the medication, the part of you that's a vampire was successfully suppressed. However, recently was when you started experiencing more vampire-like attributes?"

"So what, I'm some half-human, half-vampire?" Kira made a disbelieving expression.

The bond between a vampire and their Mate is historically powerful, but also a mystery. Some report they could listen to another's thoughts, another that they could sense where they were and even feel when the other is in danger. In Kira's case it seemed her vampire's abilities responded to her heightened emotions as a human, a dangerous union if not balanced properly. Together, something either extraordinary or catastrophic was possible.

263

"Honestly, I'm not entirely sure, this is unknown territory, and you're the first to have survived this." Emily explained in the book, "But if you're serious, you need to understand the Stigma in order to protect yourself."

Kira put on her shirt, "What do you mean?"

"Originally, the Stigma I created was designed so that it would progressively and safely alter a subject's genetics, reverting them to their previous state." Emily paused at her desired page.

"A cure...you're talking about a cure..." the human whispered in disbelief.

Emily nodded with a frown, "But that was not what happened: Rather than revert, the Stigma caused a mutation in the vampire cells to go wild, it took over and converted human cells until the strain would ultimately kill the subject."

Understandably, Kira drew concern for herself.

"As you are human, to prevent this, I created four locks, four levels of protection, to keep your vampire from taking over the part of you still human." She turned the book and showed Kira the drawings and notes she had made. "Each level unlocked grants you more access to your vampire abilities, but it also makes you vulnerable to your vampire." The doctor frowned. "It will not be like becoming an ordinary vampire, and the mutation converts any trace of human DNA, while simultaneously replacing it with altered vampire DNA. With these locks, however, your body is given time to adapt to the new cells. It gives you a better chance of surviving."

Kira looked up from the notes, "So, as long as it remains locked, I stay human?"

Nodding slightly, "For as long as your heart beats."

Chapter Eighteen
The Last Good Thing

She watched Carmilla carry out her duties with elegance, grace, and power. Perfect in every manner. She sat upon the throne as though they made it for her and her alone. Her body fit comfortably, curved to its ancient rough edges. Though ordained with velvet cloths and cushions, tradition never stopped her from adding her own touch and comforts. The mortal stood in the throne's corner room, hiding in the shadow of one of many pillars, listening to the verdicts of the Empress's ruling.

Fair to the requests of her people, the humane who do not seek the blood of mortals. Merciless to her enemies, vampire or human alike; Kira watched the Empress separate traitors' heads from their shoulders. Their blood pooled at their limp bodies. Humans who were gave information to the Last Stand paid for their transgressions with their lives. She frowned and turned her eyes from the sight and gave the victims a silent prayer that they may find peace in their next life.

Eona stood beside Carmilla as equally disturbed by the bloodshed as Kira. She looked at the mortal and tried to make a contact, even for a moment to show this was not something she condoned. Kira was noticeably displeased, agitated even from the death, but it was not this man alone that caused her frustration. For weeks she has been on edge, has not only shown, but outright spoke, her disapproval gained unwanted attention from Eona's father.

Not that Kira cared for his, or anyone else's, opinion as of late. Eona worried that her anger would spill out towards an immortal less understanding than the Tepes. Eona would always look out for her, whether or not she wanted it, but they could not be together twenty-four/seven. What worried Eona most of all was the lack of self-preservation Kira has displayed since she learned the truth and her isolation from everyone.

Kira exhaled with a heavy breath as she could no longer stand the sight of senseless death and left outside the side door of the Throne Room. She walked the side hallway, as she did not want to draw attention nor to stay cooped up in her room. As she had already practiced archery for the day, she headed to the library. Carmilla often worked here, but with the business in the Throne Room, she would not be here for a while. Kira reminded herself many things she did here would be the last: the last she walked in this hall, the last she read books from the library, the last she would ever see some people again. Despite her anger, the festered hatred... this was where she grew up, these are the people who helped raise her; they taught her to read and write, to speak a foreign language.

Kira entered the Library and brushed her fingers along the spines of books older than her, her father and her grandfather; not that she knew who that was. She remembered when Eona her to read books and remembered how often she managed to let Kira stay when Carmilla read stories to her beloved niece. Just as humans had their fairy tales, vampires too had their own, preserved orally and in tomes, many of which Kira knew better than ones taught to mortals.

Her hand stopped at one such book. She pulled it from the shelves: *Myths and Lore of the Immortal*. She opened the book and flipped through the pages, finding the story labeled simply as *The Sun and the Moon*. She knew this story well; it was one of Eona's favorite.

It began with a man and a woman; the man was one of light, one blessed with the power of the sun who gave the world his brilliance to allow life to flourish. Humans could grow crops, see, they lived happily; seeing their happiness brought warmth to his own. But in his happiness, there was a dim of sadness those he protected could not understand. They called this man the God of the Sun, he came to have many names, in many languages, but his true name was lost to time and even his own memory. There was only one who knew this man's name, one who could understand the sadness and relieve it: a woman, one like the Sun God. Unchanging, powerful; different.

They met near a tree, whose branches were thick with green leaves, blocking out the light from beneath its branches. When he approached her, she hid in the shadow of this tree and concealed herself from the light he radiated. Eager to know her the first he had ever met such as he, the man of the Sun came too close, his brilliance blinded.

His light burned the woman's eyes and caused her to grow weaker with each glimpse of him. He felt great remorse at being the cause of the woman's pain, but it did not dissuade him from his desire to meet her. One day, an idea came to him. He dimmed his light enough so that she could peek out from the shadow of the tree.

Time passed and the Sun God craved more. While she could stand beside him, they could not touch and so, further, he lessened his light. They could be together, to love another as the mortals the man had protected and provided for. In his happiness, he did not see the effect his actions had on humanity.

The less his light shunned, the fewer crops grew, the colder it became, and the darker the world grew which caused many people to die. In response, discord grew among the humans, a people once unified in utopia fought another over the dwindled resources. For the first time in history, one person intentionally shed the blood of another.

Outraged by the abandonment of their God, the humans waited until he was away in other lands and captured their God's corruptor. They believed her to have bewitched the God to ignore and neglect the humans. They tortured her and used the fire they were gifted from God. By the time he learned of what the humans had done, it was too late: the woman was found on the brink of death and the Sun God could not bear to let her go.

Instead the God, in his grief and in his rage, slaughtered the humans who had harmed his love, to save her, the God had her drink the life currency of the fallen humans, which brought her back from the brink of death. She was saved, but was changed. The green of her eyes, which reflected the leaves that once protected her from the light shun blood red. Her teeth sharpened to fangs; she became stronger, faster, getting new powers. As a result, she was named the Goddess of the Moon.

Humanity regarded the woman with great fear, for after her first drop of blood, her thirst for their lives was never satisfied. With each person bitten, they joined her legion of darkness, granting her a people to call her own. The first vampire. The mortals wove seeds of rebellion, desiring to protect themselves and their families from the hunger of the shadows. The Sun God, horrified by what he had done, could not bring himself to end the woman he loved, nor those she protected, but he could also not allow the humans he loved and cared for to be hunted and killed. Torn by his duty and his heart, God was at a loss for what to do.

As she watched her lover, the woman saw the turmoil she and those she turned to the shadows had caused, seeing what her personal vendetta against humanity had done. She decided she would not force her lover to choose between their two people: to appease both sides; she proposed an idea: to split the world.

The light of the sun could shine brightly for the humans half the time, while the other half, her darkness, could take the rest, allowing her children to run free and unharmed. When these two times met, that is when the lovers could be together. As sure as the sun sets and the moon rises, they would be together.

Satisfied, humanity and the vampires coexisted and the two passed onto their child and their children's children the story of the two lovers. This spoke of love and sacrifice, of perseverance, and responsibility: the tale of how the sun loved the moon so much. He died every night to let her breathe.

Kira flipped through the pages of the books, the pages landing on a fable: *The Curse of the Nightraven*. She stared at the title and rolled her eyes. Apparently, Eona and Emily had a sense of humor. Kira thought to shut the book and put it away, but thought after this whether she could go back to her real name. From another person's mouth, she has heard it once in thirteen years.

Never has she spoken it aloud since her original capture. What would it be like if she said it out loud? Would it be weird? Would it even sound right? Most of her life she has lived as 'Kira Nightraven', she cannot imagine as anyone, but this. It felt that going back was becoming someone else entirely.

She read the Edda, a short poem of a single page.

Hail our Protector
You who commands the shadows
Deliver me from the oppression of light
You who drains the wicked
Teach me to relentlessly hunt my desires
You whose steps make the Earth tremble
Show me the truth of this world
You whose glowing eyes pierce the night
Fight beside me as I claim victory
You whose name we praise
Hail the Nightraven

When she traced her fingers on the page, Kira wondered if there was some hidden meaning or message for it to be titled *Curse of the Nightraven*. Was this person cursed for having so many people rely on them or were these the words of a vampire who prayed to a god and was unanswered. Was this to curse the enemies of those who spoke it or were these words themselves a curse upon the one who spoke it? She did not know; she did not understand, but she had at least some knowledge where the last name she bears came from. Perhaps the name itself was a curse, to give those who bear it great misfortune and suffering?

"It's been a long time since I've seen that." Carmilla said as she closed the door behind her.
Kira did not hear her come in as her focus was on the book, but she was not startled at the sudden noise. She turned to the vampire and leaned against the bookshelves as she held the book to her chest.

"I thought you still had a few more heads to separate from your shoulders." The mortal said in sarcastic jest.

270

Carmilla's face hardened. "I do what must be done as Empress. It is my duty to secure the safety and prosperity of my people. My authority must be respected and feared, my emotions cannot come between me and that duty."

Kira huffed, "Fear only breeds hate and resentment." She shut the book with force and slid it back into the shelves, "The war did a good enough job of that for you to add to it further." Kira added as she walked to the door.

"Is that a concern?" Carmilla's eyes narrowed, "Or a ridicule?"

Kira shrugged, her tone quiet and as detached as she could muster. "It's a warning... I won't always be there when the Last Stand is planning to attack."

"We are immortal. We will outlive their rebellion long after they have lost their will to fight an unwinnable war." Carmilla said confidently as she gave Kira a smile, "But they are not the ones who have occupied your thoughts as of late." She added knowingly.

Kira shrugged again, "I've always got something on my mind."

The Empress walked to the couch and sat, she lifted her legs to the cushions she made herself comfortable when she watched Kira.

"Indeed, your thoughts and actions have often reflected one another." Carmilla leaned on her hand, propped on her elbow on the couch arm, "But lately they seem in turmoil with one another."

"You say that like you do not know what I'm thinking." Kira smirked.

"I do not and it drives me mad." Carmilla growled with annoyance.

"Whatever do you mean?" Kira asked innocently, batting her eyes.

She walked to the couch across from Carmilla, and propped herself on the arm rest of it.

Carmilla breathed with frustration, "The Game is easy when you know everyone wants something. By then you've already won three quarters of the battle the last is only to know what specifically. I have lived for over a thousand years now and in that time I have developed the skill to foresee people's thoughts and desires. Money, pleasure, power, influence; they all crave something. It is our nature as a vampire, to crave and consume. Humans are similar in those regards, even easier to predict, but not you."

The Empress leaned into her hand, "Your desires have eluded me, that I must often guess, or use roundabout methods to know them."

"You could make life easier and just ask." Kira could not help but chuckle.

"I detest doing anything unprepared." The vampiress grumbled.

Kira struggled to hold back a laugh and coveredher mouth. She tried to play it off as a cough, but it was too late.

The Empress of the Vampire Empire, one of the most powerful beings in existence, fumbled over herself over a human... over a woman. Kira thought to herself there must either be a sincere difference between how humans and vampires show affection, or she was the first person Carmilla claimed to love. 'Claimed', as the mortal constantly puts it, helps to draw a line between the two of them, a line she needed for herself more than anything. It was easier that way. For there to be lines, to be barriers, it protected Kira, either from her own stupidity and hope or from others.

The human herself did not acknowledge whether she felt the same toward Carmilla. If Carmilla felt as she claimed, then it would only complicate things further for Kira, just like it did with Eona. Kira knew she could not afford to acknowledge those feelings because it would only make leaving more painful. It would never sway her. She knew this; the past was no longer a distant memory; no longer would she wonder about the world alone. She would live, not survive, because she knew she had paid enough for being a human in a vampire's world.

Despite all that she has endured, all she has suffered, who she is now is because of the past and who she will be in the future is because of this moment. Kira did not intend to come back and if all went as planned, after this, they would never see another again. That's why, at this moment, Kira wanted this to be the last good thing Carmilla had of her. Perhaps it was selfish and cruel to do this, to lead her on, but it could not possibly be leading on if it was not one-sided.

As she looked at the flustered Carmilla, Kira's mind remembered different parts of her life within the Palace. She was a wild animal when first brought here, as she witnessed her family be torn apart by the enemy their father taught them to fear and hate. She lived under the roof, clothed, fed by the very woman who Kira believed to be a beautiful goddess, was, in fact, an angel of death.

Introduced to the young niece of the Empress, a girl a little older than she, Kira took one look at her eyes and decided she did not differ from the other murders. For weeks, she refused to speak more than a hateful 'vampire'. She never told them her name, her age, her birthday, nothing about her family or her past.

The relationship between Carmilla and Kira began as master and slave, a position the Empress would remind the human of whenever she acted out or refused to obey. There was a point when Kira refused to bathe for days, fled from the staff and escaped their every attempt to seize her. Carmilla was often the one who cornered Kira, grabbed her by her shirt and threw her into a nearby bathroom. When Kira fought back, the vampire grabbed her by her cheeks and held her close to meet her crimson eyes. She threatened the mutt would not leave this bathroom until she was clean, even if she had to hold her under water until the bubbles stopped.

Threats did nothing but fuel Kira's rage. When she refused to comply and chose violence, Carmilla raised her hand—Kira flinched—the woman stopped. Human or not, this girl was just that, a girl, a child, and they had not been treating her like one. It was the first kindness any of the adults had shown Kira since she arrived. Carmilla lowered her hand and kneeled down to the child's height. She made a bargain. If Kira took a proper bath, then she would treat her to ice cream. A growl sealed the deal. From then on...no one ever raised a hand to the child again.

When Eona left, grief struck Kira, a pain seen and unseen, and threw the young girl into a state of depression. Carmilla herself spent hours, months of her time and attended to Kira. When she cried in her room at night, it was the Empress who was there, a shoulder for the broken-hearted girl to cry on.

When she was out fulfilling her duties as Empress, she ensured the staff made Kira get out of bed, made her eat something at every meal, and get plenty of sleep. Kira's was enjoyment to wander around the garden came out of Carmilla's suggestion for Jake to take her, to distract her, to keep her out of her spiral.

When Kira's family was torn apart, she had a face to picture, an enemy to hate and rage against. Depression can be a faceless demon. It is a void closing in, draining a person of will. Carmilla knew this. She had felt it herself when her other half was murdered.

As the girl became a young woman, Carmilla had been without a partner for a few years, her attention diverted elsewhere, outside of a personal life. If she were to be honest about how engrossed into her duties she had become, it had focused any notion of free or personal time on Kira. She was not the only one who felt Eona's absence with a heavy heart. In a way, Kira's presence acted as a filler for Carmilla's departed family. It was more than that, however, a feeling, a connection. The vampire held from her to Kira.

For the first couple years Carmilla attributed this feeling to perhaps being motherly. As she had no children of her own, Eona was a daughter to her, having sworn she would take care of her sister's daughter no matter what. She thought she failed in this promise, having been unable to save her from a heartache, but for a vampire, these aches heal— especially for one as young as the Princess. With Kira she thought it also reflected her mothering toward Eona onto Kira, but it was not so. Carmilla realized the true extent of what her connection was when she saw Kira and Jake among their friends in a bar by chance.

There she witnessed Kira kissing another woman. Though it appeared to be a drinking game as they were all highly enamored, Carmilla was not. Logically she knew it was a game, she knew it was meaningless, but a twist in the Empress's gut made her realize; jealousy. Her inner vampire emerged, the personification of desire and instinct showing itself after all these years of careful control. The vampire's mouth watered, hungry to devour the woman before her eyes, to take into herself all that the woman was and ignite the passions. It was then Carmilla knew she wanted Kira; she needed her and would do anything to make it happen.

The years since then seemed to have flown by after that first night. The first night when the women became inseparable was originally an arrangement. Carmilla had called Kira to her room, a place she had only been in the room a few times to deliver food or wine and had only stayed once when she experienced terrible nightmares. When she entered the room, she was nervous. She thought she must have done something wrong, but it threw her off when she entered to find the Empress warmly invite her in and offer wine from one of two glasses on the coffee table. Kira was suspicious for certain, but at that point she had only learned enough of the Empress to avoid her wrath. She had only studied the Game secretly for the past year and mainly learned from Jake.

Carmilla sat in her chair and offered Kira a seat across from her, but was politely declined. The Empress took a sip of her own glass and sat as though she were on the throne. Elegant, refined, powerful; her presence was authoritative, dominating, but here that feeling was not as prevalent. She had lessened the intensity of her strength, but Kira knew what she was capable of which did not make the immortal's presence any less nerve-wracking.

At first the conversation was kept light, Carmilla asked about Kira's day-to-day activities and how that she had approached graduation if she had any aspirations. Guilty, Kira admitted she had not thought about anything more than continuing what they expected of her and becoming a full-time servant among the staff. Carmilla dangled her glass between her fingers, her crimson eyes glittered with a hunger Kira had seen before. She got straight to the point: they are women who share a similar taste. She stood, walked toward the mortal. With each step closer, the mortal backed away until she was against the wall.

The Empress had reached her hand and gently raised Kira's chin to look into her eyes. Like a lamb against a lioness, the human was uncertain and frightened; the Empress had never acted like this toward her, had never started such contact and with the look in her eyes—she feared what would be next. Kira clenched her eyes shut and jumped when she felt something warm on her lips. Slowly, she opened her eyes to the Empress's own incredibly close and realized what she was feeling. Carmilla had kissed her.

It has been nearly four years since then, and Kira now finds the distant memory funny in hindsight.

"What are you smiling at?" Carmilla asked curiously.

"I was just remembering the first time you kissed me, how different our relationship is now compared to then." Kira rubbed her neck

Smiling, "Disappointed?"

"Surprised really." Shrugged Kira.

Carmilla chuckled, "That you and I are Mates?"

"That I lived this long, actually." The mortal said honestly, a bit too casually for a normal person to consider her sane after everything.

"Did you think I would devour you?" Asked the immortal.

With a smirk, Kira gestured her arms out, "Which context are we talking about now? Because last I checked, you do that routinely.

They laughed.

Kira bit her lip as she looked at the time on the clock. "Want to go out?"

The Empress tilted her head as she raised a brow in silent wait. She needed a bit more clarification, because that could mean quite a few different things.

"Dinner." Kira rolled her eyes. "It's a human thing, I'll explain on the way."

Chapter Nineteen
A Night to Remember

Carmilla continued to show confusion, but she agreed, interested to know what Kira wanted. It was the first time she had suggested for them to do something together. They changed into casual clothes, it took longer for them to find something not designer brand for the Empress, who did not indulge in anything less than the best. Kira had to give Carmilla one of her t-shirts. Then they hid her hair in a braid and a beanie in an attempt to make her less than a goddess. That proved to be more difficult than she imagined. They drove together into the city and parked in a garage of one clubs before they left to walk the main-street.

Crowded with people, the night was young, and the people as well. Among the masses, the thousands of faces present on a cold Friday night, no one would look twice at them. They were two of the hundreds of couples and in this world, the world of the vampire, few judged who or what one loved. None dared, for who an immortal bonded with, if there was one universal and absolute law, it was to never harm the Mate of a vampire. Not unless you planned on killing both; a courtesy that helped prevent a significant amount of death in the act of revenge.

"What is this?" Carmilla asked to take the offered food from Kira.

The human chuckled, her mouth full of food. "Street food; It's called a hot dog." She swallowed as she Carmilla's suspicion of the creation's edibility, "You've seriously never had one?"

Carmilla looked at the whiner in a bun, "I have not." She took a bite, "But it's quite good."

Kira loaded hers with mustard and relish then bought two more, one a chili dog labeled a 'Chicago Dog', the other she instructed Carmilla to add condiments to her liking. To the Empress's surprise, the greasy food was quite delicious, and adding the toppings made it better. She looked at Kira with puppy dog eyes, the human smirked as she handed the half-eaten chili-dog to the woman. Carmilla took a bite. After she finished the dog, Kira noticed something on the other woman's face. She took her finger and took the mustard and licked it from her thumb with a mischievous glint in her eye.

"It is a strange feeling." Carmilla said as they walked down the street.

"What?" Kira asked, leaning closer to the woman.

"I have spent my life living the role I was born into: Pureblood of the House of Tepes; Leader of the Nightcore and now Empress. Not once have I considered what could have been, only what is; my duties, my responsibilities. Despite all my power, my abilities; my conviction to the path laid before me narrowed my sight to many things in life." Carmilla admitted as she looked out to the colors of the Christmas lights that pepepred the city in this cold December.

The human did not understand what it meant to have her life planned out for her. Much of her life has been unexpected and rapid, sudden changes and shocking truths have made it quite the rollercoaster for only being twenty-two. She could not imagine being born into such an important family, to have such responsibilities thrown onto her from birth. Carmilla has lived as they expected her to and had those expectations forced onto her is a type of chain themselves.

Carmilla looked down at Kira, "It is a strange feeling to find happiness in such mundane things. I think I am understanding why humans seem to have such fulfilling lives despite how short."

Kira curled her fingers with Carmilla's, "We call that living."

She hummed a pleased sound, then the older woman lowered her head and nuzzled it into the younger's.

"If it's with you, I think I may enjoy it."

A twist in Kira's gut forced her to fake a smile. There was guilt. She acknowledged this, hated this because in the end she would hurt someone she cared for. Deeply, Kira knew her care of Carmilla well exceeded that of a physical arrangement and that whatever it meant to be a 'mate', she felt. The parts of her heart that had been exposed by the breaking and chip away of her walls made her feel naked and raw. Years of training herself to control her emotion had this wall placed, it protected her against that which would hurt her again. With that wall, however, came the knowledge that her heart was untrained for what would come once those walls came down. Some already had which exposed her to these new uncertainties, feelings she had taught herself to deny for the sake of survival.

She had known better than to let her guard down, and yet she had done it all the same. Trust in people had hurt her in more ways than she imagined and yet still she does it. Over and over, as a broken record, half of her knows not to trust the vampire, while the other half sees these vampires as more than their nature as more than killers; she saw Jake, Emily, Wolfgang and Mablevi. People she knew, had grown up and lived with—those she would call friends. Yet her other half denies this, sees them for the atrocities they have caused the world, the pain they have caused her; that tore apart her family and left her on the tip of death frequently.

Yet she also saw a man qho desired to bring peace to humanity and acted as their protector. She saw the hopeless love behind the Pureblood Princess, a woman who grieves her mistakes and knew she had done wrong not by a human, but by her best friend. Kira sees the woman behind the Empress, a seductress who has never once lived a normal life, who sees the world the only way she knows and yet strives to understand that which she does not. She saw them as people, not vampires, makes it that much harder to leave them.

The other half... desired vengeance for the pain they have caused. Kira struggled with an internal war with herself, the heart against the mind; pulling her heart out of this inextinguishable hate. She told herself it was better this way, for all of them, but that too was a lie; Kira refused to remain when 'she' was out there, refused to stand aside and do nothing while her people suffered. Too long had she stood in silence; no longer and seeing what the Empress will do to fulfill her duties to her people... there was no way Kira could convince her to do otherwise. This was war. No matter who you saw behind the 'human' and 'vampire', it will not sway the people. So long as there are the weak and the strong... equality is impossible.

As she looked to the side, Kira smiled, slowly and tugged on Carmilla's hand for her to follow.

"A carnival?" Carmilla asked as the younger woman led her into the side street.

Dozens of vendors with food, gifts, games and fortune telling lined the area. Children ran with their parents, police patrolled, eating donuts and drinking coffee as they passed out stickers and candy-canes.

Kira smiled lightly. "When I was a kid, my parents used to take us to the annual carnival in town. We'd play games, eat cotton candy; my dad would have me on his shoulders letting me see over everyone."

Carmilla kept silent as she listened intently.

"He taught me how to use the bow and arrow, he tried to teach me how to shoot too, but I wasn't very good at it."

They walked down the street. Carmilla stopped, and bought them a treat called 'funnel cake'.

Kira chuckled when Carmilla coughed when she took a bite of a large piece with a significant amount of powdered sugar. She took a fork, stabbed it into a piece and tapped off excess sugar, she offered it to Carmilla. Cautiously, Carmilla took another bite, it was less sweet, but crunchy and oily; fried that she did not take too much of a liking to. Kira shrugged and ate the Funnel Cake by herself; Carmilla grumbled she wanted another hot dog. Kira chuckled, as she walked ahead to another stand.

Carmilla watched Kira, bright and beaming, order food and drink. The vampire's worry over Kira seemed to have been unfounded. But then again, though she could not tell what the young woman was thinking, she could see what the human was feeling. There was a sadness there, behind her smiles tonight, her anger; ever since she learned of what Eona had done to her, she has not been the same.

She had tried to keep the knowledge of Kira and the King together compartmentalized and unbiased, but it was no simple task. The Empress within her suspected the human of betrayal, yet knew the King was capable of great manipulation. Still when King attacked the Empress; Kira pushed her down, she saved her, and the King, the Empire's lifelong enemy, withdrew. Why had he done this? This was his chance to strike at the heart of the Empire, and he did not. It was then Carmilla suspected it was not her that the King had come for, but Kira. She saw them together. Kira was dirty, her hands blistered and coarse, as though she had been digging with her bare hands.

What had she been digging for?

She tried to give Kira the benefit of the doubt and the trust she deserves, the trust she had earned. Her years as a Pureblood within the Game, the Head of the Tepes family and the Empress of the Empire, have made her weary of those, not her blood. Kira was more than that, was more than a lover, than family. She was her Mate. Her Bond connected them together. Yet Kira had not acknowledged this, had not confirmed it and it blurred the line that connected them.

283

Carmilla wanted to give Kira her space. She did not understand how humans processed trauma—she had been born into a world at war. Her toys were wooden swords, her playtime was training, her gifts were new armor and weapons, her rewards were the triumph of meeting her parents' expectations; coin and land. War was her life, bloodshed was an expectation and love? Was a weakness of the mind. She banished it from her thoughts. Physical pleasure was a release, a tool, and nothing more.

Until Kira.

This young woman she brought to her house on a chance. She had said it was to give Eona a companion, but this was half the truth. It was on a chance, based on information with many black lines. She ensured none, but she knew. She eliminated the Hunters who pursued the family, after their violation of the Empress's order, they would never transgress again. As a human minor, there were few records to confirm her identity and many of those had been destroyed. Without the parents, it was impossible. Despite this, Carmilla had taken in the human to act as a companion of Eona and originally hoped to sway her through her niece, but this proved to be far more difficult than she had expected. The human had a strong will and a burning hatred that never faded.

Everything changed when Eona attacked Kira.

"I hope you like..." Kira held up cans of pop, *"Sprite* or *Dr. Pepper* because those are your choices." Carmilla grabbed the *Dr. Pepper* and one hotdog, "Now *that* I know."

"How did I figure?" Kira laughed as she the *Sprite* can and readjusted her hands with the remaining hotdog.

They casually walked through the crowd, ignored by the common people as being simply another face in the mass, another couple this night. Carmilla was not the Empress, nor a Pureblood, and Kira was not a human slave. They were a couple enjoying themselves. It was simple, peaceful, a life

Kira was supposed to have and one Carmilla never thought possible. Then again, if not for the life they live, neither would have ever met. Kira did not know if that was something she wanted or will allow herself to accept. Not that it mattered to her, 'what-ifs' were a pointless waste of time and energy because in the end they were a fanatical dream and something she would always wake to reality from.

Carmilla stopped and looked to the left where Kira's eyes had wondered. She had looked at many games, but this one had caught a special sparkle in her.

"Would you like to play?" The silver-haired woman asked as she gestured to the game.

A smile lit up Kira's face. Carmilla led the other woman by the hand and pulled out her card—the vendor scanned it with his device and explained the rules of the game. Hit the target, win a prize. Playfully Kira pulled back the cheap bow and shot the first arrow where she hit the first target and missed the next. The vendor gave her a small teddy bear: Carmilla nudged her.

"What about that one?" The vampire asked, as she pointed to the larger wolf-like stuffed animal dressed in a tuxedo.
The vendor chuckled, "Well if you hit the target with all three arrows you get the medium prize."

"And the grand?" Carmilla smirked, glancing at Kira.

"That would be the medium prize and two-hundred dollars cash prize—but it's difficult: you have to land nine bullseye shots, three at each target." He explained, as he did not believe they would take the challenge.

Carmilla turned to Kira, "That stuffed animal would look nice over the fireplace, would it not?"

With a smirk, Kira took the bow up again, "Hope you got spare arrows."

"What—" The vendor ducked.

The first arrow hit the bullseye, broken in half by the second and third. After the game, Kira walked down the street with a pleased Carmilla. She seemed infatuated by the cheap stuffed animal, like a child with a new toy. Kira didn't quite understand why.

"This is the first gift I have ever received from you." Carmilla said as she tucked the fancy-dressed wolf under her arm.

Kira had not thought of it in such a way. Neither woman gifted another with anything outside the bedroom. Often it was Carmilla buying lavish gifts for her lover to wear when in private, or subtle hints of her belonging to the Empress, like telling a secret out-loud only for the two of them to know. Kira had told no one about her birthday and for vampires who have eternal lives, their celebration of birth ceases being relevant.

"January thirty-first."

Carmilla looked down at Kira.

"My birthday: it's January thirty-first, Two-thousand-ten."

Though the creatures of the night were far from tired, the carnival met its end towards the first hour of the morning. The city knew no sleep, however; the night was older now, and the drunkards, who pre-gamed too early, began to slowly be removed from the bars and clubs. In another two hours the streets would be filled with pleasantries, it inclined those of which neither Carmilla nor Kira to deal with.

"A moment before we return home." Said Carmilla, as she halted outside the car they would take home.

Quizzically Kira watched the vampire walk to her and held out her hand. In it was a gold chain with a renaissance, brooch-looking attachment, it lacked a stone attached to it. She must have held onto this all night, otherwise Kira would have seen her purchase this. Carmilla stabbed her nail into her palm and opened a slight wound as her blood floated upward as though weightless. The blood gathered and swirled into an oval, it solidified and hardened into what looked like a stone.

This stone attached itself to the gold mount and completed the necklace.

Carmilla lifted the necklace, "For you." She said with a smile, "A part of me, to keep with you always."

Kira starred as her gut twisted in guilt. She put a smile on her face, thankful for the gift as she lifted her hair for Carmilla to clasp the chain around. It was no lie when she said she was grateful however, there was an immense pain in her chest when she put on this fake smile. She repeated to herself that this was all necessary. The human needed to, *wanted* to leave because remaining here was no longer an option, not when *she* was out there.

This, all this; the night on the town as they spent time together Kira forced herself to ignore the lie she has lived, to embrace, if only as a front, Carmilla's affection for her. This was all for the vampire, to give her a good last memory, a night to remember, so when Kira finally left, it would be on the best of terms she could manage. She would not be allowed to just walk away, not from the Palace, not from the Tepes and not from Carmilla. Kira needed to disappear completely from watchful eyes; she would betray their trust, but that was fine. She intended to never see them again.

Light conversation made the car ride quicker, particularly about Kira's birthday. A date she had nearly forgotten herself; Carmilla talked about different places they could celebrate her birthday, just the two of them. Kira declined anything extravagant. She had spent that last thirteen years not celebrating her birthday, she would prefer to not make a tremendous deal out of nothing.

When they arrived back at the Palace, Wolfgang met them at the steps, his dirty-blonde hair smoothed back, his beard trimmed and groomed to be within some manner of regulation. His arms were crossed, dissatisfied and disapproving of the giggling Carmilla and Kira were sounding as they climbed the stairs.

"How can I do my job, when you disappear into the night telling no one, and decide to take a stroll in the city?"

She hissed, his anger more directed at Kira for her obvious influence than at the Empress.

Carmilla waved him off, "I do not need to waste the time of others when I decide to take a walk in my city." Her eyes glowed. "As I recall, it was *you* who *recommended* I keep my personal and professional life separate."

Wolfgang frowned, "The guard is not there for you..." He glanced at Kira, "But to prevent others from creating rumors and discovering weakness."

"You believe my Mate to be a weakness?" Carmilla narrowed her eyes.

"To the Empress: no." He stepped forward, "But they will not attack the Empress. That title, that responsibility, is an idea. They cannot kill an idea. They will attack that which is flesh and blood: Carmilla Tepes and anyone remotely important to her."

Kira looked at Wolfgang, who seemed entirely unsurprised: Carmilla referred to Kira as her Mate. It was likely either he did not register her words or this had been a discussion before. The Commander of the Guard without a doubt disapproved of Carmilla's Mate being human, but as one who lost his, he understands it is not a choice made, but an instinct engraved in their souls. Something a human cannot possibly understand.

He knew the conversation tonight would go no further in Kira's presence so Wolfgang let out a sigh.

"In the future, give me less gray hairs and notify me first." He requested as Carmilla patted his shoulder with a smirk.

"Yes, mom." She laughed as she motioned for Kira to follow.

Wolfgang grabbed the human's arm as she began to pass him, "I will protect my family from anything, or anyone." He warned, "Even if it's from the thing they love most."

Inside Carmilla's room, she poured herself a glass of wine and offered an alternative beer to Kira. She accepted the drink and sat on the couch and watched as the winning stuffed animal was placed on the nightstand on Carmilla's preferred side. Curious, the younger occupant spoke up.

"I thought you wanted that on the mantle above the fireplace?" She asked as she took another sip of her beer.

Carmilla set the wolf down, looking back to Kira, "I thought I might enjoy waking to it every evening." She smiled.

"Oh?" Kira chuckled. "A stuffed animal has beaten me out. How tragic." She gestured dramatically with her hand over her forehead.

The elder woman shook her head and walked to the edge of the bed, then stopped and leaned against the bedpost. She watched Kira's movements, the subtle pulsing of veins, the rise and fall of her chest with every breath. And with every movement she watched, Kira did the same. She took in what she knew would be the last sights she had of this beautiful goddess. Her long silky hair loosened from a ponytail on the carrier's back. Her crimson eyes, danced with light with each flicker of fire reflected in them from the flames of the fireplace. Carmilla's long slender body. One would never know how experienced this tall, thin woman had in combat and how masterful she was with a blade.

Despite her immortal and supernatural strength, she was careful with Kira's mortal frailty. Restrained, yet powerful, Carmilla embodied beauty and brutality all together in elegance and refinement. When she touched Kira, there was an electrifying excitement that left her on edge and in anticipation. At first, she accepted these feelings and physical needs as her body's reaction to the knowledge of what was to come from these sensations. Now, it was not an acceptance; it was a desire; not for a woman's touch, but for Carmilla's.

"I know that look." said the immortal as she held the wine at her lips.

Kira did not respond.

"That *hunger*..." Carmilla walked to the seated woman and set her glass down as she approached.

Her shadow cast over Kira and covered her completely as she hovered and wore a small toothed smile. Kira was without fear. She had courage to her for being a sheep, and she enjoyed tempting the lioness.

The mortal smirked as she leaned back, "Thought you couldn't read my mind."

"My dear..." The vampire leaned down and pinned Kira beneath her arms, "I do not need to read your mind when I can sense your arousal from across the room."

"Well..." Their lips hovered a breath apart, "Whose fault is that?"

Carmilla hummed, "Ah, forgive me..." Her fangs grazed Kira's lips, "I shall remedy that now."

Kira felt weightless for a moment, a quick rush of air, and she felt the rigid stiffness of the bedpost against her back. They kissed, their eagerness and desires pent up over weeks of unwanted but respected celibacy. Their lust, their desire, their need for one another without barrier, without restriction.

The immortal lifted Kira off her feet and in turn Kira wrapped her legs around Carmilla's hips as they went together to the soft California King bed. Kira felt her back press against the mattress, but paid no mind to it. She was focused on Carmilla alone, her touch, her scent; Bearded Iris. She clenched her fists with sheets, the vampire hissed as she pulled back with panted breath. Her desire for Kira was intoxicating, dangerous even if she was not careful, but how could she resist these urges, these feelings? Carmilla wanted her. Every inch, every fiber of hair, every drop of blood. To love her as only a vampire can.

Carmilla nuzzled her face into Kira's neck, her fangs gently dragged across the mortal's flesh and sent a bolt of excitement below her waist. The scent of arousal excited the immortal all the more. She placed her knee in between Kira's legs and applied a small amount of pressure enough to cause a moan to escape the woman's mouth. Distracted by the pleasure of making her Mate come by a single touch, she did not realize the hands at her hip and shoulder.

In an instant, Carmilla found herself beneath Kira, the mortal clasping her hands around the other's wrists with unexpected strength. It was an exciting surprise.

"How unexpected." Purred the vampire, "Where did this strength come from?"

Heat gathered in Kira's neck. She felt a surge of confidence and power course through her. She felt strong, dominating, something within her called out this unknown desire to make Carmilla hers. Not once had she known this, had she experienced it, but it was not frightening and was certainly welcomed. Tomorrow would be the end of this life, but tonight she would hold on to it as one of many precious memories locked away in her heart.

"Who's saying I haven't always been like this?" Kira countered with a mischievous smirk.

Carmilla's wrists were loosened, which freed her to rise and sit Kira in her lap as she pulled the smaller woman closer and kissed her with a far from satisfied hunger. She slipped her fingers beneath Kira's t-shirt, they crawled over the flat belly of the woman eventually they unclasped the bra with her other hand that snuck from behind. Kira helped along the way. She lifted her shirt over her breasts and Carmilla grabbed the mortal's wrists, which stopped her as her shirt was just above her mouth and nose, her eyes still covered.

Carmilla traced kisses from between Kira's breasts, to her neck, "I think I like you this way." She whispered, "At my mercy..." Her free hand softly traced a line in Kira's inner thigh, "... of whether..." She pressed at the wet place of the women's jeans, "... I'll give you release."

Kira lifted the shirt over her head, but kept it around her wrists as she put her arms behind Carmilla's head.

"If you don't— "Kira barely managed without a rasp, "Then *I will*!"

With an amused chuckle, "Will you now?" She eased Kira to her side, she lifted and pulled down her jeans, before she removed her own shirt next.

"And how will you do that?" Carmilla asked with a gleam in her crimson eyes.

She wore a smirk on her lips as the attempt entertained her, one Kira was valiantly putting forth to be more dominant.

It was adorable, but not a role that suited her. Perhaps in the future, as Kira's personality seemed to at last be coming through, they could make a dominant side of her yet, but not now. It was not a weakness to be submissive. In fact, Carmilla often considered a submissive to be braver than a dominant—during sex—they will give their trust and safety completely over to another person. The vampire could not do that, she could be trusted with another, but giving herself to someone else, exposing her in such a way... was not a comfortable feeling.

"When the view I have of you..." The well-practiced hand easily passed the waistband of Kira's panties, "... coming undone..." A slight graze made the mortal bite her lip to hold back a moan, "... makes me wet, just thinking about it..." Carmilla traced her thumb along the bottom of the other woman's lip.

"Now imagine how I am... with you in front of me." She flashed a devilish smile as she knew exactly what her words did to the other woman.

Kira turned flush red she tried to cover her face and eyes, but her lover would not allow this.

"Do not hide those beautiful eyes from me." She whispered as she eased the mortal's arms over her head then saw an expression of surprise.

Carmilla tilted her head, "What is it, my love?" She purred with a hum.

"I've... never had anyone one say that..."

For a moment Carmilla cursed at herself for her lack of praises, but it was true, while she had been commented on for centuries for her beautiful flawless appearance, it became something she ignored. Flattery was a tool the novice of the Game used to gain favor. Some Purebloods, nearly the incarnation of Narcissus himself, often enjoyed these comments. Carmilla did not and so while she cared not to receive, she neglected that hearing those words meant something to others.

"Your eyes... are the deep blue of the Mediterranean. The jewels of the ocean that not even Poseidon himself could possess—not that I would allow him."

Kira giggled.

That made Carmilla smile. "As vast as the sky, they hold an entire world within them. Reflecting great storms and peaceful calms, they give life and freedom to all those sheltered within." The immortal brushed her fingers along Kira's cheek, "Were I so permitted, I would become lost within them for eternity."

"Didn't take you for a poet." Continued Kira with her giggles, as she brought Carmilla closer for them to kiss.

Chapter Twenty
The Free Choose, a Slave Obeys

December in London, England was unlike that in the Tennessee Mountains. It rained a lot more often and the cold seeped far deeper into one's bones. For Kira, however, she was numb to it because her mind and body ceased being in synchronization. In the Shangri-la Hotel, she stared outside the window and watched the city below as the rains beaded down the glass.

The Empress would meet with the council in the next few hours during the day to decrease detection. As the immortals awaited their departure time, Kira held the letter she had received by an unknown carrier in her hand. She hated the rain; she hated how cold it made her, how it made her clothes heavy and damp, it was like walking through a freezing river.

Carmilla enjoyed the rains during the summer, but was as equally displeased with the cold weather at the moment. She said they were a time of renewal as though it washed away the old and the sadness. It was an optimistic point of view Kira could not find within herself to smile about. All she could think about from the moment she stepped onto the plane was how everything was ending. This was reality, this was the waking world and in the face of the unknown she was terrified. She did not know what would come next, what would happen when she finally reunited with her other half, but she knew this was the only way.

Kira found herself, in the beginning, trying to talk herself out of this seemingly insane plan. It was too risky, too dangerous; she was justifying to stay and live her life just as she had. In the end, however, this painful twist in her gut had her concluded this had to happen, that she needed it to otherwise she would be trapped in an illusion of reality. There was no future for her among them, no future in the Palace, no future in the Empire and to think there was now was a denial of her past.

The past was where her future laid now, the memories of what once was, of what now was truly possible. This unknown future frightened her, but it was better to die free than live her life in a cage—no matter her feelings toward Eona, Kira told herself that it was complacency. If she desired the truth, desired to have an affirmation of whether these feelings were real, she would have to be free to choose whether to accept them.

This letter she held in her hands had no hidden message, no decryption to discover within an invisible ink. It was one line of letters and numbers: an address. As she clenched the folded paper in her hands, Kira did not think about the plan, about what would happen after. She wanted to keep these last two hours with those she could call friends for longer.

She left the bedroom and slipped the paper into her pocket when she went to the living room and slumped onto the couch.

"Are you alright?" Jake asked as he glanced over his cell phone. "You look pale." He added as politely as possible.

Despite being a vampire and being without the experience and understanding of the human body's ability to become sick, Jake learned to read the signs. As Kira was adventurous and wild in her youth, she often scratched her knees or stayed out too long in the cold and would catch it. While Emily would usually attend to her, Jake had been instructed to keep a better eye on Kira and to look for early signs of injury or sickness to avoid them in the future.

Kira rubbed her head. "I really don't like planes." She said with half-truth, "Between jet-lag and this shitty weather, I think I'll stay while you're at the meetings."

Carmilla was at another table and went over some documents with Eona.

"Maybe I'll hang at the bar and catch a game or something." She shrugged casually.

Jake agreed mostly. "Want to call Em and let her know? Maybe she can fax a prescription so we can pick you up on the way back?"

"Sure." Nodded Kira in agreement, "I'll text her in a couple hours, she's probably not up right now."

Jake stood from his spot and moved closer to Kira, "Wanna ditch those two tomorrow and go to the *Warner Brothers Studios?* They've got the *Harry Potter Hogwarts on Ice show—"* He stopped when he saw Kira give him a weirded-out concerned expression, "What?"

"You only came because you wanted to go see Harry Potter, didn't you?" Kira asked with knowing suspicion.

With a studder, "That—that is not true! My folks want me to get into politics they made me—"

"And the Harry Potter brochure I saw in your backpack was there when we got on the plane?"

Kira continued to poke holes in Jake's excuse, the man grumbled as he put his phone back to his side, "Talk about a Slytherin..."

"A what?" Kira did not know if that was some kind of wizard or vampire slang, but it sounded insulting.

With a sign, "We've been over this: there are four Houses in Hogwarts —"

"Hogwarts is a camp...?"

"School! The School for Witchcraft and Wizardry! Holy hell, woman! Do you live under a rock?" Jake exclaimed as he snatched his phone and showing her a picture.

Kira rolled her eyes. "My bad, I don't watch old movies—"

"You don't even watch TV." Eona added into the conversation from across the room.

Agreeing, "She's right, the staff tried to have movie night one time—fell asleep ten minutes in." Carmilla chimed in, "I quite like Harry Potter, I consider myself a Slytherin."

"I tested and got Gryffindor." Eona said.

"Figures." Jake and Carmilla spoke together.

Proudly, "I'm a Hufflepuff! Best house in the entire school!"

"How so?" Eona turned in her chair. "Gryffindors get the best and are the protagonists."

Jake turned around on the couch and leaned over the back, "Yeah, but without the Room for Requirement, provided by Helga Hufflepuff—"

"That has not been confirmed." Carmilla interrupted.

As she watched and listened to the three of them engage in a topic she knew and cared little for she could not help but enjoy it. In her heart she ached, ached for the things she would miss about these people, about this time together. She could feel like a genuine person when they were together like this, away from the Game, away from the Palace; there were no masks they had to wear in front of each other...at least not those three. Kira was different. Kira would always be different because of a single significant difference: she was human and a human, cannot survive in the world of vampires without losing themselves.

While she looked out the window she clenched her fists. *I'm sorry, but I don't have a choice.*

The Council meeting took longer than the Empress cared to deal with, the complaints and ramblings of men and women who do not wish to pay forward what is necessary to build their army. They desired to hold on to their accumulated wealth as though it will mean anything should the Pureblood King emerge victorious. Like cockroaches they scrambled to their hiding places, they were as weak and spineless as insects.

These were different people than in Carmilla's youth, rather than elder, experienced warriors. These were trust-fund babies. Brats who are a shadow of their families and their blood so diluted and thinned they are useless as tools and as soldiers. Few remain from Carmilla's youth, even less from times before when every immortal was a warrior, a fighter, battle-tested and hardened. Vampires? The Empress scoffed at them; they were money and power-hungry buffoons babbling around like a band of baboons. If the Empire was to survive... the Council would either need to change its ways and people, or parish.

"Damnit."

Carmilla heard from the back of the SUV, Jake pulling his phone quickly down and tapped the screen for the same number again.

"What's up?" Eona asked as she looked up.

Jake cursed again, "I can't get ahold of Kira."

Everyone stared at him.

"She probably doesn't hear her phone, or it died—" Eona began.

"No, no, I've texted her four times in the last two hours and this is the second time I've called her and it doesn't go straight to voicemail, it just rings." He said with concern.

Eona tried next and received the same response: nothing. It was no different for Carmilla. The second time, however, she called a different number, a member of the security team left specifically for Kira. After a few moments, her phone rung and she answered.

"Report." Carmilla hissed low, but heavy, with controlled anger.

They explained further that all that was on the bed was Kira's phone, a scarf, and a necklace. Her clothes were left in the suitcase, the suitcase, fitted with a tracking device, also remained untouched. Carmilla allowed access to additional tracking information, placed on all members of the Tepes family at Wolfgang's advice—those too were in the room.

Wherever Kira had gone, they could not track her.

"Find her." Carmilla ordered as she on the window to the driver's cabin.

Understanding her series of knocks, the driver increased his speed—suddenly the truck in front of them exploded and flipped over repeatedly. The driver quickly jerked the wheel, trying to avoid the destroyed vehicle, another explosion in the direction here the SUV drove to avoid caused his to jerk the other way, slamming into the median—a spear crashed through the window, impaled the driver and turned him ash. Without a driver the vehicle lost control and flipped into the next lane.

Kira walked in the streets of the city, the rain poured down on her coat. She left everything that connected her to them, things that she wanted to keep, to remember, but it was too risky. The life she had with them was over. If she held onto memories it would bring only pain in confusion to her later on. The past that was where her life would be, to continue the life they robbed her of and it was best to think of these last thirteen years as a vivid dream she needed to fade with time.

She walked, certain this was the right choice, that this was the only choice she could make. In the single-shoulder bag rested on her back, she had the bare minimum. Three days' worth of clothes, a few snacks, all of this was gained to prepare for this day—these were not her clothes, they were a loaner from a friend, one who too was certain of this plan, this choice. There could be no chances taken, no chance of failure, not with the costs so high; nothing could have her tracked, have her traced. Despite how secretive Carmilla may have been about having tracking devices placed into Kira and Eona's belongings... Kira has survived the Palace with this understanding in mind:

Prepare for the worst, expect nothing less.

She turned the sidewalk into an ally then turned again and slipped between a small space caught in the middle of two buildings. At the end it opened to a cove where the grass was untamed and wild, a large, ancient tree in the center. To the right of the tree, in the back of the lot, was a stone building, an enormous iron door where two others had already arrived.

Concealed beneath the overhang of the building, it shielded them from the rain and allowed one to smoke her cigarette without difficulty. The rains dampened their senses, but the splash of water from the wanderer alerted them to her presence. They turned, Kira surprised at the presence of one, much less than the other.

"You didn't think I would let you go off on your own, did you?" Emily laughed as she blew out a puff, "Gotta make sure you eat your veggies and don't die."

Kira smiled, "Yes mom." But it faded when she looked at the King, "Where is she?"

"Elsewhere." He answered incompletely.

Sirens raced by one street over.

Kira glared. "I'm not fucking around. Where is she?"

"Do not ask a question you do not wish to know." The King warned, "Ignorance is a bliss you may wish to keep this time."

In an inhuman speed, Kira snatched the King by his jacket and pushed him against the wall, "I'm done asking!"

"You wish to know?" Asked the King one last time, "She is ensuring that after today, you will never be hunted again."

For a moment Kira did not understand, "What... what does that mean?" She asked, her grip loosened, "What did you do?"

"Nothing she did not choose for herself." The King answered calmly. Another convoy of sirens passed on the opposite street.

Kira clenched harder, "YOU LET HER GO AFTER CARMILLA!" She bellowed in terror.

"For you." The King said, "She would kill God himself."

Kira dropped him and ran.

"Kira, wait!" Emily sprinted after her and caught her halfway across the cove. "You can't, they'll know you left, they'll kill you!"

The King spoke having not moved where Kira left him, "It is already too late: To the Empire Kira Nightraven is a traitor, would be hunted down and executed, if you are fortunate. Your other half did not want this for you. Will you ignore her will for that which you cannot let go of?"

Kira shot him a furious glare, "Carmilla will kill her—!"

"Carmilla will kill you *both*!" Emily tried to reason, "Are you really willing to die for this woman!"

"She's all I have left!" Kira shouted as she pulled with increasing strength.

Emily tightened her grip. "Goddamnit Kira—" She groaned loudly as she dug into her pocket. The doctor grabbed a piece of paper and pressed it against her neck.

A red-fresh burn made the mortal yelp, "What the fuck—"

"You now have complete control of the locks!" Emily yelled as she threw Kira's hand free. "If you go, you need everything you've got to win."

Eona coughed as she crawled out from the door, her leg separated from the SUV. Jake was already outside as he directed people away from the crash site and protected innocent bystanders from bullet fire with shields of ice. He used these shields, punched out spikes towards the cars the terrorists used as cover,which ignited explosions. The surviving guards circled around Carmilla and protected her attackers.

"Eona!" Jake called, "Help me with this!"

After she gathered her bearings and her leg healed. Eona moved beside Jake—with each spike he created and sent forward Eona increased its velocity with her winds. She sent a crescent of wind as sharp as steel and cut a vampire in half before it reached her aunt and rendered them ash.

"How long are reinforcements!" Eona ducked from gunfire.

"Fifteen minutes!" Wolfgang answered as she cut down a fighter with his sword. "Longer if they set more IEDs off!"

Carmilla manipulated blood to stab at her attackers and took theirs into her arsenal to throw back at the enemy. This attack was planned, organized, someone with insider knowledge of the security workings of the Imperial Guard. A traitor was among them, but who? The immortal thought of Kira, of her sudden disappearance, her intent to flee; her discovery and discarding of all tracking devices. Carmilla suddenly thought of her meeting with the King, the mysterious actions and lack of an explanation—it all pointed to one conclusion.

Suddenly a woman dressed in black fatigues with a plain tactile full-helmet, sprinted forward. She flew past the Imperial Guard with unprecedented speed and agility. She swung her weapon, a thickened metal spear jabbed forward, cutting the Empress's face. Blood spiraled around like a tornado. The masked woman flipped back and rotated the staff around her back while she knocked back the guards, she

303

stabbed a hidden blade through their chests. One by one ande decimated the guards' numbers.

Eona noticed this. She left Jake and combated the unknown attacker; her wind grasped in her palm like a sword. The Pureblood Princess swung. She stepped forward, Eona released one hand and grabbed the spear's shaft. The unknown woman drove the spear into the ground, spun around; she drove her heels into Eona's chest and knocked her back, simultaneously she avoided the invisible sword.

Ice hurled toward the woman. She left back, spun her staff like a helicopter and made snow of weaponized water. She stepped forward then moved rapidly offensively against the Empress as she swung her staff with masterful precision. Carmilla raised her hand. Blood hardened as a stone above her arm's surface, acting as a shield against the spear's attack.

"You have chosen death in coming here." Carmilla hissed, "Before you die I have one question—"

The unknown woman jumped back and avoided ice, however, was cut in her arm by Eona's wind.

"Who was it that betrayed me?" The Empress questioned as she held an open palm to her side, the solidified blood now liquid again and spiraled it around her arm.

The woman scoffed with a heavy glare, "It doesn't matter, I'm not here for them." Her voice sounded frightenly similar

Carmilla's eyes glowed intensely with anger. "Indeed, you are no doubt the King's right hand. I wonder though... will he save you from me?"

"I'm not here for him, I'm here for you." Charged the woman, she darted for Jake and kicked him hard into one of London Tower Bridges' iconic structures.

"You will not hurt her again."

Eona came next. The woman grabbed the Pureblood's wrist and snapped it; drove her heel into the shin, she snapped the vampire's leg next then kicked her across the ruined street. Carmilla appeared she backhanded the attacker into a car. Straggling gunmen open-fired whiched caused the

Empress to defend herself. The spear-wielder came around the shield, to Carmilla's exposed back—her neck was snatched, but she reacted instantly and wrapped her entire body around the immortal's arm and twisted until it broke.

Freed of the vile woman's grasp, she back-stepped to createdan opening. Carmilla's arm twisted twice over; broken and grotesque, spun back and healed itself quickly. The helmeted woman would give it no chance to fully recover. She closed the distance and jabbed her spear into the Empress's chest. Blood, dripped from the Pureblood's healing arm, shot out as spikes. They hit the attacker in her arm and leg, her neck opened last before she could withdraw defensively.

She collected her breath and knew that the longer this went on, the greater her chances of failure would grow. Failure was not an option, not here, not now. If the Empress did not die, then she would spend the rest of her life being hunted. She attacked harder, concluded in what she must do. She would kill anyone and everyone if it meant keeping her safe.

As she cast the staff aside, Carmilla jumped to the right to avoid it and found her enemy quickly behind it. Blood hardened and sharpened to a point; the attacker slid under, pivoting to face the Empress's back as she went past, grabbed the lodged spear and with the intent to drive it through her enemy's heart from the back. Wind threw her across the broken road and slammed her into the bridge's outer railing. Her grip of her spear lost several feet from her.

Carmilla did not hesitate. She gathered her crimson weapon into a lance, thrusted it with killer intent. The helmeted woman had no chance to evade. The tip of the lance closed in—the shaft shattered under the impact of the sword at its center. Its path diverted, the tip landed off target and shattered against the force that dropped on the ground. Without a connection to the Empress and her blood, any outside blood could be manipulated and lost all strength and power.

Between the helmeted woman and the Empress stood Kira armed with a fallen guard's sword. Hooded, she hid her face with a bandana grabbed on the way here. Exhausted and out of breath from running, she barely arrived in time and did not think she had the strength to put up much of a fight.

"How—why are you here!" The helmeted woman demanded frantically, "You're not supposed to be here, you should be safe—"

Carmilla manipulated the remaining blood and liquified it to spiral around her. Across the bridge, on a rooftop, the King and Emily watched the events that would transpire.

"Are you seriously going to stand there and just let them be killed!" Emily yelled at the Pureblood.

The King watched easily with his enhanced senses. "This is not my battle, but hers. She must choose..."

"Between being a human or not!" Emily asked frantically.

He shook his head, "Between two loves."

They watched Kira arm a sword against the Empress, but her grip was not steady, her legs shook, her knees weak and her heart pounded.

"Get out of here." Kira said to the wounded woman, "I'll hold them off."

"Are you insane! She'll kill you!" countered the woman as she stood and grabbed her spear while she limped to Kira's side.

Carmilla tilted her head, "I will kill you both—"

The helmeted woman pushed Kira to the side and countered the ice thrown from afar. Kira ducked and blocked a shard of blood at its center. Wind pushed her from behind and toward the Empress. She stabbed the sword into the ground to keep herself up. Carmilla diverted her attention to the spear-wielder and armed another blood weapon at her; Kira yanked the sword free and used its momentum to slam into the Empress, which knocked her off her feet. She quickly bolted for Jake, she skiied on a wave of ice and opened his

306

Achilles' tendons, which caused him to drop and avoid the spear that was aimed at him.

"You're no match for them!" Kira grabbed Jake's shirt and threw him over the median.

She grabbed the woman then pushed her back when she countered an attack from Carmilla, but the attack separated and the other woman was stabbed in the gut.

"LILY!" Kira yelled as she pushed the hardened blood back. She shattered what stabbed the woman and dragged her towards the railings.

Carmilla appeared nearly out of thin air. Kira swung, and her wrist was grabbed and squeezed until pain made her compliant. She dropped the sword; the Empress threw her across the road, her body impaled on impact against the exposed rebar of a rogue median. Kira felt as though all the air had been taken from her lungs. The pain that stabbed through her made her believe for a moment she could not breathe; her shoulder, bicep, lung, and collarbone pierced, pinning her in place.

"You son of a—"

Lily jumped up and swung—the Empress grabbed her arm and backhanded her in the face. The force had her go through a car and land an impression of her body in the door of the next.

Kira shouted as she struggled against the bars.

From one bar, the mortal's blood dropped and hit the ground then spread into the waters that rained from the sky. Carmilla and Eona's heads snapped up and looked at the only person toward the familiar scent.

"Kira?"

Lily grabbed the Empress and wrapped her arms around the Pureblood's neck. Carmilla reached up and grabbed her shoulders. She threw her across the road. Eona fronted her, armed with a blade of wind as she swung. Lily countered then kicked her, but the Pureblood Princess would not go down easy. Carmilla's attention went back to focusing on the helmeted woman.

"Stop—!" Kira gasped, the slightest movements radiating significant pain. She grabbed one bar and tried to pull it, but it would not budge. *Fuck, FUCK, this hurts*!

She watched helplessly as Eona and Carmilla backed Lily into a corner, the odds were against her. They hit Lily in the face. She came back, slammed her fist at Eona in the gut and sent her flying. Carmilla raised her hand and created a sword.

Kira pulled hard against the bars, trying to pull herself free with her body, "Carmilla—stop!"

Nothing was heard.

She's gonna kill her! Kira panicked as she pulled harder and harder and experienced some of the greatest pain in her life. *No—please no!*

"Stop it—!" Her phantom vampire stood in front of her. *You have to make a choice.*

"Come on—!" Kira released the bar and clawed at her neck. She pulled hard, "LEVEL ONE UNLOCK!"

Carmilla hesitated. An overwhelming force slammed into her and threw her against a flipped over SUV. In her face, Kira's bandana-red face roared at the Empress. With eyes full of anger, the woman pushed down with inhuman strength. Her hood was down, her raven black hair seen by all others, her wounds were closing and the few knew her identity.

"Kira? What—" The Empress was kicked and sent several feet away.

Lily ran to Kira, who growled viciously as she held her aching shoulder. She felt her flesh stretch and blood boil as her wounds stitched themselves back together. The pain only fueled her rage further.

"What—what did they do to you...?" Lily asked as she saw furious red glow on her neck, its vines stretched out on her neck and down her collar.

"What have *we* done—have *you* done!" Carmilla hissed viciously, "Was this always your intent Kira? To betray me like this, was this your game?"

308

Kira stepped in front of Lily. "Go."

"Come with me—"

"I promise..." Kira bared her fangs behind her mask, "I will protect you this time."

Lily backed away. Carmilla dashed forward, only to meet with Kira.

Carmilla created a sword of blood and hissed, "Who is this woman to turn you against me so easily?" She watched the woman flee. "If I kill her, will you return to your senses then?"

She broke off from Kira and aimed at Lily. Kira moved between them again and shattered the edged weapon with the sword.

"You will *not* touch her again!" Kira's eyes flickered another shade.

She dashed forward, swung the sword, but Carmilla foresaw her amateur skill and grabbed the blade then pulled it from Kira's grip. The young woman continued to go forward, she hurled herself into Carmilla and pushed her over onto the ground. With a fury she raised her fist, tightened her fingers and aimed—but froze. The Empress grabbed her and pushed her over before she slammed her fist into the younger's gut.

Kira groaned as she held her gut, but still got back up. She grabbed Carmilla and threw her into one of the brick towers of the bridge. Her neck was on fire, the vines spread further as an overwhelming feeling of dryness felt like a scorching desert. She gripped at her neck as she felt something else was coming to the surface, a raw, untamed instinct to fight; anger, rage, and hatred. If Carmilla left here, she would go after Lily, she would kill her.

No. Kira focused her mind, her strength as the Pureblood emerged from the debris. *I won't let you tear us apart again!* Whatever power she could use, this creature, this animal, this monster were because of them. Whatever she is now, whatever she becomes... she will do so because she will never again be powerless to save her loved ones. Kira growled slowly, her dull fangs flashed despite Carmilla being unable to see them. She will not lose her family again and if that means breaking her own heart, so be it.

"Does our life together mean nothing to you?" Carmilla asked, as Eona helped Jake to his feet, "Your humanity that you have so carefully guarded, you will throw it all away for what?"

Kira moved she swung the grabbed spear and collided with Carmilla's created sword. She bared her dull fangs, her intent and will to keep the Empress from Lily was as apparent as night and day.

"Life!" Kira shouted quizzically. "You call that a life! I was a slave! Terrified every day would be my last! I won't go back!" She pushed against Carmilla's sword with untrained, brute strength, "I won't go back to a cage!"

"How long have you conspired with the King against me?" Carmilla gritted her teeth, "Before, or after I told you I loved you—or was it before then? Have you hated and reviled my family so much your mission dictated that you slither your way into my bed chambers?"

The King watched still, "She hesitates and Carmilla is going easy on her." He said without empathy.

"You forced Kira into an impossible situation. How can she not!" Emily moved towards the edge to jump down. She could not watch this anymore.

Her arm was grabbed. "If you interfere, she will not understand the consequences of choice. One cannot have one thing without sacrificing another."

They threw Kira into a median, her body broke the concrete. She forced herself to stand. That dark feeling returned as it clawed from the depths of her mind to take hold of her. Its hands reached out and wanted to sink her deeper into its raw emotion, to take over and be allowed to run free. Kira found herself fighting two people: Carmilla and herself. She felt her reason slip, a hunger for violence against not only Carmilla, but all vampires. She knew what this was, who this was; the vampire, the feelings it latched itself onto when she turned. Her vampire would tear everyone apart without restraint and that she could not allow to happen.

"Is she really worth all of this pain?" Carmilla asked through gritted fangs.

For a moment Kira vanished then appeared in front of the Pureblood, she snatched Carmilla then threw her onto the ground near a hole in the bridge's structure. Jumping on top of her, Kira slammed her fist into Carmilla's face, then wrapped her hands around the Empress's throat. *I didn't want this. I didn't want this to happen—*

"I just..." Kira realized how tightly she held Carmilla's throat, realized how these emotions and her choice had driven her to hurt someone she cared so much for. Her grip loosened, "... wanted to be with my sister again..."

Wolfgang unloaded the rest of his magazine into Kira. She dropped, rolled into the bridges break and fallen into a watery grave.

Chapter Twenty-one
Past the Point of No Return

From the river's edge, Emily slid to a halt as she scanned the waters for any sign. Parts of the river were frozen which made visibility a greater challenge with the surface's constant disturbance from the rains. The King and the doctor went separate ways. He felt no need to aid the ex-human in locating the fallen. There was little doubt she had survived. It was one of her greatest skills, after all. He said they would meet later, he would send another for them. Emily was not so confident, She watched as the girl she helped raise be shot, watched her fall through the London Tower Bridge and hit the icy waters below.

Kira had opened the first lock, but there was no telling what the long-term effects could be if someone did not reseal it. The physical, mental, and emotional stress she had undergone while under the influence of her inner vampire was more than enough to overwhelm. It was not likely for a vampire to drown and die. Death came to them only with the destruction of their core, but Kira was not a vampire. She was something else.

They were down the river a way, beyond the first bend. Sirens wailed on streets above as they headed to the bridge, armored SUVs followed behind, reinforcements would come to a battle already ended. This was not how things were. Kira slipped away quietly, but the King... he knew that woman would go after Carmilla, knew Kira could not let that happen. He intentionally pushed her to the edge, and the doctor gave her the means to go over that edge.

He was dangerous; she knew that, more than before. Relentless in his goal to eradicate the Tepes and all vampires, he will violate all innocence. If he continued to be hell-bent on this crusade, why had he taken this long and why was he using such round ways to attack the Empress? His desire to manipulate Kira was not simply because she and the woman she went after were connected. There was something else, something he wanted to drive her towards.

She looked towards the water's edge and saw a familiar face.

"Kira!"

She clung to a broken slate of ice as she floated down the river as her life depended on it. She pulled herself out of the water and dropped on the flat surface as her breath was visible. *Son of a bitch.* Kira panted as she gripped her gut. *If I ever see that fucker again* — she groaned, then lifted her hand and saw the bleeding had lessened. Whether to the cold or to healing it was not as severe now. Wolfgang had shot her. While it was not fatal, it hurt like hell.

She gribbed her neck and found the burning pain had subsided for now, but a great thirst had rooted. Kira slowly, as she groaned in pain, turned onto her stomach and used her hand to paddle towards weaker currents. She took off her jacket to serve as a greater surface to paddle, but halfway lost the frozen coat to the same current she wished to escape. *I have to get out of the open.* Painstakingly Kira rowed herself towards the shore and went under a bridge where an aged and large drain pipe provided further protection from the elements.

She dragged herself onto the frozen rock and sludge, she turned onto her side, certain that if she went onto her back, the icy weight of her wet clothes would be too much for her to move again. She watched the slate of ice that acted as her life raft drift down the river and break apart quickly before it disappeared into the darkness below. *Jake*. Kira shivered as she clenched the rocks that bit into her palms. She forced herself again, though her strength was nearly completely depleted she knew she could not stop, not rest until in that pipe.

The closer she thought she was getting, the further the pipe seemed. Her muscles locked up, her fingers and toes lost feeling. She tried with all her might to keep going, to give herself a goal, but her body was quickly failing. *It hurts*. She saw the look of betrayal in Carmilla's eyes felt like a thousand cuts to her heart. She knew her leaving would hurt the woman; she tried her damnedest to keep the damage as minimal as possible, but she failed.

It was not only Carmilla's heartbroken, but Kira's. She had not answered when the Empress had asked if this was her ploy all along, if their lives together had meant nothing. There was no yes or no to be found. The answer was clouded and twisted into many right and wrong. She just wanted to be with her family again. Was that so wrong? To choose between all she is against who she was. It was not fair; it was not just; the world kept taking from her the things she cared for and now the person who she has lived with all this time is crumbling down around her.

Kira clenched her jaw, a low growl in her throat, her neck burned; her mouth opened, desperate for something to quench this insatiable thirst. She grabbed her neck and dug her nails into her flesh. *Lock already*! Her vampire was winning this tug of war for control, and Kira was full of great fear of what would occur. *I need—* she locked her body as tight as possible to restrict her movements.

It would be easier if you just let go. Said the phantom image of Kira's vampire. She gave the physical woman a toothy smile while she crouched and rested her arms on her knees. *If you do that, you wouldn't be in such pain.* The phantom chuckled innocently. *We could find a nice yummy—*

"Go to hell!" Kira snapped, "I won't—I'll never hunt another human!"

The phantom smiled.

"—Y!"

Who says it needs to be human?

A weight came over her, they turned her onto her back. Whether it was an enemy or a friend, she did not know at first, not that it mattered. She did not have the strength to move, let alone fight. Turned over, Kira looked at her own face.

"Over here!" Lily called behind her.

"Lily...?" Kira whispered as though she had seen a ghost.

Happily, the woman smiled as she lifted Kira onto her lap and put her jacket over her other half.

"That's right! It's me, it's your big sister Lily!" Lily exclaimed in relief as Emily quickly joined them.

She put another jacket on Kira's legs, "Hey, you little shit!" Emily laughed as she placed her hand on the Stigma, then lifted the jacket to see the bullet wounds, "You're bad enough in giving me grey hairs! I thought I was seeing a ghost with you two! Twins! Nobody said anything about twins!"

Lily and Kira chuckled, "You should have seen us when we were kids..."

Kira's sudden cough and the sound of oncoming first responders brought them back to their situation. She caught the scent of life's currency, her tattoo glowed bright which worked to restrict her vampire further from acting out.

Emily noticed this, and was calm when she talked to Lily, "She's lost a lot of blood...you happen to be A negative, do you?"

"No, and what the hell is that doing on her neck?" Lily demanded, "I thought she was still human!"

Emily pulled up her sleeve, "She is—" The Doctor bobbed her head side to side before she finished, "Mostly."

Emily took a scapel and opened her wrist before held it over Kira's mouth.

She took a deep breath, looked at Kira, who was horrified. "We don't have a choice. If you don't drink, you'll attack *us*."

In her mind, Kira cringed at the thought and it made her stomach ached at the idea of having to drink blood. It nearly made her vomit, but that was better than attacking them. With a whine, Kira reluctantly turned and let the blood drop into her mouth. As though the air had been let into her lungs, a rush of warmth and revitalization. On instinct, Kira grabbed Emily's arm and pulled it into her mouth. A few moments later, Emily placed her hand on the Stigma and locked the first seal once again.

"This will get you going for a little, but either you get a transfusion or you feed—animal blood won't help you."

After that, Emily helped Kira into a fresh set of clothes and provided a rapid first aid to her injuries that had not fully healed. They left them drenched where they were. Lily gave her sister her jacket and helped her to walk as the doctor hailed a cab. In the city, all police were on high-alert. They put an alert on screens and news everywhere to be on the lookout for members of the *Reich* and co-conspirators.

Carmilla addressed the public. Her outfit was different, and she was in the conference room of the hotel.

"Bitch didn't even flinch." Lily spat, as they paused at an electronic store, "Barely an hour and she's already in front of the camera like nothing happened."

"She has to." Kira frowned weakly, "The Empress has to show the people that she's invincible." She put more weight on Lily, "That's how the Game is played."

This cowardice attack does nothing, but proves once again there is neither honor nor responsibility in the Reich.

317

Launching this attack with innocent civilians on a historical site further shows there are no lines these terrorists will not cross.

The broadcast concluded, and the television changed to the general news.

"Least she didn't paint a target on your head. Not publicly anyway." Emily tried for positivity, but they found none.

Kira gripped Lily tighter, her strength left her and was replaced by a growing thirst, "Let's go before she does."

The rains made it difficult for vampires to notice someone with an open wound, but it did not act as a guaranteed shield. Eventually, Lily and Emily changed their positions. The doctor helped Kira to walk, while the elder sister lifted a hood over her head and a scarf around her nose and mouth when scouting ahead. They kept off of public roads and places with sizeable crowds, the trio eventually arrived in the area where the safe house lived.

Lily peaked around the ally corner, a block from the initial turn into the back door to reach the building through another. Police and several black SUVs lined the street around. Emily eased Kira to the ground against the wall, allowing her to catch some of her escaping breath. Gripping her gut, the injured woman groaned, her ability to stay conscious lessening with each passing minute.

"Hey—" Emily patted the side of Kira's face, "Kira, you have to stay awake." She inspected the bandages Kira had bled through.

"They've made the house. Time for Plan B." Lily said as she to Kira's side and saw the grave look on Emily's face.

The doctor pressed on Kira's stomach. "How far?"

"On the outskirts of the city, maybe... ten miles from here?"

With a shake of her head the doctor advised the grim reality, "Your sister took one hell of a beating for you. If I don't stabilize her and warm her up she could go into shock."

318

Lily glared, "What do you need?"

"For now, to get away from here."

Lily jumped in front of Kira and Emily and drew out a staff that extended to its full length. The sudden presence of another was neither sense nor expected, and it was entirely unwelcome. Lily prepared for the worst—the familiar vampire did not move and upon recognition Lily eased her stance and withdrew the staff.

The immortal looked at the doctor and, to a dazed Kira.

"I have a place not far from here." Urged the King.

Lily frowned, "The closest safe house is miles." Emily lifted the unconscious woman into her arms. She walked toward the other vampire, "Lead the way."

The women went into a navy-blue Honda. The King jumped in the driver's seat and sped up, heading away from the scene. After ten minutes, they arrived at a shipyard; the car parked inside a warehouse. The Pureblood moved from the driver's seat to where Emily held onto Kira; he took the woman from the doctor and moved inside, pursued by the other two.

Inside the warehouse was an open and relatively unused space, but further back was another area where a large, secured office was. Kira was set down on an operation table occupied by many medical tools and devices; weapons; supplies of all manner. Lily entered last, closing the door behind her, looking to the wall of guns.

"What is this place?"

The King helped Emily prep Kira for surgery.

"A safe house maintained off the records." He answered, "Only I am aware of its existence. In the event of an internal threat that compromised the higher ranks of the *Reich*, I have these established in every major city." He explained.

"And yet you never told me." Lily stated bitterly.

Emily removed the bandages from Kira's gut. "Argue about that later." The doctor barked as she returned to focus on Kira.

"Kira was never supposed to be there!" Lily snapped at the King, "You were supposed to protect her!"

The King shook his head. "I will not force protection onto anyone and I will not stop someone from making their own choice. You two are adults now. I cannot decide for you."

Lily clenched her fist. "I asked you, I told you! Keep her away from the bridge, keep her safe until I — "

"And if she had not come for you, you would be dead!" The Pureblood said with a hint of frustration.

Lily hesitated. Not only had she failed to kill the Empress, but also had to be saved by her younger sister. That was her job. She was supposed to be the one to protect her and all these years, even now she has failed to do that. The King was right Lily was not strong enough to battle the Empress, the Princess and another gifted vampire. Her training has been for nothing and yet... there was hope. They were finally together again.

Kira jerked up suddenly. Emily, taken by surprise, was thrown back. Lily quickly came to her sister's side, pushing her back down into the table. She yelled and struggled, snapped her dulled fangs and growled like a rabid animal. Kira broke free from another's hold and snapped her hand around the King's throat, a deep snarl came from within.

"Fucking Pureblood—!"

Emily jumped back to her feet, "Hold her down!" She ordered a sedation into a needle.

Lily and the King both pushed the flaying woman. Emily quickly jabbed the needle into Kira's arm and in a matter of moments, she was motionless. They restrained her further with leather bindings and secured her while Emily immediately prepared for operating on the rest of the woman's injuries.

"Someone wants to explain what the fuck just happened? What the hell did they do to my sister!" Lily demanded, looking to the King and the doctor for answers.

The King was the only one free to answer, "It would be best if you asked her directly when she wakes."

Kira opened her eyes to the shut off bulbs of the operating light. She budged, her muscles stiff and sore, but it was not as when she went through a few floors. It was duller; she felt more recovered, stronger and cooler overall. She turned her head and saw Lily sitting beside her, her sister jumped to her feet and rushed quickly to Kira's side.

"Hey..." Lily smiled, relieved as she took Kira's hand into her own.

Kira smiled, "Hey back." She coughed, Lily returned quickly with a glass of water.

After a few sips, they helped Kira to sit up against better judgement and held her bandaged gut while Lily supported her. Able to turn and sit on the side of the bed, Kira finally could inspect her other half.

"Is this a dream?" Kira asked as she held Lily's hand. "If it is... I don't want to wake up."

With a smile Lily, reached up and pinched the other twin's cheek.

"See." She chuckled, "You're awake and I'm very real."

A tear of joy came down the other woman's face, "I can't believe it... all this time you were alive and I—"

"I didn't know either, not for sure, until last year. But I never gave up. I always hoped that somewhere, somehow, you were alive." Lily explained, looking at Kira's neck, "Still... I guess I was too late to protect you from them."

Kira squeezed Lily's hand with assurance as she shook her head, "What happened to me wasn't your fault and right now, after what just happened, I'm grateful it did."

Lily frowned, "I didn't want this for you, to have to deal with the thirst—"

"Neither of us wanted that for the other."

Lily cringed, imaginary dog ears dropping in shame. "You can tell..."

"I can, and I don't care. No matter what we are, we are and always will be sisters. Whether human, vampire, or something else, that fact will always prevail over everything else." Kira declared as she felt these words seemed to relieve Lily, but in the woman's heart she felt a deep grief.

Lily was a vampire, though seemed she had not fully transitioned. She had not once had a drop of human blood, which allowed her to age as her sister. Maybe she did this intentionally, maybe it was because of the King, but none of that mattered: Lily was alive, her sister, her flesh and blood were right in front of her.

That reality alone made up for a lifetime of horror and pain. She had won the Game, had survived all this time and had been rewarded for it; finally. Where hope had been lost for a future, Kira was at last reunited with the past she feared she would forget. This time she had the power to protect it, to fight for it and with Lily there was one less thing to fear in this world ruled by the immortal.

"What happened at the cabin?" Kira asked, "The last time I saw you, you and mom were in the cabin they lit on fire. They dragged me away and knocked me out."

Lily nodded, "Mom... really was strong. You saw what happened to her, what they did to her."

Their mother, Anna, crawled to her daughter, grabbed her with her only usable arm, and dragged her to the trapdoor. She opened the door, Lily took her mother's hand and was eased into the darkness below.

"I love you..." she said despite the holes in her throat, "Never forget that I love you both so much." Anna let her daughter go and shut the trapdoor. Lily saw something dark move over the door, but did not know what.

The wounded girl used the tunnel's walls to keep her up, her back screaming in pain. Dirt, blood, snow and so covered her entire self; the tunnel was pitch black and only her sense of touch allowed for her to navigate. The roar of the flame echoed in the short-distanced tunnel, but it was the cool breeze of the exit, covered by wood and brush, that had her known relief.

Lily pushed the concealment and arrived right where she had begun. She around the wall of stone to see her sister motionless, over the shoulder of a vampire. She was alive. They vanished and moved into the night without giving her any chance to catch them, not that she intended to. Her sister was taken, but she was free, she would be able to get her back even if it took years. Lily thought that she may at least save her mother and staggered to the cabin, but it was already engulfed in flames.

"Mom!" She cried out over and over until her lungs gave out and her throat swelled shut by her coming tears.

She dropped to her knees, the wound to her back made her feel dizzy.

"Your mother has gone ahead of us, little one." Said a man who wore a dark overcoat and a black suit with a red tie. Lily looked up at him. Her eyes saw the red cat-like of his own and knew this man was no ordinary vampire. She took a broken shaft of her destroyed spear and tried to arm herself against him, but her body lacked the energy to do little else. The man slowly eased himself down to her height and showed his empty hands. He sensed her pain; the scent of blood and charred flesh filled his nose and wetted his palette. He ignored them with well-practiced discipline and control.

"There is nothing for you here, only death." The man said as he removed his coat and put it around Lily, "But, if you want to stop this, to stop the vampire, I will teach you."

Lily sniffled. "They took my sister."

323

"Then..." said the man with red cat-like eyes, "Take her back."

"I never even had time to bury her..." Lily admitted quietly.

Kira smiled a little. "You don't have to worry about that. It wasn't nearly what she deserved, but I was able to."

Lily noticeably relaxed and displaced great relief in knowing that.

"I've always been too scared to go back—that was the worst night of my life." The elder twin nearly whispered, "Too scared to face mom empty-handed."

Kira lifted her arm and wrapped it around Lily's neck, pulling her to have their foreheads meet, just like when they were children.

"You don't have to face anything alone ever again." Kira said with assurance, "We're finally together and nothing will keep us apart again."

Chapter Twenty-Two
The Past Unforgotten

Kira's fingers sneezed tightly around her throat. From above, one would think she was trying to kill the Empress, but Carmilla saw her where no other would. Tears hit the woman's face, tears shed by Kira, whose heart was breaking. She did not want this, did not want to fight Carmilla, and did not want to hurt her, at least not intentionally. But she had hurt Carmilla, had fractured the woman's armor where no one had before.

She fought with inhuman strength, but at the last second, her strength over the Empress wavered.

"I just... wanted to be with my sister again..."

Carmilla heard the gunshots, but did not register them until Kira had slumped to the side and slid into the break. The Empress rolled over desperate to catch her out, but she was not fast enough and watched as she went over the edge and hit the icy waters below.

"KIRA!"

Eona screamed as she sprinted to the bridge's side. Jake ran to her and grabbed her before she could go over.

"You can't help her—!"

She shouted against his hold, "Let me go—"

Jake wrapped his arms around Eona and froze her legs in place. "You can't help her! If someone sees you try to save her, they'll find out who she is!" The Noble came in front, "We can't help her if everyone knows who she is!"

Eona snapped her head to Wolfgang, "What the fuck—" She broke the ice, darting toward her father.

Carmilla caught her mid-run, before she could reach her father.

"**STOP**!" she bellowed, the power in her blood booming out.

Eona instantly recoiled against it and calmed down enough to not attack her father.

"Your father did his duty, he protected the Empress from an enemy." Carmilla said, brushing herself off. Her niece went red, "Ki—"

"Let me make this *very* clear: Forces of the *Reich* attacked—we engaged two, unknown, masked vampires. We believe one to be dead, the other escaped." Recited Carmilla, her tone and eyes a clear indicator this is the truth they will express to others, whether officially or verbally.

With reinforcements, Carmilla called for a press conference within the hour. The four vampires entered the new armored SUV and returned to the hotel. They ushered Eona and Jake into another room while Wolfgang and Carmilla went to the Empress's bedroom. As she changed and rapidly cleaned, the two of them spoke while the shower was on as a noise buffer.

"Check every camera, every recording—erase anything that identifies her on that bridge." Carmilla ordered as she looked at the dresser where the scarf and necklace were.

Wolfgang spoke, "If she truly has betrayed us, then the entire Palace and your safety are compromised."

"No." Carmilla said as she touched the scarf, "This wasn't a betrayal, it was an escape."

A knock on the door had the two of them silence themselves.

"Ensure Eona and Jake do not leave the suite." The Empress ordered, opening the door and heading downstairs.

Wolfgang instructed his men to wait outside. While the Commander of the Guard was certain he hit Kira, he was not at the angle he desired. Depending on the extent of her new abilities, vampire in nature, she could very well have survived the gunshots. The plunge into the river was another story entirely.

"What the hell were you thinking!" Eona yelled in hush tones, "If you killed her—"

"Then that will be one less threat to your life." Her father said unapologetically, "You can hate me all you want, but I will not apologize for protecting my family and cursing her for doing the same is a dishonor of her actions."

"What...?"

Wolfgang grabbed Eona as he pulled her further into the suite. "She said she wanted to be with her sister. I assume the woman she was defending was just that."

"But... her sister, her entire family—"

"According to her is dead and we know nothing about her past save for when she was brought here." The father pointed out, "Neither her name, her birth, her family, we are to take the word of a woman who not only attacked your aunt, the Empress, but you and Jake, people who were supposed to be her closest friends."

Jake sat on the couch with his head between his arms, he could not believe everything that happened in the last half hour. Everything had seemed fine. Kira had acted normal, sure she had been morse as of late, but that was seemingly justified given she learned about Eona. There was nothing out of the ordinary and yet she fought them, defended the terrorist who tried to kill them.

Yet she also protected them.

He tried to see where the signs could have been, he thought how long they had aligned her with the enemy. In spite of this, he gave her a slate of ice to act as a lifeboat down the river. Was that a mistake? Did he save someone who would only come back to kill them again? Kira had grabbed him, his core wide open and exposed, and yet she threw him across the street to get him out of the way. What was he supposed to think? Was Kira a friend or an enemy?

"We'll talk about this when we get home. For now, none of you are to go anywhere, not alone, not with a security team." Wolfgang said finally, Eona knew his tone when he concluded a discussion.

Eona went to Carmilla's room and looked for anything that may explain Kira's actions and disappearance. She saw the scarf, the necklace on the dresser, her clothes left where they were placed earlier in the day. Kira had taken nothing of emotional value with her, nothing to hold on to the memories of their time together. Did she hate them that much? Did she want to forget them? Was everything a living nightmare for her? She wanted to leave it in the back of her mind.

How could so many years of memories, of experiences and emotions mean so little? Eona had thought humans felt deeper, that because of their short lifespans, it was in their nature to hold on to memories. Was it different for Kira because she was raised by vampires, or had she changed because of what Eona had done to her? It made little sense for Kira to want to discard memories; she had expressed great fear in that, but maybe that was a lie. After all, how much did any of them know about Kira, anyway?

In all the years they were together, even when she revealed her past to Eona, at least what seemed to be the truth, she gave no names. Eona attributed that to her explaining how she felt the more she revealed to the vampire, the more she lost. What did that mean for them? Would Kira tell the Reich all she knew of them? Their weaknesses, their secrets. Would she turn everything against them in one last act of hatred and defiance? If that were so...how was she any better than the vampires she claims to hate?

Confusion and misunderstandings filled Eona's head as she tried to wrap her mind around a 'why' and 'when'.

Why did Kira leave and for how long had she planned to leave? Eona could not stand not knowing and further hated that Kira did not even bother to leave a note, a goodbye. She just left, disappeared as though her presence would have no profound effect on all of them. Maybe she knew, maybe that was the point, but Eona had no intention of leaving things like this.

Without her father and aunt's blessing, she would see Kira again.

The Empress departed the press conference as quickly as she had arrived. Posed and perfect, one would not know she had been soaking wet in a battle on historical London Tower Bridge half an hour before. She left the hotel; they had already planned to lock down the city and already they had led where Kira had come from before arriving at the bridge.

Local law enforcement, special operations and an Imperial Detachment were in route to the location, but against her choice, she elected to remain at the hotel. To Carmilla, what mattered now was protecting Eona came above all else and no matter her heart, her duty to her family came first. Besides, if she had gone, Eona would have somehow followed and Carmilla was in no mind to put her niece in danger twice in one day. As much as it pained her, their plane was prepped and ready for their departure in the next hour.

Whether it was Kira or another, someone had betrayed them and this far from the center of their government was dangerous.

"We can't leave!" Eona burst out as Carmilla instructed them to pack their belongings.

The Pureblood Princess stormed after her aunt. "Kira is still—"

"Gone, she is dead or somewhere else." Carmilla said, lacking emotion, "There is no way to find her, we will return home and that is the end."

Eona's anger towards Carmilla's indifference swelled. "Doesn't any of this bother you! None of this makes sense. Kira wouldn't do this without reason!"

"Her reason is her own, actions speak louder than words."

A fist slammed into the dresser and broke it on impact, "Did you even give a damn about her at all!"

Carmilla took a deep breath, "Kira made her choice, as Empress her choice deems her the Empire's enemy."

"But you're not *just* the Empress!" Eona hissed. "Not to me and certainly not to Kira!" she spat as she out of the room.

Carmilla went to the bathroom and collected the last of her belongings. She saw that Kira had not even set up anything. She meant to leave. This entire time, she planned to escape this life and took nothing with her. The woman rested her hands on the bathroom counters and leaned on them as she looked at herself in the mirror. All this power, this strength she had suffered for and inflicted pain with, and she did not realize she was fighting with Kira.

She had thrown the woman across the bridge, a weak, fragile human, and caused her to be impaled by rebar. In a fit of rage, she turned it against the woman Kira defended so ferociously, casting aside her humanity to protect her. She did that for that woman and not Carmilla. *Of course she did.* Carmilla thought to herself. *Who would give anything up... for a monster like me...?*

Kira had come between her time and time again, fighting against the most powerful immortal of the Empire. She dared to fight against the Empress, the Red Queen, for another woman. Carmilla did not know what hurt more: to have her love rejected in such a way or to watch it be given to another. *I was never meant to be loved; I suppose.* The woman sighed. *Not by my parents; even my niece hated me now.*

The mirror cracked.

That's fine though, I'm used to being hated. After all, it's what my parents wanted: to raise a vampire who would be feared and obeyed without question. The perfect soldier. Carmilla clenched the sink. *It was too much for me to hope that something would be different.*

They returned to the Palace on a quiet flight and a graveyard silence on the car ride from the airport. As soon as they returned to the Palace, Carmilla ordered for the four of them to go into her office. No one had spoken of Kira the entire way home. Her name became a forbidden topic for anyone to mention. Not until they returned to the safety of the Palace. As safe as it could be for now.

In the library Eona and Jake were instructed to come alone and to listen and not speak. Inside, Wolfgang shut the door and locked it. He activated a device that distorted all electronic devices, be they cell phone, tablet or spy gear. Once satisfied, they secured everything in the soundproof room. Carmilla leaned forward at her desk and dropped a tiny file at the front of the desk.

"Everything your father and I know about Kira."

Eona opened the paper folder and found two pages.

"Until recently, there was no way Kira could have been a spy for either the LSA or the *Reich*. What I needed to know was of a particular male in her family." Carmilla began.

"A male?" Eona asked as she looked at the paper.

Within the one paper was a photocopy of two partly burned birth certificates. At first, Eona believed it to be the same certificate twice. Both had January thirty-first, Two-thousand-ten as the date, but when she looked closer she saw there were two times, separated by one minute. While the names of the children were burned away, what was clear and untouched was the name of the mother on the certificate: Anna Harvey. The twins were born at Northern St. Louis Hospital in Saint Louis, Missouri, where Anna Harvey worked as a nurse.

On the other side was an employee photo of the woman. She was a light African American woman with raven black curly bob hair. A young woman, her records showed it registered her as 'single', but there was no name. There was, however, a next of kin, a male with the last name Harvey.

"What does this have anything to do with Kira?"

Eona asked to pass the file to Jake.

Wolfgang looked to Carmilla. As he had only seen this file on the plane on the way back, he knew little more than they did.

"Whoever this Harvey is, someone closely connected him to the King's inner circle."

The room fell silent for a moment.

"An inner circle that has allowed him to evade us for hundreds of years and a circle I believe handles the plot to kill you, Eona." Carmilla revealed, "I sent a team of Hunters to track down Anna Harvey and her family hoping to use her to find this male relative—"

Jake jumped up. "Wait, you're saying that Kira is related to the ones who tried to kill Eona when Rayann died?"

"I had no evidence to prove it. All I had was a woman matching Anna Harvey's description dead, one of her children reported dead and the other one completely traumatized and so full of hate she refused to reveal her real name." Carmilla sighed, "Without evidence, I could not risk someone learning I had a lead was possibly harboring a connection to the my sister's murderer—so I disposed of the entire team and destroyed any records involving where Kira had been found and captured."

Until recently, Carmilla had cast aside the idea of Kira's identity and simply gave her to Eona to be a companion. When Kira told the immortal her birthday, however, the Empress could not ignore the growing truth of the woman's identity. She wanted to bury it, to not allow it to change anything, but after Kira's words on the bridge she was certain now that Kira is without a doubt the daughter of Anna Harvey and is related to the man who tried to murder the two, and started a war.

332

"I am certain now that the King is also aware of this and has sought these daughters as well. For what purpose he is with them, I do not know. What is certain is this: as of right now, Kira Nightraven is missing in action, presumed dead. We do not know the nature of her departure, whether by force or choice, and until that is clear, no one is to breathe a word about what happened on the bridge."

If the Council were to discover Kira's significance and her identity, then she would never be safe. It is doubtful she is even aware of anything, that her only intention has been to be reunited with her sister. Without evidence, there is only speculation, however, and they must tread carefully. A rumor can spiral out of control and consume every attempt to protect her.

"The Council is already looking for a means to start a war with one another. Against the *Reich*, we cannot allow this to happen. We must stay united or we all will die. This is not just for Kira's sake, but for all our kind."

Jake and Eona left the room, Carmilla and Wolfgang were alone. The Empress took the file, folded it, and locked it with her own blood, sealed in a hollowed-out book. It would be better to destroy this, but this was the last record of Kira's birth and of her mother.

The Commander of the guard sighed, "You didn't tell her."

"I don't want her to become me." Carmilla rubbed her eyes, "To lose a great love and have your entire life dictated by the emotions of grief and hatred; helplessness and despair is no life to live."

"She is much like her mother. When she loves, she loves hard and long; even small things." Wolfgang smiled some, "But what of you?"

Carmilla leaned back, "What of me?"

"Come now Carmilla, marriage may not bound us as family, but we are still such. You are still my beloved little sister-in-law and I worry about you." The old wolf said as he sat down, "Kira's actions have weighed on you more than anyone: she is your mate. I know what it means to lose them."

Carmilla shook her head, "You have suffered far more than me my brother, you lost your great love; mine has simply rejected me."

"A rejection that has killed some in the past." Wolfgang reminded, the story of the sun who loved the moon that he died every night for her.

"I am the Empress first, a Tepes next and then the Red Queen, the demon of the Empire. There is no room for anything else." Carmilla said softly, "I have killed far too many to be loved."

Wolfgang stood, "If someone were to truly love you." He adjusted his suit before he walked to the door, "Then they will see the woman behind the mask."

Left to her thoughts, Carmilla turned in her chair and looked out the window to the rising sun. To the world, to her family, they forced her to wear many masks, to be perfect, fearless, merciless, but none of these were really her. They were what the world wanted her to be. When she tried to remove her mask in front of one person... that person wrapped their fingers around her neck.

For Kira, she was a woman forced to wear a mask simply to survive. She gave the world what it wanted to see, an obedient, submissive human too frightened to defend herself, cowering before the might and in awe of the vampire. She did not show anyone her face because she knew what would happen to her.

Carmilla foresaw a darkness coming, a shadow that would be cast over the world. She saw the coming of a time when bonds would be tested, spirits would be broken; when morality would be pitted against reality. Whichever side Kira found herself on, the immortal's hope was that it too, she would survive. Even if Carmilla was not by their side, she prayed that the two women she loved most in this world would find the light within the darkness.

"Let the Game begin."

ABOUT THE AUTHOR

Meghan Jones is an author who enjoys writing between work and time on the road on her motorcycle. Her lesbian fantasy and adventure novels often feature strong, complex and passionate women who are sure to leave a reader wanting more.

Meghan is in her mid-20s and lives on the east-coast of the United States. When she isn't writing she plays with her zoo of pets, spends time with her partner and trains to fight in her Armored Combat Sport.

Visit lezbeawriter.weebly.com for information on her books and contact information.

facebook.com/meghanjonesbooks

TikTok.com/meghanjonesbooks

Maxilyn Lykaios is a Marine fresh out of the Corps. Adjusting to her new life in the civilian world, Max gets a job as a bouncer at a high-end club in New-York City. While Max tries her best to get a piece of her old life from the military back, she meets Kassandra Theron, a woman unlike any other she has met before. Kassandra soon brings the Marine over to the Other Side, introducing her to the world of the supernatural, but the familiar danger also brings an unfamiliar risk: secrets of Maxilyn's past threaten to surface, placing the women in grave danger.

-Children of the Night-

Printed in Great Britain
by Amazon